Amos Yong

10/22/19

The Kerygmatic Spirit

The Kerygmatic Spirit

APOSTOLIC PREACHING IN THE 21ST CENTURY

Amos Yong

Edited by *Josh P. S. Samuel*
Reflections and Afterword by *Tony Richie*

CASCADE *Books* · Eugene, Oregon

THE KERYGMATIC SPIRIT
Apostolic Preaching in the 21st Century

Cascade Books
An Imprint of Wipf and Stock Publishers
199 W. 8th Ave., Suite 3
Eugene, OR 97401

www.wipfandstock.com

PAPERBACK ISBN: 978-1-4982-9817-9
HARDCOVER ISBN: 978-1-4982-9818-6
EBOOK ISBN: 978-1-5326-5697-2

Cataloguing-in-Publication data:

Names: Yong, Amos, author. | Samuel, Josh P. S., editor. | Richie, Tony, author.
Title: The kerygmatic spirit : apostolic preaching in the 21st century / Amos Yong, edited by Josh P. S. Samuel, with reflections and an afterword by Tony Richie.
Description: Eugene, OR: Cascade Books, 2018 | Includes bibliographical references and index.
Identifiers: ISBN 978-1-4982-9817-9 (paperback) | ISBN 978-1-4982-9818-6 (hardcover) | ISBN 978-1-5326-5697-2 (ebook)
Subjects: LCSH: Preaching | Pentecostalism | Pentecostals—sermons | Sermons, American.
Classification: BX8762.Z6 Y66 2018 (print) | BX8762.Z6 (ebook)

Manufactured in the U.S.A.   OCTOBER 23, 2018

To
Bob & Nancy Jonsson
Ralph Herbert & Anita Killebrew
Steve & Tara Overman
~ Preachers after Pentecost ~

Table of Contents

Preface

I consider this a fourth volume in a series published by Cascade Books, following my *The Dialogical Spirit* (2014), *The Missiological Spirit* (2014), and *The Hermeneutical Spirit* (2017). Whereas the previous three are largely reprints of previously published journal articles and essays, this one is a collection of previously preached sermons. However, as I do not write out my sermons, the book you hold in your hands results from the hard transcription work of volume editor Josh P. S. Samuel. I had met Josh at a Society for Pentecostal Studies meeting before and knew he had worked in his doctoral thesis on Pentecostal preaching and worship, so I inquired about his interest in helping me get these sermons transcribed for publication. Along the way, Tony Richie, a Holiness-Pentecostal Church of God (Cleveland, Tennessee) pastor and theologian who has been a co-conspirator in many things Pentecostal-theological, agreed to include some perspective as a seasoned Pentecostal preacher.

The appendix provides a full list of Yong sermons preached since 1999, a record that I began to maintain electronically in that year. Most of the sermons since 1999 exist in outline and note form electronically, far fewer are archived either in audio or video format, and even of the latter bunch, far fewer are of the quality that enabled transcription. In my last move (from Virginia to California in the summer of 2014), I threw out handwritten notes that I had kept for the dozens of sermons I had preached prior to 1999, reaching back at least to the mid-1980s when I traveled with Bethany Bible College's "Team Ministries" group that went out to churches in the Northern Bay Area on weekends.

The published version of the sermons in this volume were transcribed and edited initially by Josh Samuel and then edited again by me. The audio of fourteen of these sermons are made available by Fuller Theological Seminary on Soundcloud at http://bit.ly/amos_yong_audio

for those interested in listening to their delivery beyond reading their content. Three of these fourteen sermons, numbers 2, 9, and 12, are available in video format on Youtube at http://bit.ly/amos_yong_video. Unfortunately no usable audio or video archive of sermon 3, preached at All Nations Church in Minneapolis, Minnesota in March 2010, remain.

Editorially for the printed sermons in this volume, we have attempted to be consistent regarding the following guidelines:

- The grammar has been smoothed over and punctuation decisions have been made keeping readability and comprehensibility chiefly in mind.

- Brackets indicate added text, usually by editor, not found in the recordings.

- Ellipses indicate words, phrases, or portions of the recordings not preserved in the transcriptions.

- Footnotes have been added (identified as being from the editor when by Josh Samuel) for explanatory, contextual, and content purposes.

- Numbers have been spelled out mostly, except when referring to scriptural chapters and verses or to large figures.

At the end of my first year in youth ministry (on 5 June 1988), the Fairfield Assembly of God youth group gave me a farewell gift, a name-engraved, leather-bound, thin-line edition of the New International Version (NIV) of the Bible (1978; rev. ed. 1983), that I preached from for approximately the next two decades plus. The first few sermons in this book used the NIV. However, for my theological publications, I switched over to the New Revised Standard Version (NRSV) of the Bible and in the last few years, have been preaching from the 2006 pocket edition published by Oxford University Press. Most of the scriptural quotations in this book are noted as being either from the NIV or NRSV, although on occasion other versions are cited and will be identified as such. Note also that the transcriptions of scriptural passages attempt to preserve what is spoken, and these do not always match verbatim the published version.

Acknowledgments

I (Amos) wish to thanks to Robert Graves and The Foundation for Pentecostal Scholarship for a grant that facilitated transcription of the sermons.

I am grateful for the collegiality of Josh Samuel, especially his labor of love in helping me get this collection of sermons into print and his expert analysis of my preaching vis-à-vis the wider scholarly literature in this arena, and the pentecostal preaching tradition. I also appreciate Tony Richie; I am thankful for his long friendship and grateful for his partnership in all things Pentecostal and theological.

Thanks also to Nok Kam, my graduate assistant here at Fuller Theological Seminary for help with various aspects of the manuscript, including proofreading, conforming to preferred publisher style, indexing, etc.

Robin Parry and others at Cascade/Wipf & Stock were professional at every turn; I am grateful to have this as the fourth installment of books on method I had not set out to write but that have emerged over the course of my publishing essays and articles, in various venues. The first three—*The Dialogical Spirit* (2014), *The Missiological Spirit* (2014), and *The Hermeneutical Spirit* (2017)—have focused on theological, missiological, and hermeneutical methods respectively, all from my pentecostal perspective (albeit one that is connected to the Day of Pentecost narrative in Acts 2 as much as, if not even more than, any aspect of the modern Pentecostal movement); this volume is suggestive for homiletical methods, although readers should be forewarned that outside of one class on preaching during my undergraduate years over thirty years ago, I have no formal training in this arena.

I am grateful to my wife, Alma Yong, for her patience, love, and support, all of which makes my scholarship, and ministry, possible.

This book is dedicated to three preacher couples. Robert (Bob) and Nancy Jonsson were pastors of Olivet Baptist Church in Crystal,

Minnesota, which Alma and I attended during our tenure at Bethel University from 1999–2005. Bob invited me to preach regularly and had us involved in his small group. He has epitomized to Alma and I what "pastor" means. We continue to miss his and Nancy's friendship, and pastoral care.

Ralph Herbert was pastor of Great Bridge Presbyterian Church (GBPC) in Chesapeake, Virginia, where Alma and I attended during most of our years at Regent University in Virginia Beach, Virginia (2005–14). Anita Killebrew was his associate pastor for most of those years and she married Ralph in 2012. I was more or less active at GBPC over the years, including publishing my *Who Is the Holy Spirit: A Walk with the Apostles* (Paraclete Press) from out of a year-long study in Sunday School with a group of faithful members. Ralph came from an Assemblies of God background but got his Doctor of Ministry at Fuller Theological Seminary. Alma and I always enjoyed listening to Ralph and Anita preach (Anita preached regularly, even before they were married), and were edified by their messages.

Last but not least, Steve and Tara Overman are pastors of Faith Center, a Foursquare affiliated congregation in Eugene, Oregon. I have not had the privilege so far of hearing Steve preach, but I have preached at his church twice (unfortunately those messages were not available for transcription), even as Alma and I have been hosted by him and Tara in their home. I consider Steve one of the most theologically astute Pentecostal pastors—no one else I know among this group reads philosophers and theologians like Raimon Panikkar and Maximos the Confessor!—and he has been unflagging in his support of educational initiatives in the Foursquare Church.

It's not just that I have tremendous respect for these preachers but that they are also the kinds of friends that are gifts to Alma and me. This dedication does not presume that they would be in agreement with every thought expressed in the pages that follow.

* * *

I (Josh) would like to first thank Amos Yong for inviting me to be a part of this book. I have admired Amos for many years as one of the outstanding Pentecostal scholars of our day. As I've got to know Amos better, what I've come to further appreciate about him is that he is gracious, down-to-earth, and has a great sense of humor. I have enjoyed listening to his sermons and engaging with his approach to preaching, particularly because of my interest in Pentecostal theology and homiletics. I'm also grateful for Tony Richie, who I got to know through this project. Tony not only provides excellent insights in this book, but demonstrates both scholarly insight and pastoral concern. Thanks also goes to the staff at Wipf and Stock for their support with this project.

I am also grateful for the many pastors and professors who have encouraged me in my preaching and in my studies of homiletics. Thanks to Pastors Easaw Philip and Craig J. Burton, who gave me opportunities to develop my preaching within the churches they led as senior pastors. Also thanks to the professors who helped me grow in my knowledge of homiletics: David Kennedy, Paul Scott Wilson, Glen Taylor, Stephen Farris, Michael P. Knowles, and Steven M. Studebaker.

I am also grateful for my mom, Kunjunjamma (Molly) Samuel, and dad, P. Stephen Samuel, for their ongoing prayerful support of my ministry. While my mom did not formally preach in many pulpits, she preached many sermons to me at home and introduced me to important preachers. My dad's father, P. M. Samuel, was a minister I did not get to know very well, but whose ministry provided inspiration to me as a preacher.

Finally, I'm thankful to my family at home. Thanks to Joyce M. Samuel, who not only supports me as an incredible wife, but graciously offers detailed analysis and feedback on my writings, including my introduction in this book. And thanks to my kids, Josiah, Jeremiah, and Joanna, who encourage me in so many ways, as young children can.

* * *

I (Tony) am particularly grateful for an enduring and personally enjoyable friendship and partnership with Amos. Over the years I have found him to be a brother with true Christian graces. His professional commitment is only exceeded by his personal humility. I am thankful for a new and, I hope, lifelong friendship with Josh Samuel. Josh has made this work all the richer with his radiant attitude and resourceful participation. It is my special privilege to work with both Amos and Josh on this volume.

Of course, I cannot imagine completing this project (or any other) without my long-suffering but loving wife, Sue Richie. I appreciate my precious parishioners at New Harvest—especially Pastor Danny Davis, who often, together with Sue, bears the brunt of my load—and my colleagues at Pentecostal Theological Seminary, especially Lee Roy Martin who is a preacher par excellence, more than words can say.

When working on this volume I often thought of my students such as Michelle Smith, Drew Eastes, and others who for me exemplify great Pentecostal preaching for the coming generation.

Next to incomparable gratitude to our gracious Lord, I am grateful to be a part of a family of Pentecostal preachers. On both maternal and paternal sides of my family there are numerous aunts, uncles, and cousins as well as my own nieces and nephews who followed the call to preach the glorious gospel of our Lord Jesus Christ. I specifically note my father, Andrew Richie, who has been preaching now for nearly sixty years; my sister, Pastor Sharon Grooms; and, my brother-in-love, Pastor Jeff Odom. Their ministries have enriched mine immeasurably.

Introduction

Situating Amos Yong's Preaching

Josh P. S. Samuel

Like some of you opening up this book, I was introduced to Amos Yong through his many impressive scholarly publications. So when he contacted me about editing a book on his sermons, I responded affirmatively. I was eager to work with someone who has been an exemplary Pentecostal scholar, with an ethnic background that is underrepresented in North American scholarship. We share some commonalities, for I too am a Pentecostal, I enjoy scholarly pursuits, and I come from an Asian (Indian) background. Furthermore, I am enthusiastic about the subject of preaching, as a Pentecostal, as a preacher, and a student of homiletics.[1] Though Yong is well-known for his vast theological scholarship, there is little in the scholarly record so far about his approach to preaching.[2] This project addresses this lacuna variously.

First, it is important to hear the heart of a Christian scholar expressed through the venue and ministry of preaching. Quite often scholars are stereotyped as "ivory-tower theologians": people who talk a lot about theology within the walls of some seminary ("cemetery," lay-people joke!), but are unable to connect with others outside their scholarly world. Amos Yong is not one of those theologians. In fact, most people who hear and/or read his sermons will realize how capable and effective he is

---

1. My book, *The Holy Spirit in Worship Music, Preaching, and the Altar*, includes substantial work on Pentecostal preaching.

2. Though see Yong's three-part article, "The Spirit and Proclamation."

at communicating to a broad audience. Theological studies are not just for mere speculative theories—theology is for proclamation.[3] Theology delves into God and his world, so it only makes sense that theology leads to a proclamation to others on what God might be saying to our world today. Amos Yong models this for us in both his scholarly discourses on theology and in his ministry of preaching. In this book, a wide audience will have an opportunity to delve into how he translates his theological views into preaching.

Furthermore, this volume offers the church an opportunity to gain perspective on preaching, not just from any scholar, but from one of its most prolific theologians of the twenty-first century. Yong has written extensively on numerous theological themes, as an author or editor of over four dozen volumes and hundreds of scholarly articles in journals, books, and other venues.[4] Regrettably, in the twenty-first century, theological scholarship has been divided across fields like biblical studies, systematics, and homiletics in such a way that scholars with specialization in one area are deemed incapable of addressing themes outside their arena of expertise. While it is understandable that specialists can offer unique insights into their domains, we can neglect matters related even to our own fields of study when we do not hear from outsiders who approach our disciplines with different lenses. In earlier times, theologians did not fail to address issues related to preaching, whether it be Augustine, Martin Luther, Jonathan Edwards, or Karl Barth, and the church has reaped those benefits.[5] I am certain that the church and the guild of homileticians will benefit from Amos Yong, one of today's leading theologians, as he lends his voice in this sphere.

A third reason why this work is important is because it gives us opportunity to hear and engage Amos Yong's sometimes highly dense theological work in a more accessible format. This book is a helpful introduction to some of his theological views. As a Pentecostal, Yong addresses the work of the Spirit often. Where he departs from some

3. Forde, *Theology is for Proclamation*.

4. For a full bibliography through 2012, see Vondey and Mittelstadt, eds., *The Theology of Amos Yong and the New Face of Pentecostal Scholarship*, 275–82; Yong keeps his author's page on www.amazon.com updated with both authored and edited publications.

5. To see how a variety of theologians, such as Augustine, Luther, Edwards, and Barth address homiletics, see Lischer, *The Company of Preachers*, 277–92, 115–19, 120–25, 423–32.

traditional Pentecostals is in his much more holistic approach to how the Spirit operates in our world today. Mention the work of the Spirit in some traditional Pentecostal contexts, and themes like Spirit-baptism, the gifts of the Spirit, and signs and wonders typically come up. And while Yong mentions these themes, he does not limit the work of the Spirit to these areas. The sermons in this book indicate how we might understand the full scope of the Spirit's work, for instance, among migrants/immigrants (sermons 1 and 3); in healing (sermons 2, 5, 9); in relationship to politics (sermons 4 and 9); among the marginalized (sermon 4); among people with disabilities (sermon 5); in relationship to the resurrected Christ (sermon 6); in repentance and forgiveness (sermon 6); in prayers, lament, songs, and ministry (sermon 8); relating to signs and wonders (sermon 9); for justice (sermon 9); relating to gentiles (sermon 9); in the Old Testament (sermon 10); in suffering (sermon 14); in silent, desert experiences (sermon 13); with regard to the life of the mind (sermon 12); in mission and hospitality (sermon 11); in vocation and the natural environment (sermon 10); and in the difficult experiences of life (sermon 15). The sermons thus showcase important but neglected ways the Spirit's activity should be understood. While many of these themes have already been addressed in Yong's theological scholarship, the pages to come reflect his repackaging them as homilies for congregations and lay believers. And for those who may have already read his theological works, these sermons model how scholars might translate their sometimes highly technical language for those outside the guild.

Last but not least in recounting the reasons for this book is that it provides us with an Asian-American homiletical voice, one still relatively absent in the guild of preaching. Amos Yong was born and raised in Malaysia, and eventually immigrated to the United States in 1976. Eunjoo Mary Kim's work on Asian American preaching is relevant here, but her focus is primarily East Asian, associated with China, Korea, and Japan, and engaging with the influences of Confucianism, Buddhism, and shamanism.[6] With its majority Muslim population, Malaysia is distinct from the other three countries Kim addresses.[7] Matthew D. Kim also addresses Asian American preaching in a short article, but its scope overlaps with Kim's, covering Chinese, Japanese, and Korean culture as well.[8] Two

6. See Kim, *Preaching the Presence of God*, 6.

7. See sermon 4 in this book, where Yong explains how Malaysia is a Muslim country.

8. Kim, "Asian American Preaching," 200.

Southeast Asian Pentecostals have addressed issues related to preaching, albeit their immediate context is muted and the North American Pentecostal horizon more palpable.[9] Now it is clear that most of Yong's influences related to homiletics comes from the Pentecostal tradition, and he makes little of the Asian American dimension or context of his own preaching practices. While we will discuss some of the influences on Yong's preaching later, it is still noteworthy that we have here one of the first books of sermons by an Asian American theologian. Perhaps future work will delve more deeply into this aspect of his preaching in particular and on the unique aspects of Asian American Pentecostal (and evangelical) preaching more generally.

Before getting to Yong's sermons, it is helpful to put his approach to preaching into context. One helpful way to do this is to examine the ethos of preaching within the tradition to which he belongs. I will limit this discussion to North American Classical Pentecostalism—"Classical" being the qualifier scholars have used generally to refer to those Pentecostal churches and denominations that have roots in or connections to the Azusa Street revival in Los Angeles in the early twentieth century—and will focus especially on this tradition's emphasis on the Spirit's work in preaching. While unable to get into every aspect of Pentecostal preaching, I will highlight what is deemed as typical of this homiletical tradition. Given Yong's Pentecostal background, including his ministerial credentials with the Assemblies of God (USA), a Classical Pentecostal denomination, the Spirit's work is central both in his scholarship and in his preaching. So when he includes or excludes dynamics oftentimes associated with Pentecostal preaching, it likely reflects intentionality on his part. To better understand Yong's approach to preaching, particularly as it relates to the emphasis on the Spirit in Pentecostal preaching, let us see what he embraces or distances himself from with regard to these elements of Pentecostal preaching: Spirit-baptism, the anointing, supernaturalism and the altar call, extemporaneous preaching, the use of call and response, and the inclusion of both passion and intellectual rigor.[10]

9. E.g., Leoh (Malaysian), "Ethics and Pentecostal Preaching," and Chan (Singaporean), *Liturgical Theology*.

10. I discuss many of these themes in my book, *The Holy Spirit in Worship Music, Preaching, and the Altar*. Here I bring Yong's perspective into conversation with these themes, in a fairly literal way, I might add. I conducted a Skype interview with him on 6 September 2017. In the rest of this introductory chapter, any direct quotations from or ideas attributed to Yong that are undocumented or not footnoted otherwise derive from this interview.

Spirit-baptism ~ First, a key expectation among many Pentecostals preachers for effective preaching is a special experience with the Spirit—normally Spirit-baptism. Consider the history of the Pentecostal movement. The Azusa Street Revival, considered one of the most influential centers for early Pentecostalism—particularly for Classical Pentecostals—emphasized the importance of Spirit-baptism for effective preaching. The Pentecostal teaching on Spirit-baptism arises out of Christ's promise in Acts 1:8, when he stated: "But you will receive power when the Holy Spirit comes on you; and you will be my witnesses in Jerusalem, and in all Judea and Samaria, and to the ends of the earth" (NIV). When the disciples eventually experienced this Spirit-baptism, the Spirit came upon them all while they were praying in the Upper Room, and all of them spoke in tongues. Thus, what has typically been taught among Classical Pentecostals about Spirit-baptism is that one receives power to witness with this experience—and like the disciples who received this baptism in Acts 2:4, Christians will also subsequently speak in tongues as a sign of being Spirit-baptized. Following this experience, the book of Acts (Acts 2:14–41) recounts Peter's bold preaching that resulted in about three thousand people becoming followers of Christ. While Peter denied Christ three times prior to his crucifixion, Pentecostals would be quick to point out that Peter was now a bold witness to Christ as a result of his experience of the Spirit on the Day of Pentecost.

Leaders at the Azusa Street Revival distinguished between an anointing and Spirit-baptism. They explained that an anointing is an experience of the Spirit available to all Christians. And though they acknowledged that preachers would benefit from an experience of the Spirit through the anointing, they asserted that Spirit-baptism enables Christians to experience greater results in their preaching.[11] Spirit-baptism was so important that they argued that this experience was more crucial than a great theologian's sermon. In Azusa's official publication, *The Apostolic Faith*, one writer stated that "God does not need a great theological preacher that can give nothing but theological chips and shavings to people," for an experience of Spirit-baptism is the credential needed for preaching.[12] Might Amos Yong be considered a "great theological preacher," in that negative sense that Azusa participants articulated? Would his experience of the Spirit be deemed sufficient for what Azusa Street participants considered

11. *Apostolic Faith* (February–March 1907), 4.
12. *Apostolic Faith* (October 1906), 3.

crucial for preaching? Before we answer that question, consider some other contemporary Pentecostal leaders on this subject.

Consider the present-day Classical Pentecostal movement, particularly the Assemblies of God (USA)—the denomination Yong belongs to—which highlight the experience of Spirit-baptism. The Assemblies of God (USA), on their official website, state:

> The doctrine of the Baptism in the Holy Spirit is our distinctive. This truth explains the passion and power of our witness. Jesus promised His followers they would receive power from on high so that they would be His witnesses. We believe this truth is just as relevant today as our Fellowship continues to take the gospel message around the globe.[13]

Witnessing is an important dimension of preaching, whereby the preacher witnesses to Jesus Christ.[14] Charles Crabtree, a denominational leader in the Assemblies of God, wrote a book entitled, *Pentecostal Preaching*. Therein, he too, like Azusa Street participants, acknowledge that Christians may experience an "enduement of the Spirit" for ministry—which might possibly be deemed as the anointing among Azusa participants.[15] But Crabtree states that those who have been baptized in the Spirit, would experience "greater works"—results—from their ministry, particularly of revealing Jesus and supernatural results[16] (I expand on the issue of results momentarily).

We must consider Amos Yong's views on Spirit-baptism, not just in light of his Pentecostal background as an Assemblies of God credentialed minister, but also as a Pentecostal scholar. First, regarding his own personal experience, he explains that he is a "card-carrying AG guy," and experienced Spirit-baptism, as Classical Pentecostals describe this experience, as a teenager. Conversationally, he describes that experience of Spirit-baptism as "powerful," "impacting," and "formative," and as a Pentecostal theologian, he grants that Spirit-baptism and the tongues experience "should be expected."[17] And it is this experience that is one of

13. "Baptism in the Holy Spirit" at https://ag.org/Beliefs/Our-Core-Doctrines/Baptism-in-the-Holy-Spirit (accessed on January 19, 2018).

14. See Long, *The Witness of Preaching*.

15. Crabtree, *Pentecostal Preaching*, 30–31.

16. Crabtree, *Pentecostal Preaching*, 36–37, citing John 14:12.

17. Yong has "testified" to his experience of Spirit-baptism as a scholar (see his *Discerning the Spirit(s)*, 149), and has also published his own Pentecostal theology of Spirit-baptism in various venues (most recently in *Renewing Christian Theology*, ch. 4).

the reasons why he continues to keep that Pentecostal label. He admits that this experience "makes a difference in your life."

Yong, however, further shows how Acts 1:8 connects Spirit-baptism with being a "witness," which may be displayed in many ways, not just verbally. Though the experience of Spirit-baptism will make a "difference," he states, "it's not the kind of difference that we can quantify or even . . . qualify, in saying: 'Here's how you are as a preacher, let's get you speaking in tongues, and then we'll see you here as a preacher.'" Thus, Spirit-baptism, in the context of the book of Acts, and the resulting experience of being a "witness" could unfold in a variety of ways, not just verbally, or with other signs, wonders, and gifts of the Spirit. For even those 'incredible moments in ministry' that classical Pentecostals claim are unleashed by Spirit-baptism are also experienced by those not baptized in the Spirit in the Classical Pentecostal sense. Yong considers, for instance, Billy Graham's incredible influence without any acknowledged experience of Spirit-baptism, as Classical Pentecostals would describe it.

Rather than viewing Spirit-baptism as the route to "successful results"—such as more conversions, people at the altar, and other supernatural manifestations—Yong points out that the word for "witnesses" in Acts 1:8 is the Greek word *martures*, a word from which "martyr" derives. The book of Acts contains the witness of people like Stephen and James, who experienced martyrdom in their witness. Spirit-baptism identifies believers with the life and ministry of Jesus the Spirit baptizer, which includes the suffering of Jesus who hung on a cross.[18] Thus, Spirit-baptism is not just related to achieving conventionally defined positive results at the altar. Rather, one's witness in preaching may engender suffering. It will not somehow transform a preacher from Clark Kent to Superman, certainly not if such is presumed to be accompanied by the kinds of manifestations acclaimed by Classical Pentecostals.

Amos Yong admits that an encounter with God through Spirit-baptism will undoubtedly make a difference in one's life. He is unwilling to argue, however, that it is some type of formula for more effective preaching. Rather, Spirit-baptism empowers one's witness, which may be expressed in a variety of ways and may include different types of results, beyond some of the traditional ministry activities and results often expected by some Pentecostals. How many preachers have left the pulpit feeling like they have failed to preach with excellence, because their ministry did not

18. Yong, *Renewing Christian Theology*, 96. Yong tackles the subject of martyrdom and suffering as it relates to the Holy Spirit in sermon 14.

engender the type of results some have expected within the Pentecostal-Charismatic tradition? Yong's insistence that being a "witness" includes so much more than what Pentecostals have claimed, ensures that preachers have expectations for preaching that are more consistent with the experience of the early church in Acts.

The anointing ~ It is important to briefly indicate how Pentecostals distinguish Spirit-baptism from the anointing, when it comes to preaching. As stated earlier, the early Pentecostals at the Azusa Street revival distinguished the experience of Spirit-baptism from an anointing. A fresh anointing was always necessary for a preacher, whereby they might feel the Spirit's "power going all over" them, so that they are led by God to preach.[19] This need for a fresh anointing of the Spirit, whereby the Spirit leads the preacher "in the present moment" of preaching, is also consistent with contemporary Pentecostal leaders' views on preaching.[20]

With regards to Yong's approach to an "anointing" as it relates to preaching, he is generally reluctant to associate the anointing—the activity of the Spirit—with any special feeling in the preacher while preaching or the seemingly positive results from preaching. Rather, the anointing is something a preacher should be experiencing throughout his or her life, even through what may appear to be mundane. So the anointing is not relegated to that moment of preaching, but the Spirit-filled life should involve all aspects of the preacher's life, be it in those moments of study, outlining, praying beforehand, having conversations with others, and beyond.

Yong's views on the anointing for preaching helps fellow Pentecostals approach preaching in one very important way: he steers Pentecostals away from attempting to "work up" that anointing in preaching, which is sometimes the stereotype of Pentecostal preaching. Being anointed is not relegated to how loud one may preach, the glow on one's face, the results following the preaching, or how people are led to feel,[21] but is predicated on a life that is yielded to the Spirit's work in all aspects of one's life. Rather than put so much pressure on preachers to excite the emotions while preaching, the preacher is rightly focused on being yielded to the Spirit in

---

19. *AF* (June–September 1907), 2.

20. E.g., Crabtree, *Pentecostal Preaching*, 202; Holm, "Cadences of the Heart," 19.

21. For instance, Ragoonath explains that among various other things the anointing includes for Pentecostal preachers, he explains that they often speak "with a higher pitched voice," "his facial expression begins to grow; sometimes the congre-gation [sic] can see the presence of God upon the preacher" (*Preach the Word*, 171).

all aspects of one's life, so that the preaching is a more natural expression of what one has been living out in one's day-to-day life.

Supernaturalism and the altar call ~ A key expectation, especially in light of some Pentecostals' views on the benefit of Spirit-baptism, is the "supernatural demonstration" of God's power—possibly during, but most often following, the preaching—through an altar call. Pentecostals, particularly those who have taken the time to articulate what Pentecostal preaching is about, regularly argue that Pentecostal preaching includes— or at least expects—a supernatural demonstration of God's power in response to the sermon.[22] While a supernatural demonstration of signs and wonders might occur during the sermon, the most obvious dimension of a corporate worship service where Pentecostals expect supernatural results is during the altar call.[23]

An altar call is that moment when the preacher closes the sermon and invites hearers forward to an altar to respond to their message, typically for extended prayer. Altar calls are not unique to Pentecostals; people like Charles Finney helped popularize this type of response to a sermon during the Second Great Awakening (1790s), in what was then referred to as the "anxious seat."[24] Pentecostals, however, have included the altar call so often that one Pentecostal homiletician, Aldwin Ragoonath, argues that you do not even have "Pentecostal preaching" apart from a call to the altar.[25] Daniel Albrecht, a scholar of Pentecostal liturgy, indicates that the altar call is one of the three key components of a Pentecostal corporate worship service—alongside preaching and worship music.[26] Why is the altar call so crucial to Pentecostal preaching, and all of the Pentecostal corporate worship service? It is because it is during that altar time when people respond to the sermon, that people might experience "signs and wonders," miracles, healings, Spirit-baptism, and a general encounter with God—all experiences of God highlighted in Pentecostal spirituality.

Classical Pentecostal leaders concur on the importance of the altar call and the expectation for supernatural results within Pentecostal

22. Ragoonath, *Preach the Word*, 37, 75; Crabtree, *Pentecostal Preaching*, 135.

23. Crabtree, *Pentecostal Preaching*, 39.

24. Carwardine, *Transatlantic Revivalism*, 8; see Wolffe, *The Expansion of Evangelicalism*, 73.

25. Ragoonath, *Preach the Word*, 37.

26. Albrecht refers to these three as "three primary rites" (*Rites in the Spirit*, 152). I address these three key elements of a Pentecostal corporate worship service also in my book, *The Holy Spirit in Worship Music, Preaching, and the Altar*.

corporate worship. Crabtree states that the Pentecostal altar "is a focal point of faith, a point of contact between a person and God, the place where the Spirit's power begins the process of transformation. For Spirit-filled preachers, for those whose eyes of faith are on the altar, it is the capstone, the supreme reward for the many hours of prayer and study."[27] Crabtree argues that those "who do not believe in altar calls do not serve their constituency well,"[28] and since the "supernatural" is what sets Pentecostalism apart from any other evangelical entity, he stresses the necessity of expecting the supernatural: the altar, then, is important since it provides an important context for the supernatural to be experienced.[29] The expected result, of course, is the supernatural, typically: the experience of salvation, Spirit-baptism, healings, and miracles. If one has "the supernatural" as the goal of one's sermon, particularly at the altar, it undoubtedly affects the development and delivery of the sermon. A call to the altar for the experience of the supernatural has been highlighted by Pentecostal leaders and scholars of Pentecostalism as crucial to Pentecostal preaching, which is why it is important to consider Yong's views on this subject.

So where does Amos Yong's approach to preaching, the so-called supernatural, and the altar call relate to what other Pentecostals have concluded? Yong admits that he uses altar calls irregularly, which is related to his views on the Spirit's work, the supernatural, and his expected results for preaching. When you read or listen to his sermons, you will notice that a number of his sermons conclude with a short prayer by himself. Yong does not normally invite people forward to pray for some "supernatural demonstration," as some Pentecostals might hope for. However, those times that his sermons (particularly those included in this volume) include prayer at an altar it is often at the request of a leader hosting the worship service.[30] More often, Yong concludes his sermons with a short prayer through which he invites hearers to pray with him

---

27. Crabtree, *Pentecostal Preaching*, 202–3.

28. Crabtree, *Pentecostal Preaching*, 150.

29. Crabtree, *Pentecostal Preaching*, 135–37. Another Assemblies of God leader argues that the altar call is an important part of Pentecostal preaching, not only because it is biblical, but also because it "works"; see Trask, "Pentecostal Preaching and Persuasion," 180–87.

30. E.g., see the end of sermon 12, "The Life in the Spirit and the Life of the Mind," preached at the National Education Symposium, Life Pacific College, San Dimas, California.

for specific matters raised in his sermon. This reluctance to include altar calls as might typically be found among some Pentecostal churches is intentional, and relates to at least three theological issues.

The first reason Yong is reluctant to regularly use altar calls as a Pentecostal preacher, relates to his position that it is a mistake to understand Pentecostalism in terms of supernaturalism because this relies too much upon a modern binary that divides between the natural and supernatural.[31] This binary equates the "supernatural" with the work of the Spirit, but then fails to acknowledge the work of the Spirit with what may not be considered "supernatural." And much of Yong's theological work, including the sermons in this book, reveal why this binary is not only unhelpful, but it is not accurate. For the Spirit does work in what some may deem as "natural." As mentioned above, his sermons in this book address the work of the Spirit in aspects of life such as healing and miracles, but he also delves into how the Spirit works in various ways, such as in migrants/immigrants, politics, intellectual thought, vocation, and the natural world—not merely with realities typically associated with the "supernatural."

Secondly, the altar may not be the best place to respond to a message on some of these topics—the response may be best experienced in one's day-to-day life at home, at work, and generally beyond the confines of a church sanctuary. A call to an altar often relies on an emotional appeal, and Yong often does not want to merely elicit responses only at this level. He wants to get his listener to ask questions about the topics he addresses that they may have never considered before.

Finally, Yong admits that his work on disability has likely affected his approach to his views on the role of the altar call for experiencing the "supernatural." He argues that it is important to distinguish between healing and curing. Cures has to do "with removal of the symptoms" of an illness; healing, however, relates "to the salvation of God eschatologically inaugurated in the person and work of Christ."[32] Healing can happen in anyone's life, which includes wholeness and salvation. Curing may or may not happen; and even that same person who has been cured will eventually die. Thus, the ultimate healing experienced at the resurrection, because of Christ's redemptive work for humans, is most significant. Furthermore, relegating healing to the supernatural curing of people with

31. See also Yong, *Spirit Poured Out*, ch. 7, which elaborates on this false dichotomy of nature/supernature bequeathed by Enlightenment modernity.

32. Yong, *Renewing Christian Theology*, 211.

illnesses or disabilities not only minimizes healing but also potentially minimizes the value that those with illnesses or disabilities bring to the church. Yong rightly states that when ministries are developed *with* those who are disabled, not just "to or for them," "the church becomes a liberating community precisely by overcoming the traditional barriers that have divided the unimpaired 'us' from the impaired 'them.'"[33]

Yong's approach to the altar call has significant implications for one's preaching, which we should heed as preachers. Expanding one's views on the work of the Spirit in preaching beyond just expecting what may be deemed "supernatural" at the altar ensures a more holistic approach. The pressure to "deliver" results at the altar, often leading to manipulation, can be avoided, knowing that there are more ways that a congregation should respond to a sermon. Furthermore, no longer would those who may come in a wheelchair, for example, be deemed as the most important person to receive prayer at an altar. While persons in wheelchairs might desire prayer, they should be viewed more so as partners in Christian ministry. In fact, that person in a wheelchair may be the one most helpful to pray for others. Yong helps preachers, particularly those within the Pentecostal-Charismatic tradition, to correct and expand their views on how the Spirit is active and how a congregation should respond to a sermon.

Extemporaneous preaching ~ The role of the Spirit and extemporaneous preaching in Pentecostalism is also important to address. One of the reasons I was invited to engage this project is because Amos Yong does not write out his sermons for preaching, and I was asked to help transcribe his sermons. I was initially surprised to discover these sermons were not written out because one would expect a scholar would wish to communicate precisely and logically, and carefully planned manuscripts would achieve these objectives. But beyond even this, Yong is intentional about excluding manuscript notes when he preaches, even though he may carry to the platform some type of outline (as he describes in his prologue). His mentor, Robert Neville, a Methodist theologian and preacher, writes out his sermons.[34] Yong quips that he does not write out his sermons at some level due to being un-motivated; but he admits that

---

33. Yong, *Renewing Christian Theology*, 208; see also Yong, *Theology and Down Syndrome*, and *The Bible, the Church, and Disability*.

34. There are a number of Neville sermon volumes available, including *The God Who Beckons* and *Preaching the Gospel*.

it is "largely because I've never been close to reading my sermons, it's just not the thing to do in the Pentecostal tradition."

Not writing out sermons has a long history in the Pentecostal movement.[35] For instance, at the Azusa Street Revival, leaders did not value using manuscript notes for preaching, due to their desire for the spontaneous leading of the Spirit while preaching.[36] This approach was not only taken during the early years of the Pentecostal movement, but continues to be reflected among some of the leaders within the Pentecostal movement today, like Crabtree for example. On the one hand, Crabtree acknowledges the importance of putting together a manuscript of the sermon. He admits that one of the weaknesses of Pentecostal preaching has been the "reluctance to write out sermons"; writing out sermons is an opportunity for preachers to study the Word and carefully articulate the message "under the guidance of the Holy Spirit."[37] On the other hand, he admits that he personally does not preach with notes; he argues that how one uses the manuscript is ultimately "immaterial," other than it allows the preacher to sufficiently prepare.[38] One important reason that Pentecostal preachers prefer not using a sermon manuscript during the delivery of the message among Pentecostals is that it ensures the sermon is delivered with a sense of spontaneity. And this spontaneity reflects the value of providing opportunity for the Spirit to move "in the moment," so that a preacher is not so stuck to the notes that they are unable to change direction as the Spirit leads in that present moment of delivery.[39]

Yong's unwillingness to make use of manuscript notes during sermon delivery finds precedence in the Pentecostal tradition he belongs to, though his difference from most Pentecostal preachers is notable (if you'll excuse the pun). With an extremely deep and varied theological vision, Yong is quite capable of addressing numerous theological issues. Thus, if he does not stick to "the script," he has much to offer from the riches of his diverse theological studies. Yong does not fall into what some Pentecostal preachers might be tempted to do when they veer from

35. The early church fathers, such as Chrysostom and Augustine, also preached without notes. It wasn't until the sixteenth and seventeenth centuries among Protestant Reformers in England that the practice of writing out sermons and reading from them became more standard practice. See Webb, "Without Notes," 429.

36. Bartleman, *Azusa Street*, 62–63; Liardon, *The Azusa Street Revival*, 109.

37. Crabtree, *Pentecostal Preaching*, 193.

38. Crabtree, *Pentecostal Preaching*, 193.

39. Schmit, "Manuscript," 394; Webb, "Without Notes," 430.

sermon manuscript notes, which is to depend on the same handful of topics that they are familiar with. Growing up in a Pentecostal church context, it is not unusual to find a preacher who does not use manuscript notes drawing from such repertoires. But if, as Jesus stated in John 14:26, the Spirit brings things back to remembrance, then the deeper one is in the Scriptures on the theological tradition, the greater depth one can offer as one relies on the Spirit in one's preaching. Preaching without notes can be an opportunity to be open to the Spirit's present leading, but it can also potentially showcase the preacher's shallow approach to and knowledge-base of Scripture. Following Yong's approach, then, might be fitting for other preachers, as long as they are willing to be thorough in their theological studies.

Call and response ~ Another important dimension of Yong's style that is important to highlight is his regular use of the call and response approach to preaching, which is also related to the Spirit's work in preaching. The call and response approach to preaching refers to the "pattern of verbal interplay between preacher and congregation that occurs during the sermon and shapes its delivery."[40] The participation of the congregation can showcase the Spirit's activity in the congregation, not just the preacher.

In the following sermons, it would not be unusual to hear our preacher saying "Amen?" during a sermon, inviting the congregation to respond with an "amen!" And Yong does not just reserve this approach to preaching to his Pentecostal friends; he will make use of this approach amongst those who are not in a Pentecostal setting. For instance, near the beginning of his sermon at a Presbyterian church (sermon 11 in this book), he says: "Somebody say Amen. So now I'm a Pentecostal preacher, I'm going to need a little help this morning. So when I lift up my hand, give me a good old 'amen.'" You can tell from hearing these interplays during the sermon, that there is a sense of great energy among both the preacher and congregation when this happens. There is a sense that the congregation is not just passively sitting and hearing, but is participating in the sermon.

The call and response approach to preaching has broad precedent within (and beyond) the Pentecostal movement, primarily through the African American influence upon Pentecostalism.[41] William J. Seymour,

40. Smith, "Call and Response," 297.

41. The eminent Pentecostal scholar, Walter J. Hollenweger, points out the black root of Pentecostalism (*Pentecostalism*, 18–19).

an African American and one of the pioneers of the Pentecostal movement, led the Azusa Street Revival making use of the call and response form in his preaching.[42] And since the Azusa Street Revival is noted for popularizing the initial Pentecostal movement, particularly related to corporate worship, it is understandable that this approach to preaching has become more normative in Pentecostal contexts that may not even be African American.[43]

The inclusion of the call and response form in Yong's preaching is quite revealing about the influence of the African American preaching tradition upon it. He explains that when he was a student at Bethany Bible College, right out of high school, he and some of his friends would attend Faith Deliverance Center in East Oakland, California. He explains that Asian American Assemblies of God students like himself enjoyed participating in these church services at the end of the week, where they would get "charged" up, and how he observed there a three-way conversation between the preacher, organ, and congregation. His father was also a Pentecostal preacher, but did not use this call and response approach to preaching. Thus, Yong admits it's likely while at this church in Oakland that he not only began to appreciate the call and response form, but also was influenced enough by it to make use of it himself. It may seem odd to some that a Pentecostal with an Asian-American background might borrow from the African American tradition. But the Pentecostal tradition has black roots, so that an ethos of preaching developed within the African American tradition has incredible affinities within the Pentecostal movement.[44] Pentecostals who are not African American, then, who engage in the act of preaching in a way that makes use of something like the call and response form of preaching, showcase the close relationship and influence of the African American preaching tradition upon Pentecostals.

Yong argues that the benefit of the call and response approach to preaching is that it can engender communality and ecclesiality unlike any other act in preaching.[45] Preachers who feel comfortable making use of the call and response approach to preaching will find it fruitful, in that it encourages active listening and participation of the congregation. And

42. Robeck, *The Azusa Street Mission and Revival*, 117–19.

43. See also the work of African American Pentecostal homileticians Luke Powery, *Spirit Speech*, and William C. Turner, *Preaching that Makes the Word Plain*.

44. Yong, "The Spirit and Proclamation," 21.

45. Yong, "The Spirit and Proclamation," 36.

even those who find the call and response approach to preaching too unnatural for their own style, might want to use a more formal approach to getting the congregation involved by inviting questions and comments following the sermon.

Passion and intellect ~ Another important dimension of preaching worth noting, particularly in light of Yong's Pentecostal heritage and scholarly credentials, is the interplay of passion and intellect as it relates to the Spirit. Quite often, the stereotype of some Pentecostal preaching is one of hype—one in which the preacher is so passionate and emotional that he or she can sometimes minimize theological content in the message. On the other hand, scholars can sometimes be stereotyped among Pentecostals as too academic, dry, and technical. Yong, however, blends passion and intellectual rigor in ways that not all Pentecostals and scholars can. When asked about influences, Yong pointed to two homiletical exemplars. If African American preaching provided for him a holistic approach to preaching, a "fully embodied experience," where both intellect and affections are included in the act of preaching,[46] these two communicators sheds light on how such embodiment integrated both passion and intellect.

The first model preacher Yong recalls is itinerant minister Dave Roever, a Vietnam vet who experienced great suffering from the war, but used his experiences as the springboard to testify of God's work in his life.[47] Roever used to preach annually at Bethany Bible College's chapel service and stood out as "funny, engaging, and provocative." Yong's preaching reflects some of these same elements. For example, he always opens up with something humorous, reflecting Roever's sense of humor. Yong acknowledges that some of the jokes he regularly uses likely came from Roever himself.

The other preacher of note is Assemblies of God minister Rick Howard, who also taught both the book of Hebrews and Revelation at Bethany Bible College. Yong's book, *The Spirit Poured Out on All Flesh*, is dedicated to Howard (and two others). Howard's excellence in teaching indelibly marked Yong variously: 1) impressing on him the importance of scriptural exposition; 2) demonstrating how biblical exposition involved

46. See also Yong, "The Spirit and Proclamation," 21.

47. Roever's ministry website explains that while he was serving in the U.S. Navy in Vietnam, he was "burned beyond recognition when a phosphorous grenade he was poised to throw exploded in his hand." See www.roeverfoundation.org/meet_dave_roever.php.

scholarship; and 3) fusing exhortatory passion with intellectual content. Howard's ability to merge intellectual content with authentic passion stood out as distinctive from other Pentecostal leaders and preachers. Yong has adopted for himself Howard's unique approach to teaching and preaching.

A willingness to merge intellectual rigor with passion are sometimes what is lacking in Pentecostal contexts. Preachers who exhibit intellectual rigor are sometimes stereotyped by Pentecostals as lacking the Spirit's empowerment and too focused on "head knowledge." On the other hand, preachers who exhibit great passion in the pulpit but lack theological depth from the pulpit are sometimes stereotyped by Pentecostals as truly "anointed"—though the content of their sermons may all be to merely "hype" up the crowd with clichés. Integrating intellectual rigor with passion fueled by the Holy Spirit's enabling is a worthy goal for all preachers.[48] Readers of the rest of this book are invited to observe how intellectual rigor and gospel passion can converge in preaching.

Now that we have covered some of the theological and homiletical issues related to Amos Yong's preaching, we get to turn our attention to the fifteen sermons in this book. As you read them, we must be reminded of the obvious: that they were originally created for oral presentation, not written. Imagine yourself maybe sitting among the congregation, hearing what you are reading. Some context on each sermon is provided on the chapter/sermon title page, footnoted with a "*" that will clarify and provide background. Yong contextualizes his sermons to his audiences, whether with relevant illustrations, geographical markers, or even jokes. All except sermon number 3 in this book is linked to audio and/or video recordings. For audio recordings, please see http://bit.ly/amos_yong_audio; for video of sermons 2, 9, and 12, please see http://bit.ly/amos_yong_video.

Finally, I want to highlight two added benefits of this book. First, in the following Prologue, Amos Yong provides helpful biographical information to help understand him as a preacher. Yong also puts forward a theology of preaching especially relevant for our day in the Epilogue. Thus, we not only get his sermons in this book, but an inside look at his life and views on preaching, which will prove valuable for those interested in Yong's life, ministry, and theology. Second, Tony Richie agreed to provide valuable reflections on our colleague's ministry of preaching.

48. I address this in "The Spirit in Pentecostal Preaching" and *The Holy Spirit in Worship Music, Preaching, and the Altar.*

Richie is not only a scholar and theologian who teaches at Pentecostal Theological Seminary (Cleveland, Tennessee), but is an ordained bishop in the Church of God (Cleveland, Tennessee) and full-time senior pastor at New Harvest Church of God in Knoxville, Tennessee. Richie is one of those voices within the Pentecostal tradition who offers both scholarly and pastoral insight—his perspectives on Yong's preaching is valuable in that this book straddles both the church and academic worlds. Richie offers reflections interspersed throughout the sermons, as well as in the afterword. And beyond Richie's thoughtful intellectual insights, Richie is a genuinely caring and thoughtful leader, characteristics that are evident in his writing.

It is my desire that as you begin your reading and/or listening of Amos Yong's sermons, may you not merely read/hear a famous scholar preach, but receive the word of the Lord for you today through the power of the Spirit.

Prologue

Some autobiographical perspective perhaps best sets the stage for the reading of the sermons to come.[1] I will begin with some of the personal details, shift to discussion of my sermon preparation and homiletical style, and then make connections between my preaching and my scholarship. Those interested in the content of the sermons can surely go straight to the first chapter. I hope there will be treasure discernible there and in the rest of the book, but the evident shortcomings throughout might be illuminated by the fact that these messages have been delivered through nothing less than a "clay jar" (2 Cor 4:7a). These few pages preceding those homilies, then, clarify why that is the case.

The Vocation of a Pentecostal Preacher

My father was a Pentecostal preacher, credentialed in the early 1960s with the Assemblies of God in Malaysia, long before I was conceived. My earliest memories were of his pastoral work in a small village, Taiping. Then in 1969, he moved to take up the pastorate of Glad Tidings Assembly, the congregation associated with the Bible College of Malaya, in one of the suburbs of Kuala Lumpur. This grew to become a vibrant ecclesial community, no doubt invigorated by the many students present who were zealous in working out their initial calls to ministry.

My parents moved us to Stockton, California, in 1976, to take up a small "home missions" church under the Northern California-Nevada District of the American Assemblies of God, serving primarily Chinese-speaking immigrants in the Stockton area, but operating bilingually since

---

1. I agree with McClendon, Jr., *Biography as Theology*, and here in this book I therefore suggest an autobiography-as-homiletics approach, at least in this portion of the book that is the prologue.

the children preferred English. This was always a small and struggling work, so that my coming of age during my teens left me with the feeling that church work and pastoral ministry was challenging and unrewarding. The glory of the larger congregation in Malaysia had faded against the realities of immigrant life and religiosity in California.[2] I did not foresee myself following in my father's footsteps.

But during my high school years, I gradually became the de facto leader of the small youth group. We had a strong Bible quiz team that competed against other immigrant churches, and out of that a tight-knit group of youth emerged. It was during my junior year, then, that I acquiesced to be open to the ministry if that was what God had in store for me. I therefore went to the more-or-less local—125 miles and a two-hour drive away—Bethany Bible College, also affiliated with the Assemblies of God, and devoted myself to completing a degree in ministerial studies.

Although Bethany closed in 2009, my four years there, from 1983–87, were transformative. I took a wide range of ministry-preparation courses, including hermeneutics and homiletics. During the fall term of my sophomore year, I wrote a 150-page hermeneutical study on 1 Peter 4:1–6, learning about exegesis in order to lay the groundwork for pulpit ministry.[3] During the spring term of the final year of my bachelor's degree, I applied for and received my ministerial credentials with the Northern California-Nevada District of the Assemblies of God, and two weeks after graduation—and one week after we got married—my wife and I started as youth pastors at the Assembly of God Church in Fairfield, California.

Our experience as youth ministers did not go as well as planned for a variety of reasons, not least because our cross-cultural marriage (Alma is of Mexican American descent) was not something we were adequately prepared for. We left after one year dejected, and took time off to get to know one another and attempt to secure our marriage on a better foundation. It has now been over thirty years of marriage and, while our relationship is not perfect, we are grateful for the gifts of grace and love afforded to us. But the first years were surely difficult. I enrolled in seminary (Western Evangelical Seminary, then George Fox Seminary, and now recently Portland Seminary) in part because I was not sure how to proceed in the ministry in light of the challenges before us, but I knew that I could at least study and be a good student!

2. I returned to revisit these aspects of Asian American immigrant Christianity later in my, *The Future of Evangelical Theology*, ch. 6.

3. Yong, "Persevering through 1 Peter."

My seminary studies in a non-Pentecostal environment raised questions that I did not have answers for at that time. At one point, I went to the Northwest District office of the Assemblies of God—we were then living and serving in a church in Vancouver, Washington—and the questions I countered with during the interview process led the church officials to tell me to figure out answers before taking next steps to move from being a licensed to an ordained minister with the denomination. I eventually made my peace with the Assemblies of God,[4] but by then I was much further down the theological path toward academia, with the result that I have never returned to attempt to "upgrade" my credentials. As a licensed minister, however, I am legally authorized to baptize, marry, bury, etc., so my primary location in theological education has not required ordination.

My ecclesial resume after Fairfield includes the following "stops": informal associate pastoral work at Turning Point Christian Center in Vancouver, Washington, from 1990–95; formal (partially paid, even!) associate pastoral work at New Beginnings Christian Fellowship (Assemblies of God) in Mansfield, Massachusetts, from 1996–98 (while I was a doctoral student at Boston University); and active lay ministry at Olivet Baptist Church (Baptist General Conference) in Crystal, Minnesota, from 1999–2005 and at Great Bridge Presbyterian Church (Presbyterian Church, U.S.A.) in Chesapeake, Virginia, from 2006–14. During the fifteen years in Minnesota and Virginia, I was given the opportunity to preach at both of these churches on various occasions.

Over the last three decades as a credentialed Assemblies of God minister, however, I have also been active in a wide range of pulpit supply activities. Bethel University, where I taught theology from 1999–2005, regularly would send me out to churches in the Baptist General Conference (now Converge: https://converge.org/) who would call in to the ministry office when they would need a preacher. As my publication record expanded, I would receive various invitations to preach from churches whose pastors realized that I was in town for conferences or other scholarly or academic events. In short, although I have not served as a senior pastor of any local congregation, I have been honored to be given the opportunity to preach over the years in many different churches and contexts.

---

4. My *Renewing Christian Theology* is based on the World Assemblies of God Fellowship's Statement of Faith.

Sermon Preparation and Homiletical Style

As a Pentecostal preacher's kid—and then later a Pentecostal missionary-kid—I grew up listening to all kinds of Pentecostal sermons. I imbibed two scriptural truths in these formative years: first, "But you will receive power when the Holy Spirit has come upon you; and you will be my witnesses in Jerusalem, in all Judea and Samaria, and to the ends of the earth" (Acts 1:8), and second, "open your mouth wide and I will fill it" (Ps 81:10). The former instilled in me the sense that verbal proclamation of the gospel was dependent on the anointing and empowerment of the Holy Spirit while the latter suggested subordination of human preparation to divine initiative. These were received as complementary truths so that even though we were trained at Bethany to prepare our sermons,[5] the more important ways to get ready were to nurture the spiritual life.

From that perspective, I have never written out my sermons but have always worked off notes. Although the steps that I have taken to get these notes together has developed over the years, the basic elements can be identified here in logical order if not always unfolding in chronological sequence. First, I take into account to the degree possible the context of the anticipated sermon. What do I know about the congregation or audience, how large is it, how long are sermons usually, what is the occasion if more specific than a general Sunday (e.g., is it New Year's, Mother's Day, communion Sunday, and so on)? What is the "season" for this context? If in a church, what have the members been going through recently, or has there been a series that the pastor has been preaching through lately? I will usually attend to these contextual matters, even if I find ways to connect to these realities via themes that are also central to my theological work (on which more in a moment).

Second, then, my Bethany Bible College days impressed upon me that Pentecostal preaching was not antithetical to expository preaching, so the next step is to identify a scriptural passage as the focal springboard for the sermon. To be sure, Pentecostal expositions of Scripture may not be recognized as such by those in other ecclesial traditions, but the point is that we were at least taught to stay as close to sacred writ as possible. We learned about the differences between *exegesis* and *eisegesis*, wary about our Pentecostal predilections toward the latter imposition

---

5. My homiletics class included classical Pentecostal sources as well as more ecumenical manuals, including Methodist theologian Killinger, *Fundamentals of Preaching*.

of our own ideas on the scriptural text and always seeking instead the former practice of deriving our message from the Bible. If we were to gain respectability within the evangelical circles with which we are allied, Pentecostal emotionalism needed to be disciplined by sound exegetical and expository preaching. A growing number of us are recognizing that the lines between exegesis and eisegesis are not as hard and fast in reality as in theory,[6] but commitment to the authority of Scripture usually means that few of us will take license with the text unless the openings are discernible therein.

Third, then, my Bible college training gave me some tools to unpack the text in question. I had a year of biblical Greek and a semester of biblical Hebrew, but the latter never played a major role in my own scriptural study even as the former was facilitated as much by English-language resources than my fluency in the original New Testament language. In any case, I read commentaries, and consult other helps to understand the background and literary genre of the text I feel compelled to focus on.

Then, I draft an outline of notes, more often than not attempting to follow the text and then connect the text to contemporary realities and issues. Earlier in my preaching career, these would be handwritten, on three- or four-inch by six-inch sheets of paper (I had many of these still saved in my file cabinet), but in the last almost two decades drafted electronically and then printed out for the delivery.

Last but not least, preparation involves internalizing the outline as much as possible. I used to practice preaching through my sermons beforehand, although I do that much less now. Yet the goal is to have a good sense of the major movement of the sermon, ensure that the important points are memorized, and know where I ought to be going, all in order to minimize dependence or reliance on the actual notes that I will bring to the podium or platform with me. Throughout, but not least in these moments of final preparation and internalization, this process is enveloped in prayer, for me, for my listeners, and for our interaction.

Homiletically, in terms of preaching format and style, the following are noticeable characteristics or elements.[7] Start with a joke or story that connects with the audience at an affective and interpersonal level. Pentecostal call-and-response is a regular part of my repertoire; even for

6. The overarching frame within which I situate myself vis-à-vis this fine line between exegesis and eisegesis is articulated in my book, *Spirit-Word-Community*.

7. More theoretical perspective is provided in my essay, "Proclamation and the Third Article."

non-Pentecostal audiences, I oftentimes will invite their (limited) participation through allowing expressions of Amens at different moments of
the sermon. Alternatively, hand gestures are effective means of inviting
response, for instance, putting the hand behind the ear in order to summons audience reaction. Avoid looking to the notes that I bring, if at all
possible, so that I be as focused on and engaged with the audience or
congregation as possible. Be sure to meet my listeners where they are at,
appealing regularly and frequently to local news or realities, connecting
with what is happening in the community, perhaps linking to developments in the service prior to when I got up to preach, etc. Lastly, seek to
move my listeners toward a decision, whether intellectually, emotionally,
or practically.

As it is likely that I will be introduced as a scholar or theologian, that
is presumed but not otherwise something I make much of. To be sure, I
will draw occasionally on the Greek (less so the Hebrew) and will surely
attempt to situate the scriptural text in its original historical context. But
these are translations from the scholarly to the ecclesial, with the focus
on accessibility to laypersons and relevance for their lives, to the best that
such can be discerned.

Apostolic Preaching—Then and Now

As I have published mostly as a Pentecostal theologian, I have also come
to recognize my vocation as a Pentecostal preacher. When addressing
Pentecostal churches or audiences, then, my goal is to open up another,
perhaps more intellectual, dimension to Pentecostal sermonizing than
they might usually be used to, but without neglecting the Pentecostal
style. When addressing non-Pentecostal contexts, on the other hand, I
give permission for others to inhabit for those moments a more Pente-
costalized space and experience that they may have previously shared
and miss or than that they might be used to. To accomplish both goals,
I usually preach from out of my scholarship and theological efforts. This
can be observed best by following the trajectory of my publications, at
least those that have attended to scriptural themes and topics.

For starters, my fourth monograph, *The Spirit Poured Out on All
Flesh: Pentecostalism and the Possibility of Global Theology* deployed a
Lukan interpretive frame.[8] More specifically, it is the book of Acts—the

---

8. Yong, *The Spirit Poured Out on All Flesh.*

immediate scriptural site for understanding the Day of Pentecost, which is at the heart of the modern and contemporary Pentecostal message and way of life—that provides the structure for what I present as a Pentecostal theology with global purchase. Luke's second book thus provides the frame for my Pentecostal and pneumatological soteriology, ecclesiology, and theology. On the one hand, it might be said that my Pentecostal theology is a theology of and from the book of Acts; on the other hand, it might also be said that Acts is the canon-within-the-canon that opens up to the wider scriptural horizon.

This Lukan-imagination or Acts-hermeneutic is developed next in the political theology project that finds its culmination in two books: *In the Days of Caesar: Pentecostalism and Political Theology*, and *Who Is the Holy Spirit? A Walk with the Apostles.*[9] The former includes one subsection on Luke-Acts (sometimes Luke, sometimes Acts, sometimes both) that appears in the third section of each of the five chapters that constitute the constructive argument for a Pentecostal political theology. The latter also cover the terrain of political or public theology, but does so as a series of Bible studies, starting in and working through the book of Acts' twenty-eight chapters in order, but punctuated in every other chapter of *Who Is the Holy Spirit* with what is in effect a reading backward, i.e., by reflecting on the Third Gospel. The point there is to follow the apostolic experience unfolding amidst the *Pax Romana* while recognizing that their commitments were informed by their memories of Jesus, his life, death, and resurrection. Together, however, these books effectively written—albeit published within a few months of each other—develop the Lukan theological vision, even if extended in the direction of political and public theology. Important to register in this regard is that the political is a reality intrinsic to the apostolic experience, even as that means that the scriptural accounts provide a lens through which to see, and a reality through which to inhabit, contemporary political life and witness.

The last book I will mention is also the most recent predecessor to this series of my "Spirit" books: *The Hermeneutical Spirit: Theological Interpretation and the Scriptural Imagination for the 21st Century.*[10] In many respects, these are companion volumes: *Hermeneutical Spirit* lays out the interpretive principles related to my reading of Luke-Acts in particular while *Kerygmatic Spirit* shows how these interpretive commitments are

---

9. See Yong, *In the Days of Caesar* and *Who is the Holy Spirit?*

10. Yong, *The Hermeneutical Spirit.*

exemplified in preaching and proclamation of the gospel. The other reason why they ought to be read together is that two thirds of the sermons
in this book (from sermon number 6 onwards) come from the years
2014–17, even as more than half of the chapters in the other book derive
from this same period. In other words, these volumes together provide a
window into my reading and preaching of Scripture, Luke-Acts specifically but also beyond these scriptural sections.

To be sure, much of my other published books involve significant
forays into Scripture. *The Bible, Disability, and the Church: A New Vision
of the People of God* is effectively a biblical theology of disability and provides the broader backdrop to appreciate at least one of the sermons in
the coming pages (number 5 below).[11] Perhaps more widely pertinent is
Renewing Christian Theology: Systematics for a Global Christianity, which
connects scriptural interpretation to dogmatic theological loci: each of
the eleven doctrinal chapters includes two biblical sections—one about a
biblical character and another being a treatment of one New Testament
book (Gospel or letter, etc.) that provides the most direct point of scriptural entry into the theological or doctrinal theme being treated.[12] Yet
while both volumes illuminate the scriptural hermeneutic that undergirds my homiletical endeavors, neither is as widely relevant for the full
scope of the present book as the others mentioned above.

I should emphasize that rhetorically and stylistically, I teach very
differently than I preach. In my pedagogical mode, I am most comfortable
in seminar format, adopting a Socratic methodology that foregrounds
dialogical and exploratory mutuality. In a sense, the call-and-response
dynamics of Pentecostal sermonizing is also conversational, albeit the
Pentecostal preacher in me embraces without hesitation a more direct
communicative posture.

In terms of content, however, those who are familiar with my theological *oeuvre* should be able to recognize that Amos Yong the teacher
and Amos Yong the preacher are working in the same theological field.
If Yong the teacher is in some respects a methodological restorationist
that looks back to the apostolic narrative and seeks to receive that testimony for contemporary reflection, then Yong the preacher is also in
those same respects a hermeneutical primitivist that draws from those

---

11. Yong, *The Bible, Disability, and the Church.*

12. Yong and Anderson, *Renewing Christian Theology.*

apostolic wellsprings to resource Christian faithfulness and discipleship in the present era.

For those who come to this book first and foremost not because you are familiar with my theological work and more because you are interested in what apostolic preaching means for today, my prayer is that you may discover that and perhaps much more, specifically that you might recover preaching not only about but also in the Holy Spirit.

For both sets of readers, I will meet you again on the other side—the epilogue—to see if we might be able to distill certain overarching principles about apostolic proclamation for the third millennium.

1

Hitchhiking Hellenist 2

Acts 7:58 — 8:1

West Ridge Community Church, Pittsburgh, Pennsylvania, 1 March 2009*

[Host pastor introduces the preacher, sharing their common background at Bible College, his father's missionary work, and the influence of missions on Yong.]

Are you ready to receive from the Lord this morning [interjects during host pastor's introduction]? Praise the Lord! It's good to be with you here this morning. This is my first visit to Pittsburgh. We've driven by Pittsburgh before on the freeway, right? But that's not really experiencing Pittsburgh. Hallelujah!

Well, as we were collecting the offering early this morning, your pastor was expressing the glory of the Lord! Amen? I was reminded of a story of a pastor who had been a couple years with the congregation. He had been brought in to pastor this church from out of town. Been there a couple years, and getting ready to launch a capital campaign drive. So,

---

* The pastor of West Ridge Community Church was Bill Bolin, one of my roommates at Bethany College of the Assemblies of God in the mid-1980s. During one of my visits to the Association of Theological Schools in Pittsburgh, I was invited to minister at West Ridge. Bill was preaching through the book of Acts and the previous week spoke on Stephen, who he called the "Hitchhiking Hellenist." My title, then, sought to follow Bill's lead, albeit focusing on the end of Stephen's life.

he got up before the congregation one morning, and said, "Church, the Lord's been speaking to us, we need to learn, been going now for a couple years, and we need to learn how to sit and crawl as a church." The church said, "Make us crawl, Rev, make us crawl." "And after we learn how to crawl, church, then we're going to have to learn how to stand." "Make us stand, Rev, make us stand!" "And after we learn how to stand, we'll have to learn how to walk." Somebody said, "Make us walk, Rev, make us walk!" "And after we learn how to walk, we'll have to learn how to run!" "Make us run, Rev, make us run!" "And in order for us to run, we need money!" "Make us crawl, Rev, make us crawl!" [laughter among congregation].

I know a lot of you have your Bibles with you this morning. If you do, I'd like you to turn with me to the book of Acts, chapter 7. Your pastor has got his sermons up on the church website, or his own website. And I was waiting on the Lord last night, or yesterday afternoon, . . . thinking about what the Lord would have me share. Hellenist Hitchhiker.[1] What a marvelous image. And the sequel is what you're gonna hear this morning. Hellenist Hitchhiker 2. Now if you've watched the Star Wars series . . . Remember that Star Wars series? Where, you know, each successive movie, it doesn't quite go in chronological, right? You know, you make a few different twists and turns, you catch up, fill in the gaps a little bit. Well folks, Hellenist Hitchhiker 2 is like one of those plots this morning, right? I know you have sort of been introduced to Hellenist Hitchhiker 2. But today we're going to go back and pick up a little bit about the early moments, the emergence, the introduction of Hellenist Hitchhiker 2.

We're going to start in verse number 57, in the seventh chapter of Acts:

> [57]At this they covered their ears and, yelling at the top of their voices, they all rushed at him, [58]dragged him out of the city and began to stone him. Meanwhile, the witnesses laid their clothes at the feet of a young man named Saul. [59]While they were stoning him, Stephen prayed, "Lord Jesus, receive my spirit." [60]Then he fell on his knees and cried out, "Lord, do not hold this sin against them." [As Yong spoke Stephen's declaration in verse 60 loudly, he says as an aside:]—Probably wasn't that loud. I imagine that he may have barely breathed that out.—When he had said this, he fell asleep. [8:1]And Saul was there, giving approval to

---

1. Clearly, for much of the rest of the sermon, I referred to Stephen as the "Hellenist hitchhiker" rather than the "hitchhiking Hellenist," which was the original title of the sermon, following Rev. Bolin's original title.

his death. On that day a great persecution broke out against the church at Jerusalem, and all except the apostles were scattered throughout Judea and Samaria (NIV).

Bow with me in prayer this morning. Spirit of the living God, you who enabled Stephen to cry out, you who enabled Stephen to call out, you who enabled Stephen to forgive, and you who was on the shoulder of Saul: abide in our time. Abide in our moments this morning. Be here with us this morning, and transform our hearts, in Jesus' name. And all God's people said, Amen. And Amen.

Well, you know a little bit about Hellenist hitchhikers, don't you? I think in your pastor's sermon, which I, . . . now, you've got to understand, right: I wasn't here for the original Hellenist Hitchhiker 1. How many of you were here for the original Hellenist Hitchhiker 1? Now I see some of you weren't here for the original Hellenist Hitchhiker 1 either, right? So, what I've got was a sort of the script, without the fancy lights, without the amazing stunts that go along with the movie. Isn't that what happens in church? Somebody say Amen! Alright!

So, I've got the bare script of Hellenist Hitchhiker 1, but we know from the movie, the original release, that of course Hellenist Hitchhiker 1 concerns these people: Stephen and Philip, who were Hellenists, right? And what are Hellenists, as you know from Hellenist Hitchhiker 1? They are folks that grew up in what's called the Jewish diaspora around the Mediterranean world. Jews, who for one reason or another, over perhaps even a few hundred years had been [sent through] exile around the world, around the Mediterranean world. And they've grown up in these other cultures, they've grown up learning how to speak in probably two or three or four languages, just to survive. And they were certainly fluent in Greek.

And of course, a lot of these Hellenist Jews would come back periodically to the homeland, Amen? Come back to visit their long-lost—or maybe not lost, because if they were lost I supposed they would not be visiting, right?—but they would come back to visit their relatives. And in fact, we know that Acts chapter 2 was precisely one of those occasions. One of these wonderful feast days in which diaspora Jews from around the Mediterranean would make their way back to Jerusalem to celebrate the Feast of Pentecost. And of course, we know what happened on that day, when the Lord poured out his Spirit upon all of those Jews who gathered from all around the Mediterranean world. But Hellenist

Jews were Jews that were conflicted. On the one hand, they belonged to the wider world. On the one hand, they had learned how to plant gardens and grow crops. They had learned how to be successful, they were fluent in the language of the Empire. They had sort of accommodated themselves to some degree, and made it in the big world. But yet they were Jews, weren't they? Hellenistic Jews were conflicted. They came back to Jerusalem. Why? Because of the promise of the temple. They came back to Jerusalem because it was the promise of the Lord to one day restore the land to Abraham, Isaac, and Jacob, and their descendants. Somebody say Amen! They longed for that time. They yearned for God's bringing about the fulfillment of the covenant promises. The land, the temple, and the blessings. So, they bided their time. They kept their ear to the ground, waiting for news of the Messiah. Why? Because the Messiah would be one who would deliver Israel from its enemies, Amen? The Messiah would be one who would not only deliver Israel, but would vindicate Israel from its enemies. Now delivering is just this one thing. Casting out the foreign rule from land is one thing. To vindicate, however, means to justify. It's to say "My promises are not in vain." To vindicate is to demonstrate to one's enemies, that this is still my chosen people. So, it's not only a matter of eliminating the Romans from the land, but it's a matter of vindicating the law, the promises of God. Hellenists were a conflicted people. On the one hand, successful in the wider world. On the other hand, still perhaps hoping, longing: "Maybe if not me, it will be my grandkids that will get back to the land at some point."

Hellenist Hitchhiker 1 involved the ending of the life of one of these Hellenist Jews, as you know. His name was Stephen. Our passage this morning starts with, or picks up sort of in the middle of Hellenist Hitchhiker 0, which you never heard that sermon, I suppose. Picks up right in the middle of the sermon of Stephen's. And it said they dragged him out of the city. They stoned him: "These witnesses," verse 58. How many of you here are witnesses this morning? Amen? "These witnesses laid their clothes at the feet of a young man named Saul." Now, who were these witnesses? Well, they're actually other Hellenist Hitchhikers. If you turn the page, and go back to the first part of chapter 6, the middle of chapter 6, it introduces Stephen's ministry. Now of course, there [is an] irony about these Hellenists like Stephen, right? The apostles had anointed and prayed upon them, blessed them with the Holy Spirit to go out and to serve tables, so that they, the apostles, could focus on the preaching and the praying and the ministry of the word. But instead, the Holy Spirit empowers this Hellenist Jew, Stephen, the preacher who proclaims the gospel. Verse 9 says this, "an opposition arose, however, from members of the Synagogue of the Freedmen, . . . Jews from Cyrene and Alexandria as well as the provinces of Cilicia and Asia." But what [or who] were these Hellenistic Jews? Hellenistic Jews, that in this case, were specifically Jews that had been slaves but also had received their freedom? The Empire had a number of different policies for dealing with what's called expatriate slaves, slaves that had been in one part of the Empire, and were allowed to return to their homes.

Some of you might be familiar with the history of the African Americans in North America. The country of Liberia was set up precisely as that kind of a program, in order to allow Africans, who had been brought as slaves to America, to go back to Africa. These freedmen represented a kind of policy, like what happened with the Liberian experiment.

And of course, these freedmen came back to their homeland. Why did they come back to their homeland? Well it's the promised land. It's the land of the covenant. It's the land given to Abraham, Isaac, and Jacob. And maybe, just maybe, in our lifetime we will see, and hear, and experience the deliverance of the Messiah. Somebody say Amen! They were there. They had replanted themselves in the community. But they began to argue with Stephen. In fact, verse 11, they persuaded some men, saying "we've heard this Stephen speak words of blasphemy against Moses and against God." They stirred up the people, and elders, and teachers of the law. They seized Stephen and brought him before the Sanhedrin. They produced these witnesses, that we saw in verse 58, who testified: "This fellow never stops speaking against this holy place and against the law. For we have heard him say that this Jesus of Nazareth will destroy this place and change the customs that Moses has handed down to us." Here were zealous, Hellenistic Jews. They were zealous because they had been enslaved, but they had sensed the hand of Yahweh upon their lives, who had got their freedom for them. And now had allowed them to return to the land of promise. They were optimistic. Cautiously so. They were looking for the deliverance of the Lord.

But now here was one of their own members, another Hellenist Jew, who represented not this conservative Jewish posture toward the tradition. But he represented what was a threatening Jewish approach. And in fact, people like Stephen represented those Jews who had appeared to have gotten too comfortable in the Diaspora. Why? Because they were willing to sort of minimize the importance of the law. Why were they willing to do that? Well, they were being adapted to the wider culture. They had become successful in the wider world. And now they were willing to sort of compromise, just a little bit, the distinctive Jewish commitments and values and culture. In fact, these Hellenistic Jews, like Stephen, they were even saying that the temple wasn't even all that important after all.

Now if we're going to really preach the gospel that was handed down to us, from the prophets and from Moses, should we be minimizing the role of the temple? Should we be minimizing the laws that were handed down to us? Because that threatens what? The covenant promises of God. We would be very cautious to do that, wouldn't we? Well, this is an intra-Hellenist debate, as you can see, right? How many of you know what I'm talking about, right?

You know it's kind of like, I'm called a 1.5 generation Asian American. You know what that means? It means I was born . . . here's what it is. First generation folks are those who move to the [new] country when they are sort of older. That's what my folks are: first generation Asian Americans. Second generation Asian Americans are kids who were born in America to Asian parents. I'm not a second generation Asian American, I came here when I was ten. So, that makes me a 1.5'er. I didn't come when I was old, but I wasn't born here either, right? So, they gave us a label: I'm a fraction. And you know how this goes, right, if you're taking about communities, in what's called a diasporic situation, right? The first generation is real concerned with what . . . ? Preserving the way in which we used to do things. You better start speaking Chinese, "excuse me mom what did you just say?" Right? And of course, by the time you get to the 1.5'ers and the second generation, what are we all about, right? Give me my iPod! Somebody say Amen, right? Okay? I mean, it's about, I worked hard when I was a teenager, to do what? To get rid of the accent my parents gave me. Hello! Right? Why? Because it's about what? It's about fitting in, isn't it? It's about not sticking out like an . . . Asian American.

Now, how many of you know, unless there's some Native Americans in here, Amen? We're all diasporic. I mean, and we got some folks from some really strange countries, like California. And strange folks in California, we'll see how the second generation, right, adapts to this country called Pittsburgh. Okay? Now diasporic experiences are filled with these kinds of tensions. We're learning how to adapt to a new environment. And of course, the more we become like the new environment, the less we lay hold of the way we used to be, before we got to the new environment.

The debate amongst the Hellenistic Jews was precisely about what really is distinctive about being a child, a descendent, of Abraham, Isaac, and Jacob. What is distinctive about the promises, the law, and the covenant that was given to Moses? What is it about this temple? What does it represent? Is it a cultural artifact? Or is it what the histories tells us? The place where the glory of the Lord descended amidst the people of Israel? You've got the conservative Hellenists, like these freedmen from the synagogues around the Mediterranean, who were holding a hard line. They didn't want to compromise the importance of the temple, they didn't want to compromise the law that was given to Moses and the prophets! They didn't want to compromise their faith, that they were the elect of God!

But their cousins, Hellenistic hitchhikers like Stephen, and like Philip, they had actually seen that, you know what? God had dispersed us through this exile from six hundred years ago in our history. And yet God has been faithful, even when we were in Cilicia,[2] even when we were in Rome, even when we were in Arabia. We didn't have the temple. But we had the presence of Yahweh, and the word of the Lord. And we met in our synagogues, and we poured over the Scriptures, and God met us there! And Stephen begins to preach this message, which you heard about a couple weeks ago. And he tells of the God of Abraham, Isaac, and Jacob, who is not a God who was limited to the Palestinian region. In fact, the God of Abraham was with Abraham when he went down to Egypt. The God of Abraham was with Abraham's descendants, as they grew up in Egypt. In fact, the God of Abraham was with Moses, who learned from the wisdom of the Egyptians. Hellenistic Jews like Stephen had begun to see and observe that the God of Abraham, Isaac, and Jacob is not the God who is merely limited to this land. But yet a God who somehow in his providential wisdom, in his inscrutable capacity to bring about and redeem, even [in] the worst of experiences—that's what exile is—God can meet us in places where we wouldn't have "thunk" he was at. God can meet us in situations that are so dire in our lives. God can be there.

And so Stephen begins to preach, the Holy Spirit came upon him, unfortunately, for the poor fellow. Because remember, they had accused him of speaking against the temple, right? They accused him of speaking against the law. Well he didn't quite speak against the law, in his sermon. But as you know, he made the mistake of speaking against the temple. And he said at the end of the sermon. "The Most High does not live,"

2. Editor's note: The recording indicates that Amos says "Cicelia" throughout the sermon, an obvious mispronunciation that is corrected in the text.

verse 48, "in houses made by men. I have *seen Yahweh in the far off regions of the Mediterranean world!*" Somebody say Amen! Even maybe in Pittsburgh? Hello? "*I have seen Yahweh fulfilling the promises of the prophets!*" In places that we thought were impure, because they were inhabited by a people of impurity.

Of course, he was talking about gentiles, right? Of course, he is talking about the Romans and the Greeks, who Yahweh was supposed to vindicate the Jews from, right? Of course, he was talking about the folks that the disciples in Acts chapter 1, remember now, after they had been with Jesus three years, they had to listen to him, they then saw his resurrection. They sat with him for forty days, as he opened the Scriptures about Moses and the prophets. And after the forty days . . . this is how slow his disciples were; they said: "So Lord now, thanks for these six weeks of teaching, this is great. But is it now time for you to restore the kingdom?" C'mon! Remember that? Chapter 1, Acts. What are they still waiting for? Vindication! They are still waiting for Yahweh to bring about the promises, according to their understanding of what those promises were. And of course, Jesus, Jesus, he would probably say, "After like six, seven weeks of like, solid, Bible school teaching here, you know? You know what, you just hang on guys. Don't worry about that kingdom stuff, you know. Umm. I'm just going to give you the Spirit, and we'll just let the Spirit take care of things." Somebody say Amen! Hello?

Stephen was full of the Spirit. Philip was full of the Spirit. And as folks full of the Spirit, they had experienced the power of God in places where their more conservative, Hellenistic Jewish brethren didn't think God could work! Hellenist Hitchhikers, like Stephen and like Philip, had perspective. Perspective from having engaged the Hellenistic world. They had the kind of perspective that allowed them to re-read and reinterpret, and make new sense of the promises of Yahweh. And that these promises from Yahweh for the restoration of Israel, maybe didn't just mean only the restoration of a government. Maybe it didn't just mean only the restoration of a certain geographically defined piece of property. Maybe the promise of the restoration of Israel, as was already suggested in the early part of the book of Luke, would include those who we thought were outside the covenant to begin with. And Hellenistic Jews, Hellenistic hitchhikers like Stephen and Philip, had seen inklings, they could see through a glass dimly. And their hearts were beginning to pitter-patter. They began to sense, that "Hey, we're on to something here! God is doing a new thing in our day! How are we gonna follow this? Well, we're going to preach it, we're going to proclaim it! Oh no, here come the stones! Lord, help me!"

Philip, of course, saw what happened, right? He says, "well, our conservative freedmen Hellenistic Jewish hitchhikers, who have returned to Israel, are not going to be our allies. I'm moving." He goes into Samaria, right? Hellenist Hitchhiker 1 involves this bold and brazen and inconceivable idea, that somehow the Samaritans, the common Samaritans [were involved]! And of course, we know that [though they are mentioned] in verse 1 of Acts chapter 8, even the apostles didn't believe that, did they? They were held up in Jerusalem, they were waiting: "Well now the Spirit has come, we're still waiting for the redemption of Israel, the restoration of the land, the vindication of the people of God!" It takes some Hellenistic hitchhikers, folks with some perspective, with some vision, and with some boldness—and with some *Holy Ghost*—to handle the stones, to risk [visiting] the Samaritans, to even hang out with Ethiopian eunuchs? Why not? If God can work in Cilicia, and Rome, why can't he work in Ethiopia? If the good news is for Jews that are dispersed into the farthest regions of the Roman Empire, why not into the lowest regions of Empire? Philip had enough perspective. He didn't see it all clearly. But he saw enough to be faithful, to take those little steps, and of course, when he couldn't take the big steps, God just whisked him, right? Said "all right, I can't get to that Ethiopian guy too quickly, I'm going to get you there like pronto."

Oh, by the way, we're supposed to be talking about Hellenist Hitchhiker 2 today, aren't we? We're sort of just reminding us of Hellenist Hitchhiker 1. Hellenist Hitchhiker 2, though, was one of those Hellenist Hitchhikers. It was a fellow named Saul. He was there. There's pretty good evidence to think that Saul was part of, one of those who had close relationships with, the Sanhedrin. Perhaps had been in deep conversation with, relationship with, those freedmen. The synagogue of the freedmen. In Acts chapter 22, Paul tells us that he was from Cilicia, Tarsus. Paul was a Hellenistic Jew, fluent in the language of Empire. But he was one of those who had come back periodically to celebrate the Feast of Pentecost, who had learned at the feet of one of the greatest of the teachers of the conservative movement. He was with the freedmen, the synagogue's freedmen. And it says in chapter 8 verse 1 that he was giving approval to the stamping out of these heresies that would threaten the law, that would minimize the role of the temple, and that would call into question God's elective sovereignty to choose the people of Israel as his own. Hellenist Hitchhiker 2, Saul, was ready to defend the older ways.

Now, before we start to think that this is a matter of Jews against Christians, if you have your Bibles, you can turn with me to Acts chapter 15. You need to realize that this huge debate within the Hellenistic circles is also debated within wider Jewish circles. It was a very, very deep issue. About what does it mean to be the people of God, the called and elect people of God. Chapter 15, as we know, is the Council of Jerusalem. In fact, as you hopefully know by now, most of the rest of the book of Acts has to do with how the early followers of the Messiah, most of whom were Jews, how they began to see that the promises of the kingdom included not only the restoration of Israel but the blessings of those were beyond the covenant originally.

You know, the gospel into Samaria, the gospel into Cornelius's household, which you'll talk about in a week or two, and of course the Jerusalem Council. All of these provide us insights, windows into the early Jewish wrestling with a hard question. What does it mean to be the people of God? Some men came down, in verse 1, from Judea to Antioch; [they] were teaching the brothers, "Unless you are circumcised according to the custom taught by Moses, you cannot be saved." But verse 5, then some of the believers who belonged to the party of the Pharisees stood up and said, "The gentiles must be circumcised, and be required to obey the law of Moses." In other words, they were followers of Messiah, who also were influenced by, let's say, this conservative Hellenistic Jewish position that wanted to defend the conservative interpretation of the law and of the temple. And it is precisely now, an intra-Messianic debate, an intra-Messianic discussion. Where do we go from here with our understanding of the good news?

As they stoned this first Hellenistic hitchhiker, he cried out, "Lord Jesus, receive my spirit. And do not hold this sin against them." You know, God answered his prayer. The God whose world is his heart, answered his prayer. Because there was another Hellenistic hitchhiker that was there. He had blood on his hands. He approved. And he wanted to stamp out what he thought was a lie. But this first hitchhiker said "Lord, do not hold this sin against them." The conservatives felt so strongly, that according to the law, the way we get the forgiveness of sins is through sacrifices in the temple. That's why the temple was so crucial. But this Jesus fellow, who these Hellenistic hitchhikers had somehow come into contact with, he was forgiving sins, without any sacrifices. Somebody say Amen! And he was also not quite stoned, but you know the story. And he also said, "Father, forgive them, for they know not what they do." That is the gospel, isn't it? The God who will forgive the sins of Diasporic Jews, some of whom yearned for the restoration of the temple, in order that they can accomplish all those sacrifices that they had been putting off all these years and centuries because they didn't control the temple. And it's kind of like getting forgiveness of sins on credit, you know? When you haven't quite done the sacrifices, but yet you hope and believe and pray that God will restore the temple someday so you *can* do all those sacrifices. But these hitchhikers, like Philip and like Stephen, had seen the mercy, the grace, the generosity, the boundless love of Yahweh. And even when he is receiving the stones, he says, "Lord, do not hold this sin against them." Then God says, "Okay, I'll just take this other Hellenist Hitchhiker. And you know what? We're going to redeem this life. We're going to redeem this message. We're going to bring something powerful out of this life who goes to his death, saying, 'Lord, do not hold this sin against them.'" Hallelujah!

Out of Stephen's martyrdom, comes other Hellenistic hitchhikers *unleashed*. They go into Samaria. Somebody say Amen! Out of Stephen's martyrdom comes other Hellenistic hitchhikers, *unleashed* to really carry the gospel to the gentiles. Somebody say Amen! Amen! I mean isn't that what Yahweh told Ananias about the fellow that he was supposed to go lay his hands on? This fellow is going to take the gospel to the gentiles! Somebody say Amen! Out of Stephen's martyrdom you have, even the redemption of the education of Gamaliel in Hellenist Hitchhiker 2! Somebody say Amen! The gospel for Hellenist Hitchhikers, Amen? I'm a gentile. We have a need for Hellenistic hitchhikers, right?

Pastor Bill told you part of my story. A woman, a Caucasian woman, feels a call. Another Hellenist Hitchhiker. Number 975 million, or something like that. Feels the call to go to another part of the Hellenistic world, right? Malaysia. Ministers. Learns the language of the Chinese. Ministers, and then years later comes back and plants churches in northern California. And calls pastors to minister among those Chinese-speaking people. Folks, you know as gentiles we often forget what an incredible story this is that we're a part of. Look at all the blood that was shed. Look at all the debates and . . . folks, you got Hellenist Hitchhiker 3, 4, and 5 coming up in the next few weeks. Pay close attention to how *intense* these disputes were. How *intense* these debates were about what does it means to be the people of God? What does it mean to receive the promises of the covenant? What does it mean to be a people of the Messiah? Oh, you have two, three, four very, very different visions of what that meant. And I'm grateful to be here with you this morning. The result of the gospel going forth into the Hellenistic world has included us, you and I, among the seed of Abraham. Malaysian-born Asian American. Californians. Yeah! Why? When this Hellenist Hitchhiker said, "Lord, do not hold these sins against them." It covers my sins, it covers your sins. And God listened to him. And God says, "You know what, I'm in this business of redeeming lives, even though this life has gone down. I got all the Hellenistic hitch-hikers of God!" Amen?

You gonna be a Hellenist Hitchhiker today? Are you one who is go-ing to bear witness? Be careful. Sometimes, like those witnesses we saw, sometimes we mistake a certain perspective of our experience, and think it's God's perspective. And sometimes we bear false witness. I don't think most of us do that intentionally. And even if we did, God will not hold it against us, Amen? So, long as we say, "Lord, doing the best I can. In this case I feel like this is wrong, and I need to speak out against it. I need to resist it." And we do that with fear and trembling. Maybe none of us have stoned other Hellenistic hitchhikers, but maybe we've bore false witness. But the good news of the gospel is that it's also possible for us to bear true witness to God's graciousness. And the bearing of that true witness is the announcement to others, "your sins are forgiven." You don't have to be a Jew, you don't have to be a Hellenistic Jew, but you know what? We're all diasporic, we're all in the exile. We're all away from home. And all of us are looking backward to the good old days, and we're looking forward to the things that God will accomplish, Amen? The God who is a forgiving God, takes broken lives like mine, and like yours, and says, "You know what, I'm in the redemptive business! I'm in the business of taking Hel-lenistic folks and gentiles and cleaning them up! And then, sending them off to Samaria and Ethiopia and the ends of the earth, like Pittsburgh." Oh, I'm sorry [laughter]. And who are those folks in this "ends of the world" that it's your privilege to declare to them: "Father, you have not held their sins against them"?

Bow with me in prayer this morning. O Lord. These stories are about you and your love that knows no boundaries. You and your inscrutable will, who took Jews from around the Mediterranean world, and used them to teach the older generation something new about what your Holy Spirit is doing. We thank you for grafting us into this story. We thank you for inserting us into this narrative. We thank you for calling us, and sealing us with that same Spirit who can work in the uttermost parts of the world. And this morning, Lord Jesus, we once again lift up our hands to you. This morning, Lord Jesus, once again we receive that forgiveness of sins, of which you have been more than happy . . . because it's part of your nature, to forgive and to love. We receive that this morning. And for those of you that are here this morning, and you're wrestling with something or other, I just want you to lift up your hands, even now, and receive with me, the gracious love and forgiveness that is God's to give, and . . . not only to give, but to pour out upon us. We receive that this morning, Lord Jesus. We receive the full presence of your Spirit that confirms with us that we are your children, forgiven in Christ. And then also Lord, we receive this mandate, this mandate that went from Stephen to this other Hellenistic hitchhiker, Saul. This mandate that takes wrecked lives, misinformed lives. This mandate that comes along and sweeps us up, and draws us into this bigger story of the good news of Jesus. Catch us away, O Lord, in this story. Catch us away, O Lord, by your Spirit in this story. Lord, help us to be Spirit-empowered Hellenist Hitchhikers. In Jesus' name. And all God's people, said Amen.

God bless you.

Tony Richie Reflection—"The Diasporic Spirit"

This sermon exemplifies Amos Yong's sharp insights into the inevitably conflictive nature of common faith among those of diverse contexts. Refreshingly, it offers encouragement regarding God's superintending benevolence. And it reflects a significant Pentecostal intuition. A popular global movement today, the Pentecostal tradition had humble origins among society's marginalized and disenfranchised. There exists an internalized identity as "pilgrims and strangers" in a wayward world (Heb 11:13; 1 Pet 2:11). We are ever spiritual (and often literal) aliens/immigrants. Regardless of racial or regional specifics, affinities for an exilic ethos are embedded in Pentecostals' DNA. We have drunk deeply at the wells of "The Diasporic Spirit."

Diasporic identity arises out of shared history, language, values, and culture among groups with a disturbing sense of disconnect from their ancient homeland. When early Pentecostals enthusiastically sang "This world is not my home, I'm just a-passing through" or "I can't feel at home in this world anymore" or "If heaven's not my home then Lord what will

I do" the symbolism had a literal feel. Obviously, living as "saints in exile" can be, to say the very least, awkward, uncomfortable. Daily life is oriented by nostalgic longing for "sweet Beulah Land," the "country to which I've never been before."

Pentecostals look back to Pentecost for their heritage and ahead to Christ's return for their hope. The present tends to be more unpredictable, less manageable. However, they have one absolute certainty: God is with them as they go! At their best, Pentecostal preachers boldly proclaim the crucified and risen Christ's triumph over sinful world systems while gently reminding believers that they aren't quite home yet. Perhaps the most serious challenge is to make the trip count.

2

Through You, All the Peoples of the Earth Will Be Blessed!

Acts 3

Yoido Full Gospel Church, Seoul, Korea, 22 May 2009*

[Yong is introduced in Korean and his sermon is interpreted.]

Good evening. I have no idea what Rev. Kim just said. But I receive it by faith! It is an honor to be here to worship with you tonight. And to experience the Spirit of God alive in our midst, Amen? I want to bring you greetings from the state of Virginia in America. This is my first visit to Korea. And I thank God for the opportunity to experience worship at Yoido, which I've heard so much about from before.

My sermon tonight, is entitled, "Through You, All the Peoples of the Earth Will be Blessed." This was the verse that was in Acts 3, verse 25. It was the promise first made to Abraham. That was a long time ago. But tonight, God wants to make this promise to you. The promise is that,

* I was initially invited to give a lecture at the Young San International Theological Symposium, Hansei University, in May 2009, and then a follow-up invitation came from Rev. Dr. Young-hoon Lee, the senior pastor of Yoido Full Gospel Church, to address the Friday night congregation, which in any case was about 12,000 strong. Thanks to Rev. Nelson Kim for his expert translation of my sermon into Korean that night. It was surreal to hear the congregation's enthusiastic and regular call-and-response "Amens"—which sounded like a roar indeed, for such a large crowd—not at my cues but following Rev. Kim's translation!

to you, all the peoples of the earth will be blessed. How do I know that? Because the Bible tells me so. And the Bible tells me so, through the story of a man in Acts chapter 3 who was lame. You are familiar with this story.

It took place shortly after the Day of Pentecost, in Acts chapter 2. On the Day of Pentecost, God poured out his Holy Spirit upon the world. And the Bible says that they were all filled with the Holy Spirit and spoke in other languages. Young and old, male and female, slave and free people. This was the beginning of the miracle called the church. On that day, 3,000 people were baptized in water. Now I know many of you here have experienced this powerful reality of the Holy Spirit. You are here because God has touched your life and your heart and transformed you. Many of you have experienced the miraculous power of the Holy Spirit. Just like on the Day of Pentecost. Amen!

But here was this man who had not yet been touched by the Spirit. How many of you know of a friend or a relative or a co-worker, who has not yet met the Holy Spirit? This man was crippled from birth! And daily, perhaps, every other day, he was carried to the temple gate to beg. We know that he had been living for forty years in his condition. He was poor and he had no options in his life. If his friends made it to his house, they would take him to the temple gates. Other than this, we don't know much about him. We don't even know his name! Here was a literal nobody in society. How many of us feel like nobodies sometimes? But I want you to know tonight that God cares for, and is concerned about, every person. Even for this man who was a nobody.

As God is pouring out his Spirit all around the world, he is still looking for the nobody. God is not just at work "out there," he is looking for the nobodies right here. God is not only looking to save the world, he is looking to save you and me! And even if not many people know your name, guess what? God knows your name. No matter what our condition is, even if it's been for forty years, tonight God can touch us. Even if you feel that you are out of options tonight, so was this man, but God touched him.

Here was this forty-year-old man, and today was his lucky day. Why was he lucky? Because Peter and John had no money. You know, if Peter and John had money, they might just have given him the money. But they didn't have money. Instead, they stopped and they said, "We don't have any money. But we have one thing. We have the Holy Spirit. And we have the power of the name of Jesus. So, in the name of Jesus Christ of Nazareth, rise up and walk!" And they gave this man something better.

They announced the forgiveness of his sins, and they gave him the Holy Spirit. The gift of the Holy Spirit for him, and for us tonight. And as they touched him, this man's feet and ankles became strong. And he jumped to his feet, and he began to walk. And the people were amazed.

How many of you here tonight believe that God is still in the miracle-producing business? How many of you believe that God can still use nobody fishermen like Peter and John, tonight? All they had was they had spent time with Jesus, and they waited for the Holy Spirit in the Upper Room. How many of you know tonight that this same Holy Spirit, who filled Jesus, is also at work here in our lives? The Bible says Jesus went out and healed the sick and freed all who were oppressed of the devil, by the power of the Holy Spirit.

But there's something even more significant about this man's healing. We are told that this man followed Peter and John into the temple courts. How many of you realize how significant that is for this man? For years and years, he had been sitting outside the gates. He could only watch people go into the temple. He could only hear the singing coming from out of the temple. And then he would see people leave the temple, having been touched by the presence of God. But he was a crippled man! And his physical condition prohibited him from entering into the Holy of Holies.[1] For days and for days, and for years and for years, he could only experience the presence of God, second hand. And can you imagine him, longing in his heart? "God, how I wish I myself could experience your touch." But today was his day to receive that touch. Today was his day when Yahweh personally invited him into the temple courts. Before he had no options to go in before the presence of God. There was no possibility, because he was prohibited. But today he was free! On his own legs! With his own hands! With his own voice! Why do you think it tells us that he went walking and leaping into the temple, praising God?

How many of you know, today, that God would want to set you free from whatever boundaries keep us from experiencing his touch? How many of you know tonight that God desires to remove all the barriers that keep you from fulfilling his call on your life?

For this man, it's not only a medical miracle. But more importantly, it was a breakthrough in the law. It was a transformation of his life. And what God can do tonight, is to also change our lives just like this man. God wishes to take us from a position where we are bound, to a position

1. Editor's note: Only men from Aaron's line who were not disabled could be high priest and enter into the Holy of Holies (Lev. 16; 21: 16–23; Heb. 9:7).

where we are free. God wishes to take us from a position of being crippled, to a position of walking and leaping and praising him.

Luke, in telling this story, is making an allusion to the prophet Isaiah. In Isaiah chapter 35, verses 5 and 6, it says this: [read only in Korean by the translator]. Amen! You read it. Hallelujah! The prophet Isaiah did not know about this man. The prophet Isaiah never saw into the future; this man sitting outside the temple gates. But the prophet Isaiah said there will come a day when the lame shall leap like a deer! And that is the day of the Messiah. That is the day of the Christ, the Anointed Son of God. That is the day when the fortunes of Israel will be turned around. What is the prophet Isaiah talking about?

In Isaiah chapter 35, the context concerns the exile of the nation. They were sent away to a foreign country. They were no longer in their land. And the prophet is speaking about the visitation of the Lord. When the Lord comes, the eyes of the blind will be opened. When the Lord comes, the ears of the deaf will be unstopped. When the Lord comes, the lame shall leap like a deer.

Now how many of you know, that the person who wrote the book of Acts, also wrote the book of Luke? And how many of you know that in the book of Luke it tells us that the eyes of the blind were opened? And the ears of the deaf were unstopped? And you know why? Because the Lord had come. The Messiah had come, filled with the Holy Spirit! This was the day of the Lord! And in the Day of Pentecost sermon, Peter said, "All who call upon the name of the Lord shall be saved." In other words, it was coming to pass, what the prophet Isaiah foretold. When the Lord would come, Yahweh would reign once again. And the land would be redeemed and restored from Israel's enemies. Once again, the desert will become bountiful. Those who were excluded will now be included. The wilderness will be transformed. The deserts turned into streams. This is the prophet Isaiah's promise of Israel's miracle.

And how many of you know that in Acts chapter 2, that promise begins to come to fulfillment? Because that is the day of the outpouring of the Spirit upon all flesh. That is the day of the outpouring of the Spirit upon the nation of Israel, to *redeem* the nation of Israel. This was the man's lucky day! He ran into the Holy Spirit. Who was in the process of redeeming Israel. And in the process of redeeming Israel, the Holy Spirit would also touch individual lives. The Holy Spirit would also transform individual destinies. The healing of this lame man confirmed that God is in the nation-restoring process. God has not forgotten his promises to the elect. And the healing of this man shows that God is remembering. He did not know this. But the promise to Abraham, . . . hundreds of years ago, was for him that day.

And as he went walking into the temple, leaping and praising God, the people were amazed! And Peter started to preach. This sermon was in the presence of this man. This sermon was inspired by this man. Peter didn't even know this man. But he knew that God had made the promise to Abraham. That through you, all the nations of the earth will be blessed. And tonight, we're again listening to this story of this lame man healed. We are celebrating his healing. And how many of you know that through the power of the Spirit's healing in his life it is now available to us, tonight? Through him, all the nations of the earth will be blessed.

God has poured out His Spirit around the world. God has poured out His Spirit, here in Korea. I have read much about the powerful revivals here in Korea. And you are part of the witness of God's outpouring of his Spirit. But how many of you know that revivals are both for personal salvation, but also for the nations?

This lame man's healing were confirmation that God was in the process of redeeming the nation of Israel. Can you believe tonight that God can do through our lives, what God can do through our lives, has implications for our nation? Is it possible that God will touch our lives tonight in a way that has implications beyond what you and I can dream about? Is it possible that through each one of you God has even a plan to touch your nation? Let's not doubt the power of God.

You think this crippled man at the gate knew that through his life God could transform a nation? We still don't even know his name! But God is in the nations-saving business.

From a distance, I have followed God's blessing of your country. How many of you know the message Dr. Cho has been preaching over these many years?[2] It is the triple blessing that God has promised us. But how many of you know also that this blessing God has promised us is also for our country? This lame man was healed so he could participate in God's larger plans. These are God's plans for our communities. These are God's plans for our society. These are God's plans for Korea. And can you believe, even that through Korea God will touch the rest of the world? How many of you know and support missionaries from your congregation,

2. My visit to Korea involved presentation of a paper giving my own assessment of the theology of Paul Cho Yonggi, the founder of Yoido Full Gospel Church; this was later published as: "Salvation, Society, and the Spirit."

that have gone to the ends of the earth? How many of you pray for these missionaries, that have gone to the ends of the earth? How many of you believe that God has raised up South Korea, in these last years, not just to bless its citizens, but to fulfill the bigger purposes of God?

There are lots of problems in the world. But how many of you believe that God is a greater God? And the man whose name we do not know got up, walked, and leaped, and praised God. And by doing so, he fulfilled the promises of God for his people. That is both the promise and the challenge of this man's healing today.

Peter, in this sermon, in Acts chapter 3, did call for a decision. This man was an example of what God wanted to do. But God is also, through this man, calling others. In Acts chapter 3, verses 19–21, it says this: [read in Korean by the translator].

Notice, first, the call to repentance. "If you want," this is Peter, "if you want to participate in God's restoring of the nation, repent." If you want to not just be spectators watching this man, repent. If you want to participate in the messianic activities of Jesus, repent. If you want to be one of those through whom all the nations of the earth will be blessed, repent. Because when you repent, your sins will be wiped out. When we repent and turn to God, we are given a new life. After forty years, this man had a new life.

His repentance had caused him to be able to do things he could not have done before. This lame man's sins were forgiven, and he was allowed into the temple courts to praise God. Repentance and the receiving of forgiveness of sins allows us to participate in God's work. Repentance allows us to participate in the times of refreshing from the Lord. These are times of blessing from the Lord. This is the triple blessing of which Dr. Cho preaches.

But maybe it's also the blessing, that God says, in verse 21, to restore all things. The Spirit has been poured out to accomplish the fulfillment of this promise. Our repentance and reception of God's forgiveness makes it possible to participate in this restoration.

God is concerned about our individual lives. But God is also the God of the nations. And God is also the God who seeks to restore all things for his glory. How many of us tonight are willing to be mobilized by the Holy Spirit, to be God's servants? How many of us are willing to be vessels of God's blessing for the world?

Maybe God has placed a dream in your heart about something big. Maybe God has given you visions for things that you might want to accomplish for his name. Why would we be surprised if we have dreams and visions? Didn't Peter say on the Day of Pentecost that when the Spirit of God is given we will have dreams and visions?

Don't say to yourself, "But I'm a nobody." That's who God uses! God uses crippled men! God touches them. God heals them. God forgives them. God calls them. God gives them the Holy Spirit. And then these nobodies become God's servants! And they become God's agents of change.

Isn't that the life example of Dr. Cho? You have heard his testimony from when he was younger. And he was on his deathbed. But God met him. Through him, all the nations of the earth are being blessed! God called him to do the great things that he could not have imagined fifty years ago.

God is always in the business of taking nobodies and making them God's bodies. Before Abraham was called by God, he was a nobody. But God said to him, "Through you, all the nations of the earth will be blessed." And you know his story. He lived until a hundred years old, and he said "God, where's my blessing?" He could not have imagined how God would fulfill this promise to him. But yet, this man Abraham became a world-changer.

And this lame man, who was sitting at the gate Beautiful, was now someone who inherited the promise made to Abraham. And now he had become a mediator, through whom this promise would go to other people. His healing had become the occasion to remind Israel that God intended to save them, and that God intended to save the world.

Cause you know the story of the rest of the book of Acts, right? That the gospel was supposed to go to the ends of the earth? And how many of you know that we live in Acts chapter 29? We are continuing to experience God's saving of the world. The book of Acts tells us this story, that God has not forgotten Israel. But through a carpenter from Nazareth, God is fulfilling the promise made to Abraham. Through a bunch of fishermen, Peter and John, God is fulfilling his promise to Abraham. Through individuals like this unnamed man, God is fulfilling his promise to Abraham. Because we're not the ones who are special. But it's the power of the Holy Spirit, whom God has poured out on all flesh.

So my question for you, tonight. Are you willing to be that nobody that God is calling to do great things? Are you willing to dream bigger than just your personal blessing tonight? Are you ready to be God's servant for this church? To be God's servant for your community? To bear witness to Jesus in your society? To testify to God through your life, for your country? And maybe even be somebody through whom the whole world is touched by the love of God? Is it possible that through you all the nations of the earth will be blessed? Is it possible that tonight there is somebody, maybe many people in this room, through whom God will bless the nations? Is it possible that there are ministries here tonight through whom the times of blessing and refreshing will come upon the world?

Why not? It's the promise of the Scriptures. If it's just up to us, forget it! But with God all things are possible. For the lame man. For nobodies like me. For nobodies like you. But yet, God makes it possible. That even through your life, God's blessing will come upon the nations, Amen! Do we receive it?

Let's put our hands up to the Lord. And say, "Lord, if it is in your power, according to your will, may you take my life. May you touch my life. May you strengthen my feet. May you lift up my hands. May you put praises upon my lips. And Lord, all I want to be is your servant. That whoever you want to bless through me, may you do that. In the name of Jesus. By the power of the Holy Spirit, Amen."

Tony Richie Reflection—"Blessed to be a Blessing"

Amos Yong preaches that God's redemptive purposes are characterized by inclusivity and instrumentality. These rich concepts resource a panoramic vision of divine redemption accomplished in Jesus Christ, by the Holy Spirit, with human engagement. Jesus of Nazareth was the ultimate "nobody" submitting his life to God as a blessing for all. Submission meant the sacrifice of the cross. It meant death. But death ended in resurrection. Christ's death and resurrection offered eternal life to all. Since God's gift is personal, national, and global no one need be excluded (Rev 22:17).

Divine generosity makes the Holy Spirit's grace-full presence and influence freely available to everyone everywhere. Christ's Spirit crosses all boundaries, breaks through all barriers. Economic barriers, gender barriers, physical barriers, political barriers, racial barriers, religious barriers, social barriers, or any other barriers are unsuccessful obstacles to the Spirit's superabundance. Yet responsiveness isn't automatic or formulaic. It requires repentance.

Turning away from sin's rootedness in rebellious self-will and its consequent egocentrism, and turning toward God's holy and benevolent will, includes radical willingness to become God's servants for passing the blessing to others. The intent of repentance isn't mere self-flagellation. Rather, repentance moves beyond the present broken, fallen order of existence or mode of being toward the final reestablishment of full vitality and all-encompassing freedom in complete perfection. Through Jesus Christ all creation and every creature will be forever transformed in the consummation. Until then God promises those who are already enjoying a foretaste of eschatological blessing a missional opportunity to contribute lovingly to the favor and happiness of others. In short, believers are blessed to be a blessing.

3

The Lukan Commission

The Spirit, Im/migration, and the De-Construction of Empire

ACTS 1:6–8

All Nations Church, St. Paul, Minneapolis, 7 March 2010*

I want to talk to us for a few moments here of the book of Acts. For us Pentecostals, the book of Acts is in a real sense our canon within the canon. For Luther, for example, Romans was the canon within the canon. For Luther, the book of Romans was the point of entry into the biblical narratives. For the Pentecostals, however, it is the book of Acts. In fact, for many Pentecostals, this book resonates with our hearts; we are very affective people—affective people means that we take our hearts seriously. You should too, for lots of different reasons. Now taking our hearts seriously is good for a lot of reasons. But our hearts, if you will, to use Wesley's terms, are strangely warmed when we read these words about the fact that Jesus told his disciples to wait until they receive the power of the Holy Spirit. But what I want to focus on today, Pentecostals are

* The pastor of All Nations Church, Rev. Jin S. Kim, has envisioned a multicultural congregation and had been working to lead this Presbyterian Church U.S.A. community in that direction. I preached this sermon during the time when I was first researching and writing about migration, e.g., "Informality, Illegality, and Improvisation," and "The Im/Migrant Spirit." Thanks to Timothy Lim, my former graduate assistant at Regent University, and now Dr. Lim in his own right, for initial transcription of this sermon; regretfully, the archive is no longer available.

also known today as a power religion—how many folks would like to be involved in power religion?—watch out, you get plucked in a little bit and all kinds of strange things will start to happen. And Pentecostals have been known for this power religiosity you know—the emphasis on signs, wonders, and miracles—and be careful now, too many signs and wonders and miracles and things can get really wild. But what I want to focus for us this morning is this latter part—on the power of the Holy Spirit that was promised to the disciples and would play the dominant role in the Acts narrative, enabling apostolic witnesses in Jerusalem, Judea, Samaria, and the ends of the earth.

You wished that sometimes these Bible translators would line up so that thesis statements would jump off the page. This is Luke's thesis statement in the book of Acts—this is Luke's outline, and this is the way my story is going to unfold—. . . about how Spirit-empowered followers are going to be witnesses for Jesus in Jerusalem, Samaria, Judea, to the ends of the earth; and that is how the story basically [unfolds in] the book of Acts.

And when Pentecostals read the book of Acts, they say this is about my heart, my life, this is that—this is that story—our heart, our life, our story. I am going to make it personal—how I experience the story, and how my heart has been carried in the story.

I want to talk today about Christian life, Christian faith, Christian religion if you will, not just as a power religion, but a religion of migration—Christianity as a religion of immigration, Christianity as a story of migration all the way from the earliest times.

I was born and grew up as a Pentecostal in Malaysia. I grew up sitting on [a pew] much like the pew you are sitting on. And when I was ten years old, and I got two younger brothers, the missionaries under whom my mom was saved in Malaysia had come back to Malaysia. This is the group of missionaries in whom God had placed a heart for witnessing to the Chinese people, and so one of the places she went to plant churches was in Malaysia. And then she came back to California, she was from Northern California, and she continued to plant churches. Somebody thank God for missionaries who have a heart for the Chinese-speaking people, planting churches among migrant Chinese-speaking people in California. People who have moved from Hong Kong and Southern China to California, all kinds of reasons, and each one of us have our own stories about why our parents moved or our grandparents moved, or why you moved. And each one of those stories are important. And each one of those stories, I want to invite you today, to see that they can be mapped in one sense onto this story. So, she comes back from California after planting all these churches in California, and what do you need? Pastors. So, she comes back to Malaysia, to those who had been saved in their ministry, to those who grew up as disciples, and to those called to pastoral ministry, and told them, what I want you to do is to come to California to pastor a California Chinese-speaking congregation. And that is how my parents become missionaries to the United States, to California. Now we know those Californians really need missionaries, right?

So, I am a pastor's kid and a missionary kid. I spent my high school years growing up in Stockton, California. I was an excited ten-year-old coming to America, trying to figure out how to fit in. Those of you who grew up partly as what is called a 1.5 generation, we know what it means to experience this whole challenge of assimilation. I worked hard in my junior high years to get rid of my Malaysian ascent. Already, I wore all those clothes that designated me as an immigrant. But that is my story. I went to college in Santa Cruz, an Assemblies of God College, and I met my wife. She was a Mexican American and still is, and she grew up in the Spanish Assemblies of God church in the State of Washington. After we got married, we moved up and stayed in Washington for three years to get to know her family. So, we have this Malaysian-born in Washington, and I find myself in the Pacific Northwest, those people who live in the Pacific North West have their own mentality. We lived there about eight years, and all our three children were born in Portland, Oregon, and that is where I went to Seminary, and did graduate studies, and then God opened up doors for us and we got a calling to pursue further studies to prepare for teaching ministry. We decided to pursue doctoral studies and we had the option to go back to California or to go into Boston. Why stop travelling now? So we packed everything in a twenty-seven-foot truck and drove all the way to Boston Massachusetts, where I did my doctoral work. Now that is just part of my journey. We went back to California, and came to Minnesota for six years, and I can still remember the fall of 1999, my first class, teaching introduction to theology, facing these eighteen-year-olds. The only problem was that they were all blond and had blue eyes, and I was hearing them speak, and at Bethel, it took me a whole semester wondering, what am I doing here teaching theology at Bethel. Great six years. I had students like John, Hikari, and etc.[1] We are

1. John Nelson and Hikari Nakane were outstanding undergraduate students of mine when I was on the faculty at Bethel University, St. Paul (from 1999–2005), and

just trying to make our way around the country, and at some point, God will bless us by bringing us to Hawaii.

But my heart resonates with this—most Pentecostals latch on to this—the power to witness—my focus today is, my power to witness where? There is no portion in this world where God would not leave his witness. The whole known world of the time is God's world—the world [into which] God would send people filled with the Spirit. You thought it was just globalization or the incredible shrinking world—or because job opportunities open up—that is true, and there are many reasons why you and I are here or there, and perhaps, this is just one of the many stops God has for you and me as we anticipate the future.

But this word comes to us this morning. I believe that wherever our journey takes us, wherever the Spirit takes us—that is the place for our witness—the Spirit of God will come upon you, and you will be my witnesses—whether it is in Jerusalem, Samaria, Judea, or to the ends of the earth. This morning, I have already been blessed worshipping with you, you [have] already born testimony of God for this God-forsaken land of the frozen chosen. You are an immigrant or migrant congregation. I am both an immigrant and a migrant. An immigrant is someone who moves from one country into another country. A migrant is simply someone who moves. My wife, a Mexican-American, fifth generation. She was born in Wisconsin, on a migrant trail. Every six months, her family would drive through Montana, Texas, and come home. [Her family finally moved] from Texas and landed at Washington. Of course, she has relatives, cousins, and folks still in Texas. The Spirit of immigration and migration—you and I were all one or the other or both—modernity, postmodernity, globalization . . . the nature of the world we lived in. Perhaps, there is not a whole lot of difference—this is that. . . . Our lives are at large written in the migrations and immigrations of the earliest Christians. Do you not recognize your story in Luke's story? Was Luke telling a story in a script, our stories? Can we map our migration in Luke's narration that begins in one place but moves out to many other places? And as you know, the story of Luke involves these many migrant band of folks who have come from the Mediterranean world. . . . Is Luke's story your story? Don't you represent this nation? They heard the noise, but you hear a noise—they heard a noise and they asked, what means this? What [does it] mean to do church with these flags around? . . . What

---

both were active as staff members at All Nations when I visited.

[does it] mean to sing in Korean and English?[2] What does that mean for us? Luke's story is our story. It is a story of the religion of migration.

And of course, as we continue to turn the pages in the book of Acts, the three thousand who were saved came from many different parts. Yes, and they didn't necessarily all just congregate. Some went back out right away, but many stayed. And boy, you thought we had a lot to learn with a couple hundred people from many parts of the world.[3] Can you imagine about three thousand people from around the empire with not even linguistic commonality—many of them had Jewish backgrounds, but as you know, early on in the book of Acts, there were Greek-speaking Jews and there were Hebrew-speaking Jews. And they worked hard and God blessed [them] and they bore witness in all the strange tongues. But you know [that] when we have folks from around the world come together, it is hard work understanding one another. And we see the early church wrestling with that.

And a few chapters into it, and we have all the great stuff. The Lord added daily and members were being saved. [The] Lord helps us to be ready to receive the other, the migrant, the stranger, of language, of culture, and the early church wrestled with that. They had disagreements, or better, misunderstandings, lack of communications, and so they had complaints arising. Now, that doesn't happen here, two hundred people, and everybody loves one another. But that is the world of migrants, isn't it? The world [in which] the migrant has to find his or her way, their family in a new place in a new time, with all of the pressures of life, what life has become with movements of migration. We were stable people, but yet at the same time, always people on the move, always asking, always seeking, and restless in some respects, looking for that final solution. And so we find that there was the problem of diversity. A problem not only linguistically, but a problem of culture, and a problem of fellowship. And we see, Greek-speaking, Hebrew-speaking, women, men—the Spirit will be poured out on all flesh, in Acts 2, and your sons and daughters will prophesy, and man and woman—and woman were serving, but remember, cultural dynamics, linguistic dynamics.[4] Part of the problem then in-

2. There were a few Korean families besides Rev. Kim's and one of the choruses was sung in Korean; plus, the congregational meeting space was adorned by dozens of flags from many of the countries around the world.

3. I am referring here to the approximate number of weekly attendees to All Nations during that season of its congregational life.

4. Note here what happened between Greek-speaking and Hebrew-speaking widows in Acts 6.

volves establishing a diverse board of elders. And we had people, in other words, the early church began to develop leadership in order to serve the diverse people in the body of Christ—and that is so important—which is why I am so encouraged to see what is happening here at the Church of All Nations.

Now, this is absolutely important. In order to model the ministry of diversity, leadership has to be diverse. That is why the apostles, for all the Spirit's anointing on them, they could only take the growing church so far and they needed help. They needed help from people that came around from the Mediterranean. These Judean leaders as anointed of the Spirit only spoke to a certain degree of diverse languages. They can only understand a certain degree of the cultural dynamics that had been gathered because of the strange work of God. And therefore, the leaders that had been called had to be gathered from the parts of the empire. People who spoke the languages, people who understood where the growing numbers of people were coming from, and who were able to minister in more ways than just preaching. Philip, Nicanor, Timon, Parmenas, these are Greek-speaking leaders, but they were also filled with the Spirit—where did they came from? They were migrants, immigrants, coming from here and there and from places in Asia Minor, trying to figure out life in Jerusalem, and they wrestled with it, but they could resonate with the migrant community, couldn't they?

They could wrestle with the hopes and the longings and aspirations of the immigrant and the migrant community, and they celebrated the outpouring of the Spirit in their own language. And they learn and they taught, and they bore witness not only in their own language but together, Hebrews and Greeks and Asia Minorians, and Romans and Cretans, and Arabs and Jerusalemites, Judeans, together in the cacophony of the confusion, in the multiplicity of the languages and the diversity of cultures colored their lives and practices. What they bore witness to is the possibilities of an alternative empire—one not only based upon the peace of Rome. And we should not diminish the accomplishments of the peace of Rome that enable the kind of migration, that enable that kind of movement, that enable people to take up citizenship in other parts of the empire, whereas before, you would have to get an army and kill somebody in order to do that. So, we do not want to minimize the peace of Rome, but the peace of Rome is ultimately built upon a false allegiance—the allegiance of Caesar as emperor, of Caesar as lord. And thus, as Luke tells us in his first volume in the book of Acts, "in the days of Caesar"—they came upon this migrant family in Palestine, and they came upon this migrant group of fishermen that moved from sea to sea looking for a bigger catch, and they came upon a tax collector looking for another community, in which he could enrich his own comfort. And they came upon this and that and other people. . . . And Nicanor and Parmenas and Phillip, all of whom had perhaps wandered across Asia Minor, looking for a better world. Things haven't changed much since the time of Abraham, have they? As the author of Hebrews tells us, he left looking for a better city.[5] You and I are here, and maybe we found the city. Maybe this is the new Jerusalem. Probably not. We're looking for a better city.

But today, at this time, at this place, this is the place of our witness. This is the place in which we embody the outpouring of the Spirit of Jesus Christ in all of our color, in all of our diversity, in all of our miscommunications and misunderstandings. It is in the very nitty gritty of life lived in tension that the Spirit of Peace makes it all so worthwhile. That is what we are witnesses to—the claim that this experiment on human terms does not work. But that is why you will receive understanding when the Holy Spirit comes on you, to empower you to be his witness in Malaysia, in California, in the Pacific Northwest, in the northeast, in Minneapolis, and Minnesota. The Spirit of God who brings us together, who forges us into a new people, a people constituted by our world of globalization, of migration, but at the same time a people yearning within us for the Spirit to bear witness to another world, another possible way to configure our world, a world constructed by the mechanisms of our time, but at the same time, a world wells up within us, a world that speaks a language that even we do not understand, enables us to embody a form of life that even we marvel at, and that even we have no capacity to say—how does this work? But it kind of works! And in this kind of working, therein is the Spirit witnessing about the possibility of a new world—a new world in which white and black and yellow and red and green and blue are able to experience the unity of Christ that does not cancel out the diversity of our color.

And I want to spend a few minutes on a particular migrant in the story. He is a nameless migrant. We know he came from the South, from Ethiopia.[6] And he was a migrant of some means, although he was also a migrant with certain marks upon him that separated him from other

5. See Heb 11:10, 16.

6. Acts 8:26–40.

migrants. He was a eunuch who served in the court of power in Ethiopia. He was a person of empire in that sense, a person who was of the upper echelons of . . . out-workings of imperial and global relations. A person of some status and representative of empire, but yet a person of no stature in being a eunuch. Here is an identity conflicted, betwixt and between. Isn't your identity in some respect, capable in some respect, and rejected in other aspects. As a eunuch, not being able to enter into any of the sanctuaries of the people who called themselves after Yahweh, but he was a migrant who nevertheless crossed boundaries and borders of class and socio-political privilege. He was a migrant who probably crossed boundaries and borders of race and ethnicity, and of language. He was a migrant who crossed borders of ability and disability—a person who was marred because of his bodily condition. And here was a migrant who was met by another migrant, who knows . . . where Abraham was going, and all the coming and going and you sometimes wonder, where are people running from? Are we running?—that's ok. Migrants are migrants for lots of reasons. But you know what? God is with us, Amen! You might be running from something, you might be seeking something, this is that. You are looking for something. This Ethiopian migrant found the story of another migrant and his heart resonated with him. He found the story of a migrant of whom it was said that his descendants were cut off.[7] And this Ethiopian migrant resonated with the story of the other migrant, because he was not going to have another descendant. His descendants were cut off. There was no more story after his story. Where was he on this journey to? Maybe he was looking for a miracle. Maybe he was looking for that descendent that he knew he was never going to have. Maybe he was looking for that family in which he in his social and political and economic location did not have. He had a position, but maybe he did not have a family. But he read the story of this migrant whose descendants have come and he wondered about that.

Then we have Philip, this restless guy, from East Asia to Jerusalem, hanging out with magicians, and sort of getting supernatural transportation, finding rivers and saying, "let's just jump on in." I want to welcome you to the descendants that you thought you never had. I want to welcome you into a new people—a counter imperial but no less powerful, no less appointed, and no less diverse people, a people called after the name of Jesus—a people speak as empowered by the Spirit—precisely

7. Acts 8:33b reads: "Who can speak of his descendants?"—here citing probably the Septuagint (Greek translation) version of the prophet Isaiah 53:8.

because they are migrants, a people whose movement the Spirit tracks, why? Because who comes from who knows where, and who goes to who knows where, and that is the spirit of you and of me. And wherever we may go and whatever we may see, we manifest the life of that migrant, whose descendants were supposedly cut off, who hung on the cross, in order that his blood by the Spirit could constitute a new empire—not the empire of Caesar, but the empire of service, not the empire of the global Roman dogma, but the empire of life poured out of behalf of those on the move, on behalf of those seeking, yearning, calling, crying, and hoping.

I do not have time to talk about Paul as the quintessential migrant. Half of Luke's story has to do with this migrant of migrants. Born of Tarsus, educated at the feet of Gamaliel, and then who was intentional about catching the next [Boeing] 747 to wherever he felt the Holy Spirit was taking him. Being in the world but not of it. Being cosmopolitan but yet heavenly minded. Being in the church but not bound by any historical, geographical, linguistic, social, or economic expression, empowering local leaders wherever he went. Paul understood empire, he knew how it worked, he had been trained in empire, but he was a subversive agent of the peace of Rome. Not subverting the peace of Rome, but of subverting the Roman way of establishing homogeneity, rather in enabling migrants to be who they are called to be.

Lord Jesus, be with my migrant friends as they travel your world. In Jesus name! Amen!

Tony Richie Reflection—"A Divine Dance"

Yong dramatically explicates the mobile nature of human life—and of the life of faith itself. Recall the biblical portrait of God's Spirit as ceaseless, almost restless, but fermenting, fertile motion (Gen 1:2). One is reminded of the "atomic hypothesis": all things are made of little particles that move around in perpetual motion, attracting each other when they are a little distance apart, but repelling upon being squeezed into one another. Apparently the Creator deliberately designed existence with dynamism in mind. Indeed, "living" "moving" and "being" are inextricably interwoven (Acts 17:28).

Life's movement isn't aimless. Passing through this world as pilgrims, believers nevertheless make a mark, transforming and being transformed as the Spirit enables multifaceted witness to Christ in myriad contexts.

Often there are vestiges of conflicted identity as continuity/discontinuity between where/who we have been and where/who we are going to connect with and/or collide. Attracting and repelling occur as we encounter others-in-pilgrimage too. Frequently Christ's light shines bright through the solidarity of shared diversity.

Some religions perceive cosmic history's movement as endlessly cyclical. Christianity is linear. Everything, everyone, moves toward God's definitive, consummative purposeful goal. Yet since patristic times Christian theology further suggests that in Christ the Spirit draws us into a kind of celebratory and participatory "dance" with the Holy Trinity (John 17:20–23; Luke 15:25; cf. 4 Macc 14:7). Human movement never arrives at a motionless point on a compass or at a static moment in time. Rather, the life of faith ever leads us to enter salvific encounter as an ever-ongoing, always growing—and eternally joyful!—relationship with the Triune God. Can you imagine Almighty God saying, "May I have this dance, please?" If so, what is your response?

4

In the Days of Caesar

Pentecost and the Redemption of Empire

LUKE 1:5–7; 2:1–7; 3:1–6

Pleasant Bay Church, Kirkland, Washington,
10 June 2011*

[Podcast introduction by the host pastor where Yong is preaching.]

Morning Pleasant Bay. Amen, it's good to be here with you. Thank you for the invitation. I'm honored to be here, to worship with you here this morning. And to be able to share with you this morning from the Scriptures. I do want to mention my son is here, Aizaiah Yong.[1] Aizaiah, why don't you stand and wave. Aizaiah Yong. He's on staff at New Life Church in Renton, so he's just taking part of the Sunday morning off, this morning, to be with us. And we've got friends of the family from Tri-Cities Washington,[2] so we're glad to have them with us here this morning, as well . . . .

---

* Rev. Dan Neary, pastor of Pleasant Bay (Assembly of God) Church, invited me to preach while I was out in Kirkland, Washington, teaching a class for Northwest University (also affiliated with the Assembly of God); this was not long after publication of my book, *Who is the Holy Spirit?*, and he invited me to discuss themes in the volume.

1. My oldest son, pronounced like the biblical Isaiah.

2. Referring here to then Aizaiah's girlfriend (now wife and mother of our two grandchildren), Nereida (Neddy) Martinez, and her family that lives in Eastern Washington.

If you have your Bibles, we're in Luke chapters 2 and 3 this morning. You know, I grew up as a preacher's kid, to an Assemblies of God preacher. So, I've been in the Assemblies of God for a long time. Grew up in the Assemblies of God, grew up underneath an Assemblies of God pew, as I used to put it.

And I was born in Malaysia, by the way. My dad was called to minister to the Chinese-speaking immigrants in California. So, I became . . . I moved from being a preacher's kid to becoming a missionary kid to the United States. Somebody say Amen. How many of you guys know of missionary kids to the United States? Just one I suppose. I'm going to need some help this morning. When I say, "somebody say Amen!" I better hear something alright? Otherwise we'll be here a long time this morning [laughter].

In Malaysia, when I grew up, of course, how many of you know that Malaysia is a Muslim country? So, us Pentecostal preachers in Malaysia have got to play it, if you will, politically correctly. How many of you know what I'm talking about? Amen. There are certain things you can do in Muslim countries that you can't do in other countries. And there are certain things you can't do in Muslim countries that you could do in other countries. So, one of the things that very challenging of course, is how do you evangelize Muslims? Why? Because it's against the law to evangelize or proselytize among Muslims. So, being a Pentecostal preacher's kid, being a Pentecostal, being a Christian in Malaysia, is something that we do if you want in our own private spaces. Okay? In our own private spaces. Christianity, worshipping Christ, is something to be doing in certain communities, among certain folks. But the public sphere is a sphere that is otherwise very much organized in ways that do not allow for Christians to do the kind of things that you and I are used to doing here in our country.

In fact, talking about the parade that you had, right?[3] The ability to organize something like that. The ability to go out and have a presence in a community to represent Jesus is not something the people can do just anywhere around the world, at any time. In other words, there are political forces, there are political arrangements, there are political laws, depending on where we live. We need to be sensitive to those dynamics wherever we find ourselves.

3. Earlier during the service, there was testimonial reflection about the church's participation in a local community parade.

So, in any case, growing up in Malaysia, of course, one of the things I simply thought was, "well, when the Holy Spirit moves upon us, the Holy Spirit moves on our hearts." Somebody say Amen! And sometimes the Holy Spirit moves on our tongues. Alright? And sometimes the Holy Spirit empowers us and takes us outside Malaysia and go minister to somebody else somewhere else, right? Because you can't do it to the Muslims in Malaysia, you could come to the U.S. and evangelize Muslims, right? But my point is, that growing up as a Christian Pentecostal in Malaysia, our thought was, well, Christianity, the work of the Spirit, is something that's very, very personal and private. It happens within our church. It happens among certain folks. It doesn't happen out there, if you will; you know what I'm talking about.

We had a very, very non-political imagination. A very, very non-political way of looking at the world. And for good reason. The folks who became political about their faith in Malaysia eventually got in trouble. Hello? Right? Stepping where they shouldn't have been stepping in. Going places where they shouldn't have been going, doing things they shouldn't have been doing. But as I began to read the Scriptures, I begun to see that the Holy Spirit is truly at work in ways, and outside of the walls of our church, that oftentimes we're not quite prepared to discern. And those are the things that I want to talk for just a few minutes about this morning. And in fact, I want to talk about these things this morning, going right back to the book of Luke and the book of Acts. The book of Luke and the Book of Acts, as I was growing up, were always very, very central to our church life, to the way we understood the work of the Holy Spirit. How many of you know that Luke tells us the story of the acts of the Holy Spirit? Amen? Right? we read that in the book of Acts. Some people will call it the Acts of the apostles. I like to call . . . , we like to call it the Acts of the Holy Spirit.

So, I've always gone to the book of Acts, the author of the book of Acts, to understand the works of the Holy Spirit. And one of the things the Lord has been revealing to me the last few years, as I reread Luke and Acts, is how much really of the work of the Spirit is not just limited to our hearts? Yes, it's there. How much is not just limited to our churches? Yes, it's there. But how much of the work of the Spirit really is around the world? That's what I want to talk about this morning. In talking about the political aspects of the work the Spirit.

Now when I say political, you know, I'm not talking about red state blue state. Alright? Hello? I don't know what the colors are in this church, but that's not what I'm talking about. Purple? [laughter]. All "polis" means, is the public arena, the public sphere within which we live and move and do our business. How many of us know that we live in a political world in that sense? Right? We're consumers. We are constructors. We are employees. We . . . in fact, I worked for the state of Washington for eight years. Did you know that? 1988 to 1996 in Vancouver, Washington for the Department of Social Health Services.[4] Well that's another story, maybe if I get invited back later on, maybe I'll tell you that part.

But all of us are political, in a lot of different ways, if we just stop to examine our lives, and the ways in which our lives are intertwined with the public domain. The kind of licenses we need to get, the kinds of cards and identification we need to carry. And so on and so forth.

Luke tells us the story of the works of the Spirit in that kind of political world. Notice what he says, opening up the story of Jesus in chapter 2 at the very, very front of his account of the life of Christ. "In those days, of Caesar Augustus . . . ." How many of you understand what the word Caesar means in the New Testament? It's very, very simple. It simply means nothing more, or nothing less, than *lord*. In those days, Lord Augustus. Augustus Caesar was, of course, the ruler of the Roman Empire at the time of Jesus' birth. If you turn in chapter 3, we read about this just a few minutes ago: "In the fifteenth year of the reign of [Emperor] Tiberius, Lord Caesar . . . ."

These Roman Emperors were truly lords of their empire. They were lords in . . . different ways. Certainly, they were lords in a religious sense, or at least they aspired to be lords in that sense. That is what the rights of an annual ceremonies of Emperor worship were designed to do, to extol their greatness. But they were capable of generating that kind of worship, why? Because of the things that they did, that reflected their rulership and their lordship: providing for the people, organizing peace throughout the Empire, generating prosperity across the Empire. And how many of you know, that in the ancient world there were many, many wars between nations? During this period of time, the Roman Empire was organizing [what] historians, in hindsight, have called the peace of Rome—the *Pax Romana*. The peace of Rome extended from about twenty years before Jesus was born, through about 180 CE. About two hundred years. Now, how many of you understand that in a world, in an

---

4. I started as a financial services officer, providing food stamps for Washingtonians before switching to being a support enforcement officer collecting (delinquent) child support for children with separated parents.

ancient world in which wars are happening all over the place, it is literally an amazing accomplishment for there to have been a two-hundred-
year peace across the world. That signifies, in part, what Caesar meant
in terms of the designation of Lord that these Emperors took. They were
capable of organizing that kind of peace across the Empire.

In those days, Lord Augustus issued the decree that a census should
be taken of the entire Roman world. Don't underestimate the force of this
description. The entire Roman world, in this designation, means nothing less than the entire world! This was the *world*! He issued one decree.
And guess what happened? The world jumped to attention. He issued
one decree to take a census. Now what do you think these censuses are
for? Just to count heads? To see how many people are having babies the
last couple of years? No! The censuses are designed to extort government taxes. The censuses are designed to enable the government, in this
case Lord Caesar, to be able to determine from [the various] regions how
much taxes are gonna flow into the Empire.

Now, of course, these taxes were used, obviously, for some good. I
mean, think about all the roads that were created that allowed the apostles
to go out on the highways and byways to spread the gospel throughout
the Empire. Somebody say Amen! In the days of Caesar, the apostles were
able to do that because of the roads that were built. Because of the protec-
tion that the peace of Rome allowed for travel across the world, which
was unheard of in those days. I mean, you risked [danger by] going out
of your country before the peace of Rome. Going out of your enclave to
be hit by bandits. But if the Roman centurions and armies are around
then your travel is much more safe. Taxation was the word. And Caesar
Augustus had the kind of power and the kind of authority to issue one
decree, and the world jumps to attention.

Joseph went up from the town of Nazareth, in Galilee, to Judea, to
Bethlehem, the town of David. In other words, for census-taking, everybody had to report back to their hometowns. Think about all the massive
travel that this one decree stirred up, when everybody starts packing their
bags to go on and get counted. This is the power of the peace of Rome.
This is the power of the polis. This is the power of the political. And this
is the environment within which Luke unfolds the story of your Lord and
my Lord, whose name is Jesus.

Lord Jesus appears within a bigger story of Lord Caesar. Think about
how subversive Luke's story now becomes, in telling the story of this one
Lord who appears on the margins of the Empire. In fact, while Caesar

has mobilized the peoples of the earth to go back to their hometowns to get registered, what is God up to in God's scheme of things? God is up to redeeming this Empire. God is up to working within the confines of what Caesar is dictating, to accomplish God's purposes. Somebody say Amen! That gives hope for you and I, right? I mean, you've probably heard the phrase, right? There are two things that are assured in life: death and taxes. Taxes accompany empires, Amen? Really want talk about which empire we pay our taxes to? I don't want to get us into too much trouble, so maybe we'll come back to that later if I have some time. But as Caesar Augustus is now organizing the world to fulfill his own, if you will, accounting schemes, God is up to God's redemptive business. God is up to God's redemptive business to fulfill the prophecies that, from out of Bethlehem of Judea, would come forth another Lord. Another Messiah. One who would deliver his people from, if you will, the powers and principalities of this world. Caesar Augustus, capable of ruling the entire Roman world through one of his decrees, within and through that, [set in motion a sequence of events that included Joseph], who went to be registered with Mary, following orders, living according to the dictates of the Empire, while [living] out his role as a citizen, doing so with a woman he wasn't technically married to yet, but with child. Now that had some also legal ramifications. And [then the time came] for the baby to be born, and she gave birth to her firstborn, a son. [She] wrapped him in cloths and placed him in a manger, for there was no room for them in the inn.

Now it's not Christmastime here, so I'm not going to go into that aspect of it. But I just want to point out the contrast of Luke's introducing of this story of Jesus. Set within this framework of Lord Augustus Caesar. Through one decree, ruling the whole Empire. And yet, in the margins of the empire. In fact, not even in the margins of the human world, but in the heart, if you will, of a world excluded from humans, in a manger, in a place in which there was caring for animals, domesticated animals. Here comes what God is desiring to do—to redeem the world. Somebody say Amen.

As Caesar comes in power, Jesus comes in humility. As Caesar rules with his decree, Jesus comes in his vulnerability. As Caesar extols in his riches and his capacity to extract wealth from the affluent and even from the poor, Jesus comes in poverty. As Caesar is designated by his status— as one who was capable of issuing decrees, even [as did] Quirinius as governor of Syria—statuses, roles, names, titles, labels, etc., Jesus comes, simply with swaddling clothes in a manger, for there was no room for him—not only in the inn, but in this Empire. Among the census, there was no room for him among those who would rule, according to the dictates of this world. But there was room for him because God was in the process of doing something new. Somebody say Amen. God was in the process of, if you will, working with the Empire, but from within the Empire to do and accomplish something new.

In chapter 3, as Luke continues his story. Now we've got a different Caesar. And of course, the way in which the Caesars replace one another, some of it was fairly peaceful, but others of it was quite political; we won't go into all of that. But look at the way in which Luke describes what happens in the fifteenth year. I'm in chapter 3: "In the fifteenth year of the reign of Tiberius, Lord Tiberius—when Pontius Pilate was the governor of Judea, Herod tetrarch of Galilee, his brother Philip tetrarch of Iturea and Traconitis, and Lysanias tetrarch of Abilene." I'm almost started speaking in tongues reading throughout all of that. [Laughter.]

Think about the way in which this empire is organized so tightly, so, if you will, expertly. Each person with his role in the hierarchy, each place in the hierarchy secured. Now, this is what you'd call a well-organized government. Somebody say Amen! How many of you understand it is better to have a well-organized government than an anarchical one? Amen? Well-organized government—good for most things. This is a very, very well-organized polis. They don't call it the peace of Rome for nothing. The Romans were able to do what they did for two hundred years precisely because of this level of organization. They were able to bring people in, to rule in the local levels, that they knew would have allegiance to the higher-ups. Of course, sometimes when the local rulers were in it for too much of themselves, then they would be replaced, of course. And that might cause a bit of problems, but that's politics as usual. Somebody say Amen. But Luke is describing politics as usual. But more than that. Luke is describing the story of God's redemptive work within the polis. It unfolds within this massively organized system that we now know in hindsight, to be called the peace of Rome. While Tiberius was going about his thing, being Lord over the Empire. While Pontius Pilate was lording it over his region of the empire in Judea. While Herod was lording it and Philip was lording it, God is up to God's redemptive business. Somebody say Amen. That's encouraging!

Sometimes when I think about the ways in which our world is organized, I think, "Lord, what good can come out of this matter of organization?" And I read Luke chapter 3 and then I see that the word of the Lord came to John. This was this renegade cousin of this Jesus fellow that we read about in the previous chapter. Remember that story? The word of the Lord came to John, son of Zechariah. If we have time this morning, I don't think we will, but Zechariah, as you know, in chapter 1 of Luke, had a son late in his life, right? His wife, Elizabeth, was barren for much of his life. And it was through this stigmatized family that this cousin of Jesus was born. And this cousin of Jesus, already being raised by a-little-bit-more-elderly parents, if you will, not the normal folks, you know? When he's running around with his five, six, fifteen-year-old friends in the deserts, his parents couldn't quite keep up with their parents. But it was this John who was in the desert, it says. And he went into all the country around Jordan preaching. Think about how Luke so brilliantly describes the scenario. It's kind of like, you know, the song that talks about well, you know on this day of Christmas, when all through the fields everything was in order.[5] All the ruling governors were in place. And there comes God's subversive and redemptive work. Coming from out of the desert, coming from out of one who eats locusts and wears who knows what. I mean the latest stylish clothes, of course, from the latest fashion designers, from the desert, of course, into the heart of Empire preaching the gospel of repentance. Again, God's redemptive work coming from margins, coming from the mangers and the deserts of the world. Places where you and I would not look for the next decree! Where you and I would not think to look for the next major breakthrough in the polis. God is doing something new. It gives me hope. Somebody say Amen. Should give us hope.

Well maybe folks in Kirkland aren't quite from the desert. But maybe our Tri-Cities friends over there are. God could still be doing something redemptive in the desert. And John came and went into all the country around Jordan preaching a baptism of repentance, for the forgiveness of sins. Now of course, when we read about this preaching of baptism of repentance, forgiveness, again we think about that work of the Spirit that touches our hearts, and yes, the Holy Spirit does touch our hearts to lead us to repentance, Amen? Yes, the Holy Spirit does bring us to a place of baptism. Yes, the Holy Spirit does help enable us to experience the forgiveness of sins. But I think there's more going on here in the polis.

The exact language in the Greek for forgiveness of sins is identical as forgiveness of debts. How many of you recognize, you remember some

5. I must have been thinking about the Christmas carol, "Silent Night," which first two lines goes: "Silent night, Holy night // All is calm, all is bright . . . ."

of the older translations? For example, in the King James, "Lord, forgive us our debts, as we forgive our debtors,"[6] right? And of course, we start thinking about that, that doesn't sound right, you know? I paid my credit card bills, I don't want the other person's credit cards bills to be forgiven. Because that usually means that my taxes go up. How many of you know that when other people don't pay their bills, and when they forfeit on their loans we get an economic recession? Right? Forgiveness of debts is not necessarily a good thing in a credit-based society like ours. But locate this polis, in which you have tetrarchs and governors and Caesars, ruling empires, ordering census, extorting taxes. The taxes are coming, not from the 5 percent of the population where you have the government, the aristocrats, and the warriors. Taxes are coming from the 95 percent of the population—right?—that are the land workers. Not the landowners; the land workers: 95 percent of the population is paying the taxes that allow this 5 percent of the population to do what it does, and to enjoy its benefits. This is the context within which this renegade, from the desert, comes in and preaches the gospel of the forgiveness of debts. This now becomes a very political message. We don't have time to read through the rest of chapter 3, but it's very clear that part of that involved the sharing of what people had. Part of that involved him telling the soldiers, "Don't take more taxes than you should." That's economic. That's public. That's polis. That's political.

When we look at what the work of the Holy Spirit was in the early church, in the book of Acts,[7] we find this same thing, right? People streamed from the countryside of Judea to the apostles. Why? Because they found that while in the countryside of Judea they were working their "whatevers" off to pay and to be extorted by the government in their taxes. All of a sudden they came to the apostolic environment in which it said that they worshiped together daily and were filled with gladness and praising God, sharing with one another, and none of them had need, because what? God provided for all their needs through those who had.

The forgiveness of debt was taken seriously in the early church. This is a radical movement of the Holy Spirit. So radical that they could only pursue it for a short period of time, before a number of other factors undermined that. And you'll find out more about that in my book, if you get a chance to look at that.[8]

6. Matt 6:12.

7. The rest of this paragraph riffs off Acts 2:42–47.

8. Referring to *Who Is the Holy Spirit?*

By the way, I'm not quite sure I feel comfortable about this book being out there, you know. Because I remember the story about Jesus, you know. He went into the church and he saw that the people were buying and selling things. Maybe we should've taken it outside the church. [Laughter.]

But John preached the baptism of repentance and the forgiveness of debts. And when we think about the baptism of repentance, we internalize it as a way in which we demonstrate our following after Jesus. I think it's a bit more than that. Through baptism, we're now born into a new community, a body of Christ. And we acknowledge now, not just our following Jesus. That sounds so, you know, nice. But we acknowledge our *allegiance* to Jesus. Somebody say Amen. How many of you realize that acknowledging our allegiance to Jesus in a world in which somebody else calls himself Lord is subversive? In which somebody else calls himself the ruler of the world, that's treason. When you acknowledge, "No, I bow my knee not to Lord Caesar, but I give my allegiance to Jesus of Nazareth."

When John comes now preaching a baptism of repentance for the forgiveness of sins, he is now preaching a politically volatile message. A message capable of arousing the masses to turn their allegiance from one who says [he can], and to some degree has manifested the ability to provide for peace and prosperity for those that are in his empire. But now, all of a sudden, a group of people are saying we turn and give our allegiance to Jesus Christ, Jesus of Nazareth. The one born in a manger, on the margins of Empire. The one [to] whom we're introduced by one who comes from the desert eating locusts and wild honey. Dressed in nothing more than sackcloth. This is the political gospel. The gospel that challenges the power, the pomp, the status of the principalities and powers of this world.

Luke, I think, is inviting us to ask: "Holy Spirit, what are you doing in our world? Not just in my heart, not just in our hearts." Yes, the Holy Spirit is at work in our hearts. Yes, the Holy Spirit is inviting us to embrace the fullness of what he has for our lives. But the book of Acts is very, very clear. "And you and I shall receive power after the Holy Spirit comes upon us." Amen? Central part of the Pentecostal message. Hope we never forget that one. But it also says, that that power will enable us to go to what? Into Jerusalem, to Judea, to Samaria, and to the ends of the earth. The ends of the earth are ones, in Luke's story, who are already controlled and circumscribed by Lord Caesar. The empowerment of the Spirit is designed to take the people of God from the desert and from the mangers of that world, to its ends. In order to do what? To represent the subversive Lordship of Jesus, amidst the empires and rulers, and the powers and the principalities of this world. That is a message that you know . . . we get pretty good maybe sometimes organizing church-growth projects. We get maybe, pretty good organizing, and I'm not saying we shouldn't, organizing social services and social activities, representing ourselves in the community. But let [us] ask ourselves the question, how are we going to engage the principalities and powers of our world? We need concerted prayer, Amen? For that, we need concerted exploration of the Scriptures together, to ask ourselves, "Lord, how do we as the people of God, who represent the Lordship of Jesus in a world that is ruled by foreign principalities and powers, how do we live out that discipleship in a way that is faithful to you, in a way that allows the power of the Holy Spirit to be manifest to transform lives?" Peasant lives. Think again about the five thousand men and women and children that flocked to Jerusalem.[9] Whose lives are transformed by the power of the gospel. Through the experiencing of community that they had never experienced before. Going from being peasants, just working for Lord Caesar, to now serving in the body of Christ, the fellowship of the Holy Spirit, experiencing community that they had never experienced before. Because of the new work of the Holy Spirit in their hearts, yes, but also in their lives, and in their community, and in their polis.

As we prepare to close this morning, I want to go to that first chapter of the book of Luke, in order to lead us to a brief moment of prayer. And in verse 5, again. Luke unfolds his story of Jesus of Nazareth, within the polis. He says, "In the time of Herod, king of Judea." Right? Judea is well controlled at this point. Herod has got his stamp, his fingers, on the pulse of what is going on in Judea. History tells us a lot about Herod and his dynasty, his uncles, his dad, his sons, has a lot of stuff going on there. But Herod was king. He was in power. And God was in the redemptive business, right under Herod's nose. God was in the redemptive business, calling upon Zechariah and Elizabeth. And of course, it says, Elizabeth had no children. She was barren, well along in years.

Imagine, of course, the social shame and social stigma that Elizabeth and her husband Zechariah experienced because of not being able to have children. You know, having children, of course, was one of the most important things that women could do in the ancient world. She never had that privilege up until this point. So, there's a certain, deep level

---

9. Acts 4:4.

of social shame and stigma that she experienced. Even that shame and stigma is socially generated, isn't it? In other words, when people have expectations of us, and in our lives, we're unable, for whatever reason, to fulfill those expectations, there is shame, there is stigma, there's a feeling of not having accomplished. A feeling of not having lived up to the standards and expectations of the world.

How many of you know that Jesus is in the business of redeeming the world and its standards and its expectations? How many us realize that we do not need to live according to the world's standards and expectations? Amen? The world creates all these expectation, all of these conventions, all of these things that are "normal." And think about how much time and energy and effort we spend in our life trying to meet the expectations of others. Don't tell me that we don't live in a politicized world. Things we buy, things we invest our time and energies, and our monies. All of that reflects our attempt to live up to somebody else's expectations. That itself is a political way of life.

How many of you are glad that God redeems us from the polis and in the polis? Sometimes God does it by allowing us to meet these expectations. In this case, Elizabeth is given the child that she longed for, that she yearned for, that she had spent years, if you will, calling out to God for. And God, through giving her John the Baptist, now has redeemed her shame, vindicated her inadequacy, put a stamp of approval on her womanhood. That, of course, is the mark of achievement of womanhood in the ancient world. Now she was fulfilled. Sometimes God allows us to meet expectations or relieves us, alleviates us, from the shame and stigma, that social expectations put on us. But other times God challenges us to overcome and undermine and be countercultural to the world's expectations, Amen? Sometimes that's the harder way to go, isn't it? But isn't that what the power of the Holy Spirit is given to us for? Amen? To enable us to bear witness to Jesus of Nazareth, the one born outside the scope of [the] Empire and its constraints.

I mean, the Roman soldiers weren't in the manger, taking count of who was being born. That's where the animals were. The one who was marginalized and excluded from the principalities and powers and its grip around the world. That's the one we bear witness to by the power of the Holy Spirit. That's a noble calling. That's a calling above and beyond which we can't just sort of, you know, nicely and easily organize. But it's exactly, I think, the work of the Spirit, to blow in our midst. It's up to us to say, "Holy Spirit, how can we follow you in our world? How can we follow you in this place, and this time? How can we bear adequate witness to you in this city? In this public space? Kirkland. Pacific Northwest of the United States of America."

Bow with me in prayer this morning. I just have three very, very brief questions to ask as we close in prayer. Do we need, O Lord Jesus, to repent of just thinking about the gospel as being an individualistic reality? Do we not need to also see, Lord Jesus, that your Holy Spirit calls us into the world, in all of its complexity? [Second,] Lord, in what ways do we live in an imperial world that might be similar to Imperial Rome? Who is Caesar, today, Lord Jesus? Do we live under your Lordship, Jesus? Or are we living under the principalities and powers and the lords of this world? And a third question: Holy Spirit, how can we make a difference in our world today? Wherever we're at, whatever we're doing, whatever our lot in life, Holy Spirit, how do we bear witness to Jesus of Nazareth in our world? Come Holy Spirit! Fill us once again. In the name of Jesus, we ask, Amen.

Tony Richie Reflection—"Symbiosis and Symphony"

Yong's sermon suggests Christians inevitably live within a political world, which is also being redeemed and transformed by Christ. Christians have (and do) reside/d in nations governed by monarchies, dictatorships, and democracies as well as communist/socialist systems. Most systems have their own set of virtues and vices. None is perfect. Some are evil. Christians do well to take a cue from exiled Israel. Jeremiah instructed Jews to labor for Babylon's wellbeing (29:4–7). Esther and Daniel demonstrate active involvement in governmental affairs under dire circumstances. And Jesus himself calls his followers to be "salt and light" in this world, a "city set on a hill" (Matt 5:13–16). These are public, and therefore, quite political, descriptions.

The city of God transcends but temporarily coexists alongside the city of this world. Distinct religious and political spheres overlap under God's all-encompassing sovereignty. *Symphonia* (mutual complementarity) between church and state is essential. Both Caesaropapism (church subjugation to state) and theocracy (state subjugation to church) have repeatedly proven misguided and destructive. The political and social significance of the gospel is clearly inescapable. All creation and its creatures thrive only symbiotically. Detached isolationism isn't an option. There are no "solitary" Christians.

Though "principalities and powers" are fallen institutions frequently requiring prophetic confrontation, government, imperfect as it is, nevertheless is a divine gift for humanity's sake. Yet a deadly danger is nationalistic deification. Government as an idol is a blasphemous, hideous, carnivorous monstrosity. Those who worship it will be judged by the true and living God. There's drastic difference between serving God *in* government and serving government *as* God. Ultimate allegiance belongs to the only ultimate Lord—Jesus Christ—and to his eternal reign.

5

Saved from Shame and Stigma

Shortness of Stature and the Gospel in a Disabled World

LUKE 19:1–10

Central Woodward Christian Church,
Troy, Michigan, 23 September 2012*

Good morning. It's very good to be here this morning, I'm grateful to Pastor Bob for the invitation to join you and to worship with you this morning. So, I bring you greetings from Virginia, from California, and from Malaysia, why not? [laughter]. . ..

The title of our meditation this morning is "Saved from Shame and Stigma," and our subtitle, "Shortness of Stature and the Gospel in a Disabled World." Our theme this weekend has been disability. And oftentimes, we think about disability in terms of how it pertains to individual

---

* Rev. Bob Cornwall came from a Foursquare (Pentecostal) church background, has a PhD in historical theology (from Fuller Theological Seminary), and is pastoring a Disciples of Christ congregation while reading my work as part of his wider efforts to weave his charismatic inclinations and sensibilities into his broader theological vision and his ecclesial practices. He explains on his blog, "Ponderings on a Faith Journey" (see http://www.bobcornwall.com/) that reading my *The Bible, Disability, and the Church* prompted an invitation to present ideas in the book to his community. I gave two talks on Saturday and then stayed over to Sunday to give the homily. The written version from which this sermon is based was published as Yong, "Zacchaeus: Short and Un-Seen," reprinted as "Short, Saved, and Un-Seen."

lives and individual bodies. I want to invite us to think, this morning, about the fact that the gospel addresses not just disability and bodies but a *world* that is broken. And oftentimes, that people with disabilities have to wrestle with all of the other issues that the world presents, that make life even more difficult and more complicated. How, this morning, we're going to ask ourselves, does the gospel addresses all of us with whatever abilities we have or do not? But in a world that organizes itself in ways that inhibit our lives, [that] does not allow us to flourish, we as Christians have long been at the forefront of providing care for people with disabilities, and that's a good thing. We should continue to do that. But doing all of these good deeds, if you will, does not keep us from sometimes internalizing the biases and the prejudices that the world fosters against disabilities and against those who may have various forms of impairment.

I want to ask us this morning, as we look into this text in Luke chapter 19, about how the gospel as mediated through the story of Zacchaeus can open up our own hearts, to how we sometimes participate in this world of bias and prejudice. And oftentimes, [we] don't even ask ourselves questions about that. Those who have you who grown up in the Scriptures know of the story of Zacchaeus, right?

[Singing] Zacchaeus was a wee little man, and a wee little man was he! He climbed up to a Sycamore tree for the Lord he wanted to see [singing ends]! Now I'm going to stop right there because they tell me that I move people when I sing—to the exits! So, before we generate any of that movement this morning, I'd just like to continue on.

Of course, Zacchaeus is a wonderful story that we've all known from growing up as well. And of course, he resonates especially with kids, right? Because they live in their short world. Zacchaeus is right there, at their level. And they can empathize, and they love climbing trees, and here was one who climbed a tree. What a cute story, it might seem from our Sunday school days. Think a little bit more, though, about as we grow older, and how we expect our short kids to get taller. And of course, our short kids do grow up, and we grow up into a tall world. And in that tall world, people like Zacchaeus are no longer just merely cute because they're little. But of course, they're fascinating because they're unlike the rest of us. Think of, for example, about the images of short people that you and I might be familiar with.

Of course, I think many of us grew up watching Fantasy Island. Remember that story? Hervé Villechaize. I mean he had a sad ending to his life, you might know. The one who committed suicide. But he was Tattoo, Mr. Roarke's assistant on Fantasy Island.

And of course, we've got a lot of other not-so-positive images of short people. Think of Verne Troyer, you might remember him as Mini Me in the James Bond series.[1] The evil short man, who was bent on conquering the world for his own nefarious purposes.

So, we've got images of short folks. Fascinating, in their movements. Nefarious, in their intentions. Why? Possibly because they see themselves as aligned against a dominant world of tall folks, who are now all of a sudden their archenemies.

Does Zacchaeus, in our story, fit our contemporary models of disability? Now we gotta be careful about imposing contemporary notions of what we understand about short persons' lives on our story. We're not given too many details into the story of Zacchaeus's life, but I think there's more there to be noticed than what we generally have. Because most of us, when we read this story, read it from a tall person's perspective. Most of us.

Now it is the case that there are other terms that the original Greek language, in that period of time, would have more appropriately used to identify someone that today we might say has *pathological dwarfism*. That's a medical term, of course, for short people. Pathological dwarfism, of course, has a range of kinds of lives and forms. Anybody under four-foot-ten, that's an adult, technically qualifies as a pathological dwarf. But of course, they could go much shorter. Pathological dwarfs, of course, range across the spectrum. There are over one hundred different kinds, subcategories, of those who have been diagnosed with this particular medical terminology. Now it's a complex set of people. People across the spectrum of pathological dwarfism bring with them a range of abilities, intellectual, not so intellectual. They bring with them a range of physical capacities. They're all short, at a certain level. But many of them suffer from crippling, physical conditions.

Now Zacchaeus seems like he would have been one of the folks on the more, if you will, capable side of the pathological dwarfist category. We don't know for sure if he was technically a pathological dwarf, because the word in the Greek that talks about Zacchaeus is the word *mikros*. And technically, it just simply means "short person." He was short. There were a couple of other terms in the Greek that might've been used. One would

1. Editor's note: Troyer starred as Mini Me not in the James Bond films but in the Austin Powers movies.

have been *pigma*; you might recognize the etymology of that term. It is related to our contemporary notions of pygmy. Another would have been a term like *nanos*. So the term *mikros* does not definitively label him as somebody that we might consider a pathological dwarf. But there are a range of references across the ancient world—from about the fourth or fifth century before Christ, to about the fifth century after Christ—that would suggest that *mikros* may have been used on occasions to refer to people that today we might identify as having pathological dwarfism. So, linguistically, Zacchaeus might have been someone that might've been a pathological dwarf. And if that were the case, then he may have been exposed to any of these range of, if you will, abilities or disabilities. He may have been an overcoming type, having climbed up the ladder, despite the challenges that he might've embodied in his own life. Certainly, as somebody who was a short person, he would've been assessed religiously in the ancient world, and particularly in the ancient Israelite world, as somebody that would have been prohibited from entering and giving the offering in the priestly ceremonies. You know there's a phrase, there's a reference in the book of Leviticus, which we talked about this weekend, to folks who are also dwarfs who are prohibited from entering into the sanctuary and contributing offerings if they were in the priestly line.[2]

So, there would have been certain, if you will, assumptions made about our friend Zacchaeus. Aside from whatever physical abilities or disabilities that he may have had to wrestle with, he had to have confronted these social stereotypes, these religious stereotypes, that would have already categorized him within a certain group of people. [People] that, according to Leviticus, for example, would have mutilated bodies of some sort or other, limbs too short in some way or other. Scabs and brokenness in their bodies, in their bones. Or other[s] hunchbacks, even, according to that Levitical text. People with blemishes in their faces, in their eyes. These were the folks that were all lumped together. As [one of those who] were blemished in the eyes of ancient Israel, Zacchaeus would have had to deal with these religious stereotypes, about folks that looked like him.

Beyond the religious stereotypes that he would've had to encounter, would've been the social stigmas attached to the lives of short people, that are, of course, a range that we are familiar with those in our day. But across the ancient world for many, many centuries, we've got all kinds of evidence from across the world about the stigmas in which short people

2. Lev 21:16–23, esp. v. 20.

were depicted. The ridicule [that] their lives elicited, because of their very visible conditions.

You know, many of us today may wrestle with or struggle with what people call hidden disabilities. Disabilities that are part of our lives, but they're not obvious. And if they're managed in the right way, we might be able to ["pass" as non-disabled and] avoid the stigma that comes with the knowledge of some of these.

Well, a short person like Zacchaeus would not have been able to hide his disability. And there would have been caricatures, there would have been discriminatory attitudes. He probably would have faced these discriminatory biases in terms of what he could've done for employment. He became a tax collector. In the first-century Jewish world, a tax collector was the lowest scum of the scum. Worse than an IRS agent today. Somebody say, Amen! Hope there aren't any IRS agents working here.

In my tradition, you know, they say Amen when the preacher preaches. Oops, there was silence on that one.

A tax collector? Why? Because you're working for the Romans. The Romans were the oppressive governmental force over first-century Palestine. I mean, you're practically, as a Jew, if you become a tax collector, you become an outcast, a pariah to the community. Well, maybe Zacchaeus couldn't find another job. Maybe his shortness of stature prohibited him from getting in with the folks in his own . . . among his own people. So, yes, he became rich. Oh, and was that even a further stigma that he had to bear! Not only was he working for the government, the oppressive government, but it's [probable that his riches] and his wealth came from these nefarious practices of tax collectors, to build their own pocketbooks, before passing on to the government what was theirs. You see that he repented of that, in a few moments, don't we? So, we know that's what he did. He was rich, but his wealth came from the benefits; we call that today, extortion of the people. Perhaps he had just given up, and said, well you know if that's the way people are going to treat me, I'm going to take advantage of my position, as an extortionist, I mean, tax-collecting agent. I'm going to get a better life, the best I can. Those are part of the stigmas that pertain to lives of short people.

[There are] lots of studies today about the lives of short people. And short people continue to wrestle with the stigmas of the dominant tall society. There are lots of short-people groups around the country, and in some parts of the world, that allow for [a] community of folks that are like-minded, and like-appearing, if you will, amongst short folks.

But there are lots of short folks who aren't even a part of these groups. Why? Because for them, it—to gather together with other people that are their height—is a reminder to themselves about their own condition. A condition in which they have internalized an identity of self-deprecation, that is self-stigmatized because of what they have experienced growing up: the laughter, the ridicule, the rejection. And many short people live isolated lives, lonely lives. They can't go out and mix around with the real world of tall people. And they can't bear to be amongst their own folks, because it's too much of a harsh reminder of the world [they] inhabited.

Might we be able, as we look at this story of Zacchaeus, however, to adopt maybe his perspective? I want to suggest to us in the few minutes we have this morning, what I would call a shortist reading of Zacchaeus. You might be familiar, if you've been around your pastor long enough, that there are different kinds of readings of the Bible, like a feminist reading. Well we're going to adopt a shortist reading of Zacchaeus this morning. I want to point out a few things about this text from maybe a short person's perspective that us tall folks might easily have overlooked.

He was a man who wanted to see Jesus, but being short, he could not because of the crowd. Verse 4 says he ran ahead. Can you imagine the crowd? The crowd is observing him here. When the author says he ran ahead, so you could imagine the crowd there, and you're the crowd, we're the crowd, he is running ahead. Imagine us as a bunch of tall folks observing a short person running ahead, right? Imagine the kinds of fascination and curiosity in which we would look at, maybe even gawk at, the unique movements of those feet [and torso]. And then those feet running ahead and climbing a tree. Well, you know that even among us tall folks, after a certain age we stop climbing trees. Hello? Why is that? Well, not only because we don't want to fall off, but it would be unseemly for an adult to be climbing a tree. Somebody say Amen! We've got certain presuppositions, certain biases about climbing trees after a certain age. Oh, how funny it would be. Look at this short man, squiggling along here, oh, he's climbing a tree! Can you imagine, maybe the giggles, and maybe just the outright laughter as the short man makes his way ahead of the tall crowd. Stretches and struggles and gets up into the tree. This despised . . . not only is he just a short person, it's him! This despised tax collector who is a part of this oppressive system. "Look at him! Look at him go!" He wanted to see Jesus.

And I heard the reading of Scripture this morning, as you did. I hope you did, where Jesus said, "come on down." And it says he scrambled down.[3] Can you imagine the crowd looking on, and observing this interchange. Here is this short person who had struggled to get up this tree, and now he is scrambling down. Oh, wouldn't that had been a sight? Wouldn't you have like to see that on TV?

The desire to see Jesus had led him to expose himself to the ridicule that perhaps he had gotten used to. It was considered undignified for a grown man, not just to climb a tree, even to run. You know, unless you are part of a marathon or something. How many of us just sort of go gallivanting around? Too dignified for tall folks. But his physical condition would've associated him with all of these negative aspects. The crowd began to say that after all of this amusing site, "Oh look, he has gone to be the guest of a sinner!" Yeah, of course he was a sinner, right? Extortioner, to be more precise. But he's probably a sinner in more than one respect. [The] first-century world assumed that sinners were physically marked. Remember the question that was asked in John chapter 9 of the man who was born blind? And the disciples came up to Jesus and said, "Lord, who was it who sinned? This man or his parents, that he was born blind?" Well, obviously, Zacchaeus was a sinner. I mean why else would he be so short? Why else would be so marked? Why else would he represent, in his body, the signs of greed? The signs of nefarious intents? I mean, aren't those the stereotypes that we associate with certain bodily forms,[4] including those of shortness? And we have failed to recognize Zacchaeus's full humanity as a dwarf, haven't we? I mean, when we look at the history of translations and interpretations of this passage, many well-intended tall people in their readings of this passage have minimized the shortness of Zacchaeus. Or they have spiritualized—yes, yes, yes—we're all short in the sense that we can't see Jesus! Somebody say Amen! But of course, that minimizes Zacchaeus's particular challenges, his particular shape of life. And it removes it from our consideration. We sometimes want to be so politically correct that we failed to recognize the very particularities that mark every one of our lives. Or we so spiritualize it. But I want to suggest, on a shortist reading of this passage, that we can learn a few things from Zacchaeus.

Zacchaeus is not about to allow the conventions of this world and the prejudices and the biases of this world to hinder him from seeing Jesus. We assume that people with disabilities are all in need of our

3. The NRSV says: "So he hurried down . . ." (Luke 19:6).

4. See Parsons, *Body and Character in Luke and Acts,* ch. 5.

charitable acts. That they're all helpless and awaiting somebody's help to come along. Well, Zacchaeus is not gonna wait for that help to come along. He is going to exert himself, he is going to run ahead, in spite of the fact that people are looking. He is gonna climb a tree in spite of the fact that people are laughing. He is going to see Jesus. He's gonna exercise his agency. He's gonna pursue the desire of his heart.

How many of us recognize that regardless of whatever abilities we may or may not have, we have desires? And we have agency. And Zacchaeus, of course, knew that he needed to repent. Repentance is for all of us, whatever the level of our abilities. Zacchaeus reflects that regardless of what we can or can't do, regardless of our height, regardless of our size, regardless our capacities, he recognized the Lord: here and now, I give half my possessions to the poor. And if I've cheated anybody out of anything, I will give back four times the amount. Luke, in telling the story, begins to challenge all of his readers' assumptions about what shortness represents: the sinfulness associated with it, the small-mindedness that are attributed to this small stature, etc. And it begins to expose all that; hey, look, these are our prejudices [too]. And then come both remarkably powerful and redemptive words from Jesus: "Today salvation has come to this house, because this man too, is a son of Abraham." Now that's a good time to say Amen folks. For that first-century Jewish readership or that crowd, how could it be that such an evil person, how could it be that such a marked sinner, could even be declared as having received salvation? What a powerful and redemptive statement. "Today this man, too, has come into the grace and the goodness of God." That would have exploded all of the prejudices, biases; it would have shined the light now back on to the heart of the crowd, who had their own assumptions about their own salvific stature. And Zacchaeus is lying beyond the pale, on the outside of that community. Jesus now has embraced him. Zacchaeus becomes one of those few disciples who have a marked, physical condition, for whom now Jesus calls, without healing [or curing] according to our assumptions about what it means to be whole.[5] There are lots of other folks that Jesus cured and touched and made, if you will, non-sick. He didn't add another foot to Zacchaeus physically. He called him. He received him. He embraced him. And he pronounced the salvation of Yahweh upon that home, upon that life.

5. See also Yong, *Theology and Down Syndrome*, ch. 8.

And that leaves the rest of us asking ourselves, do we need to be saved today? Maybe we haven't been extortioners like Zacchaeus, but maybe we need to be saved from our biases, from our prejudices, from our viewing others through the stigmatized lens of a conventional world that values certain forms, that values certain images, that excludes people like Zacchaeus from within our communities. Maybe the question for us this morning is, Lord not how can people like Zacchaeus be saved, but how can *we* be saved?

Let us pray: Lord Jesus we ask this morning that you take this message, and that you redeem us, as you redeemed Zacchaeus. And we thank you for your redemptive work. In Jesus' name, Amen.

Tony Richie Reflection—
"The Hunchback and a Wounded Healer"

Yong's hermeneutic demonstrates that the way we read the Bible impacts how we view persons with disabilities. Unfortunately, an underlying stigma toward disability exists even in the church. But the gospel offers hope to people of all abilities. Scripture challenges churches to become more inclusive communities. Inclusiveness involves more than merely sympathizing with those "less fortunate." It requires co-suffering—voluntarily, joyfully, sharing in others' afflictions—as Christ did for us (Col 1:24). Common in ecclesiastical language, Latin's *compassio* (compassion) is literally "co-suffering." Thus we participate in Christ's Passion through empathetically embracing others' sufferings.

God created the world good (Gen 1–2). However, sin has left the world broken and disabled (Gen 3). That brokenness, that disability, grips hard at every human life. Jesus diagnosed humanity's malady as spiritual disease and described himself as the physician applying redemption's remedy (Matt 9:12). Indeed, he *is* the remedy. But Jesus isn't an opioid. He embraced the pain and thus overcame it. It is by "his wounds"—his brokenness, disfigurement, and pain—that "we were healed" (1 Pet 2:24).

So what about those who yet live among us with obvious physical and/or intellectual disabilities? Conspicuously deformed, Quasimodo (*Hunchback of Notre-Dame*) was abandoned by his family, abhorred by the public, and betrayed by the church. Incredibly, Quasimodo responded to a single act of kindness and experienced love's redeeming power. In the midst of severe suffering the Holy Spirit can impart great joy (1 Thess 1:6). Hence, Henri Nouwen (e.g., *Wounded Healer*) testified to fresh joy and peace after becoming a disability community's pastor. Although those with disabilities all too often are relegated to humanity's margins, they dwell close to God's heart. Joining them on the outskirts is moving nearer to God.

6

From Holy Ghost to Holy Spirit

Living the Spirit-Filled Life

ACTS 5:26–32

Wheaton College chapel, Wheaton, Illinois, 4 April 2014*

Good morning Wheaton College. It's an honor to be here with you this morning. If you have your Bibles with you or if you have your iPhone or whatever it is that you use to check up what we're going to be talking about this morning, turn with me to the book of Acts, the fifth chapter . . . .

Acts 5, I've entitled what I have to say this morning, "From Holy Ghost to Holy Spirit: Living the Spirit-filled Life." I'm going to start reading in verse 26 in the New King James version.

> 26Then the captain went with the officials and brought them without violence, for they feared the people, lest they should be stoned. [Aside explanation here by Yong:]—These were the leading rulers in Jerusalem, going after the apostles, who they had just locked up. And whom the Holy Spirit had released from prison, they found them now preaching in the

* I was initially invited to participate in the 24th Wheaton College Theology Conference on "The Spirit of God: Christian Renewal in the Community of Faith," Wheaton, Illinois, 3–4 April 2014—my contribution there was published as "Creator Spiritus and the Spirit of Christ"—and then was also asked to address the student body in the chapel service.

courtyard.—[27]And when they had brought them, they set them before the council. And the high priest asked them, [28]saying, "Did we not strictly command you not to teach in this name? And look, you have filled Jerusalem with your doctrine, and intend to bring this Man's blood on us!" [29]But Peter and the other apostles answered and said: "We ought to obey God rather than men. [30]The God of our fathers raised up Jesus whom you murdered by hanging on a tree. [31]Him God has exalted to His right hand to be Prince and Savior, to give repentance to Israel and forgiveness of sins. [32]And we are His witnesses to these things, and so also is the Holy Spirit whom God has given to those who obey Him."

Bow with me in prayer just for a moment. Spirit of the living God, the one who has exalted Christ, [raised] him, energized his body, we welcome you again this morning. Be in our midst this morning. May the words of my mouth and the meditation of our hearts be acceptable in your sight, O Lord, we ask and pray. In Jesus' name. And all God's people said, "Amen."

When we think about the Holy Spirit, we talk about the Holy Spirit, there usually are a number of reactions. And we find three of them in this chapter of Acts chapter 5. The Holy Spirit is mentioned three times in this chapter. Twice early on in chapter 5, in which the Spirit's work is associated with fear coming upon the believers.

If you have your iPhone you might want to scroll up, and if you have a Bible open too, you can certainly look at the first part of Acts chapter 5. That first part, the first ten or eleven verses of that, of Acts chapter 5, tells us the story of Ananias and Sapphira. Many of you probably remember that story that you heard way back when you were a child. And it was usually told in the context of, well you better tell the truth so that worse things won't befall you. You know the story. Ananias and Sapphira had brought only part of what they had sold to the apostles, but told the apostles that this was all that they had collected from the sale of their property. And the Holy Spirit is mentioned twice in Peter's response to Ananias and Sapphira. "Why has, where is it come from that it is in your heart to lie to the Holy Spirit, saying that you brought all that God has given you, when you've only brought a part of that?" And Ananias died as a result of that. His wife comes in a few hours later and we have a similar thing happening. She also had agreed with her husband to tell the certain part of the story. And as a result of telling that part of the story, she was also carried out. And it says great fear came upon the people. Sometimes when people think about the work of the Holy Spirit, they associate that work of the Holy Spirit with things like fear. Things might get out of control, and this is a judgment story. This story should inculcate some fear into our hearts and lives. I think the important point of this story, in the first part of Acts chapter 5, has to do with the fact that God was doing an amazing work.

And before Ananias and Sapphira there is a story of Barnabas, the son of encouragement; and others who shared with one another, who lived with one another, with openness and sincerity in true *koinonia*, in true love and commitment to one another. In that particular context, the Ananias and Sapphira story warns about hiding things, warns about dishonesty, warns about lying. And the work of the Holy Spirit came in judgment and brought about fear.

Throughout the history of Christianity, however, there have also been lots of other kinds of movements of the Spirit. Movements of the Spirit that people have feared or been concerned about, for a number of different reasons. It's not without reason that some of these movements have been called enthusiastic movements. People, the word enthusiasm simply means to be filled, as if by a divine presence. And sometimes when people say that they're filled with the Spirit or sometimes when people claim to walk out a Spirit-filled life, they do all kinds of strange, and what might be unconventional, or weird, or threatening things. In those kinds of contexts, within the context of these enthusiastic movements, people have been suspicious, they have been hesitant, they have been concerned. Some have feared about those movements. Some have feared about those movements because they themselves don't want to get sort of caught up in being taken over by being sort of possessed by this Holy Ghost, as they might've said it . . . the King James version translate *hagios pneuma*, the Greek, Holy Ghost. And for many of us who have grown up, sort of, in times where ghosts have negative connotations, when we read about Ananias and Sapphira, when we think about enthusiastic movements, when we think about people who say that they have been filled with the Holy Ghost, but do other things that are of concern to us, that are strange, that we're not used to, there is a certain kind of a fear, saying "I don't want to be possessed by that Spirit or that Ghost if I'm going to be led to do these things, that might be strange to me, that might be different for my church, that might cause all kinds of questions."

So there is a certain sense in which sometimes we try to keep, sort of, an arms-length from the work of the Holy Ghost. We're afraid that the Holy Ghost might come in and take over. We don't like giving control of our faculties, of our ownership of our tongue, ownership of our lives; we want to be in control. And sometimes enthusiasm suggests that we lose that control; that the Holy Ghost comes into our lives and leads us to do strange and different things.

Pentecostal and charismatic movements throughout the history of Christianity have experienced another side of this that's not quite on the order of fear, but in the order of wondrousness, unexpectedness. I understand that there are some Pentecostals here at Wheaton College. Somebody say Amen. Alright, we got a few out here this morning. Praise the Lord! It may just happen yet, that Wheaton College, whatever "it" is—there was one clap. Somebody got it. [Laughter.]

In verse 12, Acts chapter 5, through the hands of the apostles, many signs and wonders were done among the people. And they were all with one accord in Solomon's porch. So, right after you have this description of Ananias and Sapphira and the fear generated, as a result of the fact that they had been found out, and hauled away, and carried away. Then there's a mention of the signs and wonders that were done. And we know that whenever signs and wonders happen in the book of Acts, it has to do with the work of the Holy Spirit. Jesus himself was filled with the Spirit to go out and accomplish signs and wonders, and so were his apostles. Loved that song.[1] Walking in Jerusalem with the apostles. As Jesus was filled with the Spirit, as he went about doing good, and healing the sick, and casting out demons, so it says also here, in Acts chapter 5. In fact, if you go down to verse 16, the multitude gathered from surrounding cities to Jerusalem, bringing sick people and those who were tormented by unclean spirits. And they were all healed.

So, pentecostal/charismatic movements and renewal movements throughout the history of Christianity have experienced walking with the apostles, walking in the footsteps of Jesus and being filled with his Spirit, experiencing these signs and wonders. And sometimes I think many of us would say, "Well, we want these signs and wonders." And sometimes when these signs and wonders come we don't know what to do with them, because they're so different, they're so strange. We wrestle

---

1. Referring here to one of the choruses sung earlier in the chapel service, which title now escapes me.

with the role of signs and wonders, and how they played themselves out in our churches, in our histories.

So, we've got this strange relationship, if you will, with the Holy Ghost. Fear and concern and suspicion and questions, on the one hand. Rapturedness, in sort of a desiring for more, on the other hand. But yet, not quite knowing because we don't control the work of the Holy Spirit. The Holy Spirit shows up in our midst. Sometimes when we're not quite expecting it, and then we're unprepared and we don't respond appropriately. And we respond sometimes in different ways.

But I want, for the rest of our time this morning to focus on an aspect of the Spirit-filled life, that I believe should be something that we can all live into, by the help of the Holy Spirit. And that's referred to here by Peter in the passage that I read, starting in verses 30, 31, and 32. Here was a context in which again the apostles had been thrown in jail for the ruckus that they were creating, having healed the man at the gate "Beautiful" in Acts chapter 3. Thrown in prison for a while, set free again, and then they were thrown in prison again. And now the door was open and we know, of course, later on in Acts, when the doors are open, the prison doors are open, it's usually the angel of the Lord that appears. So, the angel of the Lord appears and lets them out of prison and they go back out into the public sphere, and they're preaching. And the religious leaders come after them. And again, they say, "didn't we strictly command you not to teach in his name?" And Peter's answer is what I want to focus on for our last few moments, in thinking about what it means to live a Spirit-filled life. Because this is the third time that the word, that the Holy Spirit, is mentioned in Acts chapter 5.

Peter says, "We ought to obey God rather than men. The God of our fathers raised up Jesus whom you murdered by hanging on a tree. Him God has exalted to His right hand to be Prince and Savior, to give repentance to Israel and forgiveness of sins. And we are His witnesses to these things, and so also is the Holy Spirit."[2]

I want to submit to you this morning, that there is this aspect of the Spirit-filled life which simply consists in the availing [of] ourselves to the Spirit of God to bear witness to Jesus. It's not complicated. It might be something that you and I take for granted. It might be something that you and I disassociate from the work of the Spirit. But notice that Peter says explicitly here that we are witnesses to these things and so also is

---

2. Acts 5:29b–32 (NKJV).

the Holy Spirit. The work of the Spirit-filled life, I want to submit to you this morning, ought to be no more and no less than the capacity to bear witness to Jesus.

Now I want to highlight three aspects of this message. The God of our fathers raised up Jesus, whom you murdered, by hanging on a tree. Bearing witness to Jesus is about bearing witness to the resurrected Lord. Somebody say Amen. It's a message I'm sure that we as Wheaton College students, faculty, and staff have heard perhaps all of our lives. And we might say it, we might talk it, but let us not minimize the miracle that it is, in which the Holy Spirit enables us to bear witness to a resurrected Christ. Yes, somebody can say Amen.

Let us not underestimate [this]. Again, when you think about what is happening in the book of Acts . . . . Just a few weeks before, Peter following Jesus in the dark shadows of Good Friday, denied Christ three times, denied his Lord three times. Remember that part of the story? And then a few days later [he] was hit with the reality of the resurrection, a resurrection that Jesus already implanted seeds about, and alerted them to. But that resurrection was still not something that we can rationally wrap our minds around, right? The capacity to bear witness to a resurrection is not something that you and I, in our normal ways of thinking and talking, can very easily do. That is why this is something that the Holy Spirit also has to enable. Somebody say Amen. Talking about people being raised from the dead is not something that we do in the normal scheme of things. But this is what drives the apostles from prison, back out into the public sphere. You would think after you've been thrown into prison for doing that same thing, that when you got out the next time that you would organize a more, if you will, subtle place to talk about your faith. Somebody say Amen. That's being called as wise as doves in my language. But they go right into the middle of the public square. To do what? To bear witness to the resurrected Christ. The God of our fathers raised up Jesus and has exalted him to the right hand, to be Prince and Savior. Not just resurrected Christ, but the Savior Christ, the Prince of Peace Christ. The Christ who saves, which means saves in all our ways.

The New Testament notion of salvation is rich, it's multifaceted, it's multidimensional. We're saved from our sins, we're saved from our bodies that don't work correctly. We're saved from broken relationships, we're saved from broken systems of realities in which we all live and move. We're saved from all of that. The resurrected Christ promises us a healing of our lives, of our souls, our relationships, of our communities. That's not something that you and I can bear witness to in our own language, in our own words, on our own strength. It's something that we need the power of the Holy Spirit to enable that particular witness. A witness to a living Savior, a witness to a living Christ.

Further, Christ, the witness the Holy Spirit enables, is also a witness [of the] repentance [offered] to Israel. Look at what it says in the middle of verse 31. This is a major theme throughout Luke and Acts. When you and I think about it today—most of us I assume are gentiles in this room—repentance to Israel seems like a sort of a quaint idea from way back when, that nobody really talks about anymore. But for Luke, who wrote the Gospel of Luke, for Luke who wrote this early history, this history of the apostles; they were about the restoration of Israel. They were about the renewal of Israel. It's just that what they weren't quite aware of was that God intended the renewal and restoration of Israel to open up to the renewal and restoration of humanity. And this is the message and the witness that the Holy Spirit enables. Somehow, taking the particularity of the good news of the Messiah, who had come to a particular people, the Jews, taking that message and that resurrected reality, so it makes sense to those who live beyond the borders of Israel. So it makes sense to those who live beyond Jerusalem, who lived beyond Judea and into Samaria, where relationship between Jews and gentiles were just at an all-time bad. And even, according to Acts 1:8, to the very ends of the earth. In fact, if I might say it, from the apostolic perspective, even to some place like Wheaton, Illinois, yeah! I mean if you were in Jerusalem, you couldn't get any further to the ends of the earth than Wheaton, Illinois, Amen? But that's the nature of the apostolic witness and its power. Not of its own strength. But of the witness of the Holy Spirit to enable, if you will, repentance to Israel; to enable repentance of the world, a world far beyond the border of Israel. A repentance of sins against God, a repentance of sins toward each other.

And last, but not least, to give repentance to Israel and forgiveness of sins. The witness of the Holy Spirit opens up the capacity for us to receive, and to give, and to live in forgiveness. Now you might, again, you know us growing up in evangelical and Pentecostal-Charismatic [churches], we've heard about forgiveness all of our lives, and sometimes I think we've domesticated this concept so much, we've forgotten really what it means to be able to receive forgiveness, be able to live in forgiveness.

Notice what Peter said here earlier in his passages, as he's talking to these people. We ought to obey God rather than men. The God of our fathers raised up Jesus whom you murdered by hanging on a tree. Now I don't know about you, but if I was Peter, and I'd been thrown in jail two times beforehand, talking to these same folks, and now I've been let out for a third time, and I was standing and talking to them, I don't know about you, but I probably wouldn't have put it quite the way he did. I'm not going to say, yeah, *you* murdered him. I'm might have just said something like, "Well, those other folks over there, your bosses." But this is the message of the early apostles. They're very clear. He said this here, he said this in Acts chapter 2, he said this in Acts chapter 4. There is no getting around this particular proclamation. But yet, there is a declaration of the capacity for forgiveness. Of forgiveness that was made available even to you, who murdered him. No doubt, Peter, on that Good Friday, had heard Jesus' own words coming from the cross. And said, "Father forgive them, for they know not what they do." And when Peter himself was filled with the Holy Spirit, in the next few weeks and months following, he began to understand that this was not just a Jesus thing, but this was the good news. The gospel. The gospel that allowed the declaration of the availability of the forgiveness of sins. And the gospel that allowed that gift, to be extended even to one's enemies.

For Peter, following in the footsteps of Jesus, filled with the same Spirit that Jesus was filled with, it was a challenge to live in Jesus' footsteps; to live with the capacity to forgive those who had injured [us], those who are against us, those who had thrown us in jail, those who had persecuted us. In fact, it says in the end of verse 26 that the captain and the officials brought them, but they feared the people lest they should be stoned. There was even the capacity of being stoned. And here was this pronouncement of the good news, not in and of his own strength—that's not something I could have stood in my own strength and declared to this crowd: "Oh yeah, this forgiveness of sins is available to you." In my own strength, I would have been doing other things, like planning this and that. Acting politically. Doing all those things. But for Peter, filled with the Holy Spirit, it enabled a declaration of who Jesus was as a resurrected Savior, how he invited repentance of Israel and of the world, and how forgiveness of sins was available, even to those of us who have injured the Lord himself.

I want to submit to you this morning, those are the foundational elements of the Spirit-filled life, when you are capable of announcing the gospel, and the good news of Jesus and of his work, and of the repentance that he invites, and of the forgiveness of sins that he makes available.

Which means also the promise that he will enable you to live in peace with those who oppose you. To live in ways that are nevertheless counter-conventional in our thinking. Somehow the gospel heals the gap that has opened up between us and our enemies. That's the Spirit-filled life. That's the life we are all called to. That's the life we can't step into on our own. That's the life in which we say, come Holy Spirit, enable me to walk in the way of Jesus.

Bow your heads with me in prayer. I'm going to close our time together by reading an ancient prayer[3] from the medieval period: "Come, Holy Spirit. Send forth the heavenly radiance of your light. Come, Father of the poor. Come, giver of gifts. Come, light of the heart, greatest comforter, sweet guest of our soul, sweet consolation. In labor, give us rest. In heat, give us temperance. In tears, give us solace. Oh, most blessed light, fill the inmost heart of your faithful. Without your grace, there is nothing in us, nothing that is not harmful, cleanse that which is unclean. Water that which is dry. Heal that which is wounded. Bend what is inflexible. Fire what is chilled. Correct what goes astray. Give to your faithful, those who trust in you the sevenfold gifts. Grant reward of virtue, grant the deliverance of salvation, grant eternal joy. In Jesus' name, Amen.

Tony Richie Reflection—
"Mysterium Tremendum Fascinans"

Yong's homily invites us beyond the fear of enthusiasm into affirmation of Spirit-empowered witness of the resurrected Lord. The New Testament church openly embraced spiritual manifestations (e.g. Acts 2:1–4; 1 Cor 12:7). Early church fathers Ignatius, Justin Martyr, Irenaeus, Tertullian, and others did so as well. After the late second-century Montanist sect embarrassedly overemphasized prophetic gifts, *charismata* became increasingly suspect. By the sixteenth century Luther sarcastically described a fanatical opponent as having "swallowed the Holy Ghost, feathers and all!"

Ideally, wisdom and spiritual depth dovetail. In the eighteenth century, John Wesley saw a church standing in dire need of revival. But how does one facilitate vigorous, vital faith without falling into fanaticism? The key: careful discernment between illegitimate forms of enthusiasm, often similar to psychological hysteria or diabolic spirit possession, from

3. *Veni Sanctu Spiritus*; Come Holy Spirit!

authentic "religion of the heart." The Wesleyan "quadrilateral" of Scripture, tradition, reason, and experience provides an assessment model. Another theologian/revivalist, Jonathan Edwards, similarly defended Christianity's affective character. Authentic religion is a matter of the "heart also" and not of the "head only." Moreover, Edwards carefully discerned "the distinguishing marks of a work of the Spirit of God" (cf. 1 John 4:1–6). Today Edwards's and Wesley's spiritual heirs fear formalism as much as fanaticism.

Appropriate fear of the Lord has invigorating, life-giving powers (Prov 14:27). According to phenomenologist Rudolf Otto, fear (dread/awe) of a holy God is at the root of all religion. An anthropologically universal sense of tremendous and fascinating mystery (*mysterium tremendum fascinans*) in the presence of the Holy (the *numinous*) inspires profound reverence and worship. Christians worship God by bearing witness to the Lord Jesus Christ in the power of the Holy Spirit.

7

Who Are the Christians?

The Nature of the Church

ACTS 11:19–26

Great Bridge Presbyterian Church, Chesapeake,
Virginia, 25 May 2014*

Acts 11:19–26:

> 19Now those who were scattered because of the persecution that
> took place over Stephen traveled as far as Phoenicia, Cyprus,
> and Antioch, and they spoke the word to no one except Jews.
> 20But among them were some men of Cyprus and Cyrene who,
> on coming to Antioch, spoke to the Hellenists also, proclaiming
> the Lord Jesus. 21The hand of the Lord was with them, and a
> great number became believers and turned to the Lord. 22News
> of this came to the ears of the church in Jerusalem, and they
> sent Barnabas to Antioch. 23When he came and saw the grace
> of God, he rejoiced, and he exhorted them all to remain faithful
> to the Lord with steadfast devotion; 24for he was a good man,
> full of the Holy Spirit and of faith. And a great many people

---

* My wife and I had attended Great Bridge Presbyterian Church regularly during
our nine-year stay in Chesapeake, Virginia, while I served as faculty, and then as dean,
at Regent University's School of Divinity. Over the years, I did some pulpit supply at
the church and also taught a few adult Sunday School sessions. Pastors Ralph Herbert
and Anita Killebrew had been preaching a series on the church during this time, which
theme I picked up on from the book of Acts (surprise, surprise).

were brought to the Lord. 25Then Barnabas went to Tarsus to look for Saul, 26and when he had found him, he brought him to Antioch. So, it was that for an entire year they met with the church and taught a great many people, and it was in Antioch that the disciples were first called "Christians" (NRSV).

Father we thank you for your Word. We thank you for already being here with us in our worship, for inhabiting our praise. We thank you Lord God that you promised to speak, to lead us into your truth. May the words of my mouth and the meditation of our hearts be acceptable in your sight, O Lord, we ask and pray, in Jesus' name. And all God's people said, Amen.

All right, well it's good to see you all here. Always good to be back to visit. And we always enjoy worshiping with you and are blessed to be able to share this time with you. Pastor Anita and Pastor Ralph are, I think, up in some mountain somewhere today. And they contacted me a few weeks ago and asked me and said, well we're doing, we'd like you to come and speak this Memorial Day weekend. And we're doing a series and closing off a series on the church and on the nature and what it means to be the church. Is that, kinda I think, . . . right? Although I don't want to ask who remembers last week's sermon, so I won't. But as I thought about this morning's topic, I was led to the book of Acts chapter 11. I've been living in the book Acts for a number of years. And every time I get a chance to preach, it usually comes out of the book of Acts. As I was asking the question, what does it mean to be the church? Or what does it mean to be a Christian? I was drawn to this passage Acts chapter 11 verses 19–26. And you see that as we finish reading this passage this morning, it is in Antioch that the disciples were first called Christians. So, I want to take a few moments this morning and look to see how this passage describes what it means to be Christian, and what it means to be the church.

But before we get into that can I tell you a theologian's joke? Is that okay? I'm a theologian, what other kind of joke do you want me to tell you? So, a few years ago, about two hundred to three hundred theologians gathered together for a major theological conference on the Mount of Olives in Jerusalem. They went out all week long, three-four-five days, and of course they were debating and disputing everything theological that you'd never care to know about. And so, coming through to the last day, on the last day, they had a lunch, sort of a barbecue, outside on the Mount of Olives, they're all getting their food, sitting on the mountainside just like in the old days, like Jesus' day and the five thousand. And as they are eating their food, all of a sudden in the middle of the sky, the sky broke open and then of course God appeared! Right in a theologian's conference. Hopefully you are laughing right now. And of course, God speaks out through the clouds and he says to this startled group of three hundred theologians, "Who do you say that I am?" And of course, as theologians do with a question, they called a conference. So, they huddled together and they went to the buzz in a debate, and after about fifteen minutes they un-huddled and the major theologian, came out, looked up at the Lord and said . . . read the statement, "Thou art the ontological source of all dimensions of cosmic, quantum, and astrophysical realities. Thou art the providential provider of all creatures and the purpose, the atmosphere in the hemisphere. And thou art the extra-logical ground of all ethical and aesthetic values." And the Lord said, "What did you say?" [Laughter.] Thank you! Well, we're not going to try to use all of those big multi-syllable words, thinking what it means to be a Christian.

I want to look at what Luke tells us in Acts 11. And I want us to see how he describes those who were first called Christians in Antioch. And the use of the word [in] the passive tense is not unintentional here, as you know in verse 26. And it was in Antioch that the disciples were first called Christians. These disciples weren't running around this area saying, "we're Christians." In fact, if you know much about the history of Jesus' followers up until this time, these disciples were Jews. They were Jewish followers of the Messiah. Acts 11:26 tells us that they were called Christians.

How many of you know that when somebody else calls you a name, most of the time it's not with positive connotations, right? When you get called names, it's not always positive, most of the times it's not positive. And what we see in the rest of the New Testament, sorta bears this out. In fact, most of the Christians, we'll come to this in a moment, were persecuted. They developed reputations, in fact, a number of New Testament authors had to write to these so-called Christians and say, "live quietly, behave yourselves."[1] Why? So, that all these gentiles won't have anything bad to say about you. They were already being called a bad word: "Christians." We're not used to that, right? Cause we're Christians. We don't think it's a bad word today. We have some history, right? Acts 11:26 gives a window into this first-century phenomenon. Where all of a sudden, folks at Antioch started noticing th[is] bunch of Jews, and rather than call them Jews—and of course, that was sort of a bad word for Greeks

---

1. E.g., as early as 1 Thessalonians 4:9–12, and as late as 1 Peter 2:11–17, at least according to current scholarly consensus about the dating of these letters.

too—but they called them a second bad word, if you will: called them Christians. And why did they do that? Well, I think this eleventh chapter of the book of Acts gives us some windows into how this name comes about.

Start with me in verse 19, that's where we started in our passage. "Now those who were scattered because of the persecution that took place over Stephen." Now I want to give us two or three characteristic features of those were first called Christians.

The first one is, I would say, that they are an irrepressible group. Now what do I mean by that? I see that those who were first scattered because of the persecution, and when you and I think and sit back and ask, what persecution? Well, it was the persecution of Stephen. And I'm not going to ask, how many of us have read the book of Acts recently? Cause I don't want to repeat the whole thing. I only see a few hands. I will say this, right? If you flip back to the book of Acts to about the sixth or seventh chapter you will see that there is a story of Stephen. Stephen was a Jew who had come from Asia Minor and hung out with the apostles for a while. He started engaging with other Jews about the nature of the Messiah. He started talking about a God who resided not only in Jerusalem, not only in the temple in Jerusalem, he started talking about a God who had taken the Mosaic law and had begun to expand its boundaries and its scope. He started talking about a God whose throne was the whole earth, not just the mountain in Jerusalem. And guess what that got him? It got him stoned. Remember that story when these Jews who were upset, hauled him out of the city, they took their robes off, they laid them at the foot of a man named Saul, and they stoned him for blaspheming the law, for blaspheming against Moses, blaspheming against the temple.

A persecution broke out at that time in Acts, at the end of Acts chapter 7, the first part of Acts chapter 8. And Luke, the author of the book of Acts, tells us that when that persecution broke out, the apostles, the twelve apostles—it was eleven, but remember they added Matthias in Acts chapter 1—the twelve apostles withdrew into the safety of the confines of Jerusalem, and the following took place outside of Jerusalem, outside of the city. And then persecution broke out against all those who followed after Jesus, who embraced his name and his way. And as the persecution broke out, these twelve apostles withdrew themselves into Jerusalem. They were going to wait until the emergency had blown over. They were going to wait until it was more peaceful to get back out on the streets, and talk about Jesus. And these apostles already had some experience of that. Remember the first part of the book of Acts? They were already thrown in jail, multiple times, and God had saved them. But now things were ratcheting up a notch. And the persecutors were coming at them, not just hauling them to the jail, but were coming at them with rocks.

Well, these irrepressible ones, it tells us here—my word, irrepressible—these were scattered because of the persecution. These folks, rather than withdrawing like the apostles in Jerusalem, they said, "you know, what, okay so we can't talk about Jesus in Jerusalem. Guess what we're gonna to do? We're gonna go out to Judea. We're gonna out into Samaria." And that's what they did, in Acts chapters 8 and 9. And we're going to go even further than that—they were [and we are] irrepressible—they [who were on the receiving end] of the persecution that took place over [and after] Stephen [still] travelled: "We're not going to be to be shut down. We're not going to close up shop. We're not going to cease proclaiming the name of Jesus. We're just gonna go where we have got a little bit of religious freedom to share the gospel." They were irrepressible. But they travelled, it says, as far as Phoenicia and Cyprus and Antioch. They travelled as far as Phoenicia and Cyprus and Antioch.

Now you have to understand. How many of you have seen a map in the back of your Bible before, at some point? Good, a good number of you have. When you look at those maps, of course, sometimes there will be two, three, four different versions, one of them will have Paul's first missionary journey, a second will have a second and third missionary journey, the third will be a focus on Jesus and Palestine, and so on so forth. Well that is the known world of the first century. And when you and I talk . . . the second point I want to highlight about these, who were first called Christians, was that they were irrepressible and were very, quite international, right? It says that they went as far as Phoenicia and Cyprus and Antioch. Now when you and I think about the distance between Jerusalem and Phoenicia, Cyprus, we think is not too big, right? It's kind of like going from here to maybe Nashville, Tennessee. That's not too far, right? But if you think about it from the perspective of these first-century Jews that were centered in Jerusalem . . . . Notice Luke's language. He says there in verse 20, "they travelled as far as Phoenicia."

Now you know, when you take your five-year-old little boy, and say, "Son, we're going to wake up tomorrow and we are going to drive to Nashville, Tennessee." "Wow, that's a long way away," right? We can do better when they're ten years old, say, "Son, today we're going to drive to Omaha, Nebraska." "That will take like two days, dad!" Now we're really stretching, right? Now we'll do even better than that, we'll will drive to Salt Lake City, Utah, take us three to four days. Some of you speed demons out there can probably do it in two. Now of course none of you have driven further than San Francisco, California, right? Now I've driven multiple times across the country. I understand when it says here that they traveled "as far as." From the perspective of first-century Palestinian Jews, to get to Phoenicia is crossing the whole Mediterranean ocean. You and I think about the Mediterranean world, the Mediterranean Sea. Some of us think about it, will look at it, compare it to the Atlantic Ocean, the Pacific Ocean, it's kind of almost like a little pond. But from a first-century Jewish perspective, the Mediterranean Sea was the only ocean in the world. It's the biggest one! In order to get as far as Phoenicia, somebody had to have some courage, somebody had to make an investment, somebody had to pull some cash together, somebody had to be bold enough to get on that ship. Somebody had to stay on that ship for multiple days in order to get "as far as" Phoenicia. "As far as" Cyprus. And "as far as," finally, Antioch.

Antioch, in the first-century Mediterranean world was, should I say it, [was] just the place to be. It was the third largest city in the Roman Empire, besides Rome and Alexandria. Antioch was a huge metropolitan area of 500,000 people. Of course, in our day and our time, 500,000 people, well that's just a little more than a little village, isn't it? But in first-century Mediterranean Jewish terms, Antioch was like the Jakarta, the Tokyo, the Mexico City of the world. People [were] flocking to Antioch, people were going to Antioch. That's where things were happening. That's where commerce was bustling out of the seams of the city. That's where people were moving in from the countryside.

These Jews, these who were first called Christians, were not only irrepressible, but they were also international, willing to cross geographic, oceanic, and regional, and national borders for the cause of Christ. And they spoke to no one, it says in verse 19, except Jews. Now isn't that an odd statement? Of course, not. From our twentieth-century perspective, you know, we might not have noticed that, but from our perspective it seems kind of odd, doesn't it? And it is odd, from our perspective. But from a first-century Jewish perspective, it was very natural, it was very normal. Jews traveling around the Mediterranean world don't just go hopping into the homes, in the centers, and the shopping centers, and the business centers of gentiles. Jews traveling around the Mediterranean world in the first century connected with other Jews; went first to Jewish synagogues; went first to Jewish marketplaces. You can't go to a gentile marketplace because [none] of the food that's sold in the gentile marketplaces [was] the kind of food that you were supposed to eat. Jews hung out with Jews, when Jews get to Phoenicia, when they get to Cyprus, when they get to Antioch, with its humongous group of 25,000 Jews in Antioch. That's a lot of Jews in a city of 500,000 people. Of course, they would go first to the Jews, only to the Jews. It said there that they spoke to no one, except they spoke the word to no one except Jews.

But not only were they irrepressible, not only were they international, but they were also multicultural and multilingual. Look what it says here in verse 29. Among them, among these travelers, these persecuted, irrepressible, international ones, among them were some men of Cyprus and Cyrene, who coming to Antioch, spoke to the Hellenists also proclaiming the Lord Jesus. Now that is an aberration. These who were first called Christians got called, were called this name because they began to go outside of their comfortable Jewish confines, and get into the space, the culture, the relationships, the marketplace of the gentiles. These were just some from Cyprus and Cyrene, who maybe—these, "some men"—had heard the story coming out of Caesarea.

Remember the story, a few chapters back in the book of Acts [chapter 10]? Just a couple of chapters back, where there was this apostle named Peter who had actually gone, had come out of his little hole in Jerusalem and decided, that "You know what, I'm going to venture beyond Judea, I'm going to venture even past, beyond the borders of Samaria. I'm going to all the way to Caesarea." And not only that, Peter said, "I'm actually gonna step into the house of a gentile." Again for [a] twenty-first-century perspective, we think, what's the big deal about that? But from a first-century Jewish perspective, you don't go into the house of gentiles. And Peter, of course, had learned, he had to overcome that barrier in a very difficult way. God had to appear to him in a vision, with all the animals coming down on the blanket. And then he told Peter, "Arise Peter kill and eat these animals." Peter said, "Not so Lord, 'cause I've never eaten anything unclean in my life. Why are you asking me to do that?" The Lord gives this vision three times. And the Lord says, "What I have cleansed, do not call unclean." The next thing Peter knows, there is a knock at the door, Cornelius's servants, Cornelius is a gentile centurion. The servant knocks, and says, "We don't know why we are here, all we know is that Cornelius told us to invite you to come to his house." Peter would never have gone to Cornelius's house until he saw that vision. And maybe some of these folks from Cyprus and Cyrene had heard this testimony. Maybe some of these folks had begun to say, "You know what, this Peter guy, one of the leaders of Jerusalem, he actually went to visit a gentile. And you know, I have lots of friends up there in Antioch. I have lots of friends, who know lots of friends, and they are all gentiles. And in fact, there are 475,000 of them."

Hello? Anybody here? Can you follow that? Amen? Give us a couple of Amens here, otherwise I will repeat myself. And you don't want me to repeat myself too much because I'll take a longer time to finish up.

These folks came into Antioch, and all of a sudden began to realize that, you know what, "Yeah, we should share with the Jews, but why limit ourselves? There's a whole lot more folks here in Antioch who haven't heard about Jesus." And all of a sudden, they began to see that the promise of the forgiveness of sins that Peter extended to Cornelius, "Hey, you know what, we can extend that not only to the 25,000 Jews in Antioch, we can extend that [also] to the 475,000 gentiles that are in Antioch. Why don't we start speaking to some of these Hellenists?" Hellenists is simply another word for Greeks. They were irrepressible, they were international, and they were multicultural, and they were multilingual, and they began to understand that the message of the gospel was not only for Jews. It was first, for the Jews, but also for everybody else. And that meant that they could now come and speak to those who were gentiles, and along the way.

I want us to look at two features, of what it meant for them to be called Christians, they were followers of Christ. Christ simply means the Anointed One, the Messiah. Jews prayed for the Messiah. They longed for the Messiah. They were waiting on Yahweh to send Messiah. Why? The Messiah, or the Anointed One, would deliver the Jews from the hands of the Romans, from the hands of the Herods, from the hands of the Pontius Pilates, from all the Romans agents that were taxing them and oppressing them. The Messiah would come and deliver the Jews from the hands of the Romans. And all of a sudden, some of these from Cyprus and Cyrene, some of these Hellenistic Jews, began to understand that, "You know what, the Anointed One, the Messiah, was sent not only to deliver just a bunch of Jews, but he was sent to deliver a bunch of people!" Hello? Jews or gentiles from Cyprus or Phoenicia or Antioch. That's the gospel, that's the good news. The Anointed One was sent to the Jews first, but also to the gentiles. Praise the Lord, I'm one of the gentiles. I'm going to bet most of you are too. We take it for granted.

But those who were first called Christians were irrepressible, were international, were intercultural, inter-linguistic. They said that there is the good news of Jesus that crosses these barriers, crosses these boundaries, that will take us to Phoenicia, to Cyprus, to Antioch, even to Rome. That's the story of Acts: that you shall receive power after the Holy Spirit has come upon you—that's the promise to the apostles—and you shall be my witnesses in Jerusalem starting there, and going out into the countryside of Judea, going to even to despised realms of Samaria, and by the way, you're going all the way to the ends of the earth. Right past Nashville, Tennessee all the way to San Francisco. Somebody say Amen! Thank you!

That's the good news! That the Messiah, the Christ [or Anointed One], is not only for Palestinians and Jews. For Antiochians, for Asians like me, Americans like you, Asian-Americans like us. American Asians like us and whatever else you are. Doesn't matter whether you're from Cyprus from Cyrene, or Phoenicia. This is the good news. For *all*. And they were also followers, who proclaimed and announced, it says there in verse 21, the Lord Jesus.

I want us to close. We take these words for granted. I grew up a young boy, a pastor's kid, I was saying "the Lord Jesus" in my prayers before I knew how to pray, right? The Lord Jesus. But when you're thinking and when you're talking about a first-century Mediterranean context, there is only one Lord in this culture, in this time, in this society, in this world. And that Lord wasn't Jesus, that Lord was Caesar. Lord Caesar, who paved the roads and made it possible for travelers. Lord Caesar, who kept the pirates off the oceans, to make traders be able to move from port, to enable people to catch ships from Caesarea to Phoenicia, from Caesarea to Cyprus. Lord Caesar, who following in the footsteps of Alexander the Great, had extended the domain of the Empire, brought peace to the land. That is why it was called peace of Rome. Lord Caesar, who enabled the kind of prosperity, financial, economic, and otherwise, to be spread out across the Empire, did it through taxation, that's true. But the point was that there was one Lord in the Roman Empire in the first century. And that was Caesar Augustus, later, it was Nero Caesar, later it was Domitian Caesar. But Caesar was definitely Lord.

So, when those who were first called Christians got to Antioch they recognized, however, that there is another Lord. And his name is Jesus. One who forgives our sins, the one who makes it possible for us to share the Fatherhood of God with others who don't speak our language. With others who live in other parts of the world, with others who live and who come from different cultural backgrounds, and different linguistic backgrounds. The Lord Jesus is what binds us all together regardless of where we come from or what our other identities are.

If you see here in this passage there's all kinds of identities in play. Phoenicians, Cyreneans, Hellenists, and Jews, and Barnabas the son of encouragement, and Saul of Tarsus. The way in which this kind of language identifies us, right? Most of us I would assume live here in Chesapeake. You may not know this, but you all are Chesapeakens. Hello? But most of us don't go around being really proud about being Chesapeakens, right? Some of us might take a little pride in being Virginians, maybe not. If you were born in Texas, that great country of Texas, you're definitely a Texan, right? Some of us might actually think it's important to say we're Americans! Alright! Saul of Tarsus. Saul, of the great city of Tarsus, with its history, with its tradition, with its language, with its culture, with its political power. Saul of Tarsus.

Those who were first called Christians in Antioch said, "You know what, yeah, we might be Antiochans, but that's a secondary label. Our first label is we're called Christians." Those who follow after, embrace the name of Christ, not the name of Caesar, not the name of Herod, not Pontius Pilate, not the governor of Antioch, not the culture of Cyprus—it's a beautiful culture I've nothing against Cyprus, the culture of Cyprus.

When I was growing up—I was born in Malaysia, by the way—when I was ten years old my folks moved us to California. About thirteen, when I was an adolescent, I had all those troubles that adolescents do, probably a little bit more. I was confused. I asked my dad one day, "Dad, what am I? Am I Malaysian? Am I Californian? Am I American? Am I Chinese?" He looked at me and said "Son, don't worry about all that." He said, "You're a Christian." It's not that all of those other things don't matter. I'm still Asian American my wife is still Mexican American, our kids are still confused. It's not that those things don't matter, those things matter, but they don't matter as much as what it means to give one's allegiance to the name above every other name, the name of Jesus.

Bow your heads with me.

Lord Jesus, we thank you, that you have enabled us to be called [Christians] after your name. A name originally meant for ill, but you have taken it and allowed us to embrace the name that is above every other name. A name through which sins are forgiven, a name through which salvation is made available to the ends of the earth, whether in Cyprus, in Cyrene, in Antioch, in Chesapeake, or to the ends of the earth.

Help us to live into that name, O Lord God. And we thank you for enabling us to do so. In Christ's name, Amen.

Tony Richie Reflection—"A Trinitarian Fellowship"

Yong accents the dynamic and inclusive nature of the church held together by one overarching identity in and all-consuming allegiance to its Lord, Jesus Christ. The church's distinctive nature isn't discoverable in its polity—whether congregational, episcopal, presbyterian, autonomous, or a hybrid. Rather, the church's uniqueness derives from the nature of its being.

Ecclesiology traditionally highlights three particularly descriptive biblical images useful for summing up the church's nature. First, the church is the people of God (Titus 2:13–14), portraying belonging. The world belongs to God through creation; the church belongs to God through redemption. Second, the church is the body of Christ (1 Cor 12:12–31), portraying mystical, organic union with Christ and with each member. Thus, the life and strength of Christ are imparted to believers. Third, the church is the temple of the Holy Spirit (Eph 2:19–22), portraying habitation. The Spirit indwells or resides in the church. Significantly, each image defines the church by its relation to God, specifically to respective persons of the Trinity. Furthermore, each descriptor is corporate, signifying community—a plurality of interdependent persons existing in a state of benevolent commonality. In sum, the church is a community in relationship with the Triune God. In other words, the church is a Trinitarian fellowship.

The unity-in-diversity of the Holy Trinity determines the inherent nature of the church. The church, however imperfectly at this time, yet reflects the Trinity. Therefore, the church continually exists in unity with God and with all its members while simultaneously exhibiting the joyful diversity of many tongues and many cultures. The church is a redeemed community owned by God, united in Christ, and filled with the Holy Spirit. It is essentially diverse and inclusive. It can't legitimately be otherwise. Can we?

8

Praying with the Apostles

Then and Tomorrow

ACTS 4:23-31

Great Bridge Presbyterian Church, Chesapeake, Virginia, 22 June 2014*

[The] Scripture reading today is from Acts chapter 4, reading from verses 23 to 31:

> 23After they were released, they went to their friends and reported what the chief priests and the elders had said to them. 24When they heard it, they raised their voices together to God and said, "Sovereign Lord, who made the heaven and the earth, the sea, and everything in them, 25it is you who said by the Holy Spirit through our ancestor David, your servant:
> 'Why did the Gentiles rage,
> and the peoples imagine vain things?
> 26The kings of the earth took their stand,
> and the rulers have gathered together
> against the Lord and against his Messiah.'

---

* This was the last sermon I preached at Great Bridge Presbyterian Church before we moved from Chesapeake, Virginia (and neighboring Regent University), to Pasadena, California (and Fuller Theological Seminary); the series in June was on the Lord's Prayer.

27For in this city, in fact, both Herod and Pontius Pilate, with the Gentiles and the peoples of Israel, gathered together against your holy servant Jesus, whom you anointed, 28 to do whatever your hand and your plan had predestined to take place. 29And now, Lord, look at their threats, and grant to your servants to speak your word with all boldness, 30while you stretch out your hand to heal, and signs and wonders are performed through the name of your holy servant Jesus." 31When they had prayed, the place in which they were gathered together was shaken; and they were all filled with the Holy Spirit and spoke the word of God with boldness (NRSV).

Father, we thank you for your word this morning. Your word that calls us to worship. Your word that sustains us. Your presence. We thank you that you've already been with us, [the] two or three of us gathered together in the name of Jesus. As we turn to now, to hear your word, speak to us Lord, teach us and guide us, we ask. May the words of my mouth and the meditation of our hearts be acceptable in your sight, O Lord. And all God's people said, Amen.

Good Morning. Wonderful to be back at Great Bridge Presbyterian Church. Thanks Pastor Anita for the invitation to be with you today. We're excited about this service, even though it's with a bit of mixed feelings that we're here. As some of you know, we've been members here at Great Bridge Presbyterian Church before, and have visited on various occasions in the last two years.

In 2005, when Alma and I came to this part of the country, to teach at Regent University, and moved into the neighborhood, we had three children between the ages of ten and fifteen. And kids don't stay at that age, they just keep growing and growing. And over the last few years, one of them has gotten married and moved off to pastor a church in Seattle, Washington, about three time zones away. Another one has just finished graduating from Vanguard University in Costa Mesa, California. And she's right here; Alyssa, you want to wave to everybody? Congratulations to Alyssa, the new graduate. She's just home for the summer with us. But she's got some things going on out there in Southern California. Our third one, our nineteen-year-old, has just finished her freshman year at Point Loma Nazarene University in San Diego, California. So, mom and dad have been looking for opportunities to get back out to the West Coast. My parents live in Northern California. And my wife Alma—wanna say hi to everybody? Alma's right there. Alma's parents, her mother and her family, live in Eastern Washington. And when this opportunity came open for us to move to Pasadena, we just felt it was a good time for us. And so, we're making the move with a lot of excitement. But also, a lot of . . . we've got great friends at Regent University, and of course, we know many of you here. And we hope that we'll be able to keep up with, keep in touch with you. I know that we're Facebook friends with many of you, and for those of you that we're not yet, well please keep in touch with us that way as well. And hopefully we'll get a chance to visit in the future. And hopefully Pastor Ralph and Pastor Anita will allow us to come back and share sometimes with you as well.

As I was thinking about what to share with you this morning. Pastor Anita mentioned to me that she would be speaking on a passage that we all pray every week, or you all pray every Sunday, the Lord's Prayer. And thinking about the Lord's Prayer, and think[ing] about what I would say this week, I thought that we would pray with the apostles who prayed with Jesus. I've entitled our reflections this morning, "Praying with the Apostles between Then"—Acts 4, what we just read—"and Tomorrow."

If you would like to pull the Bibles out from the pew in front of you, and turn to Acts chapter 4, we're going to follow that text a little bit closely this morning. And I wanted to pray with the apostles this morning because we know about what Jesus taught us to pray, we recite that prayer every Sunday. And no doubt, many of us pray that prayer as well, on our own time. Probably on Mondays and Tuesdays and Wednesdays, it's a great prayer to pray, somebody say Amen! All right!

Now as I thought about how the apostles would have prayed, I of course turned to the book of Acts. Any time you want to know what the apostles did, you go to the book of . . . ? You go to the book of Acts. And of course, we find out that the book of Acts—in fact, Acts chapter 4— provides us with the first recorded prayer of the apostles after Jesus had left them. Now we'll see in a moment, that of course the apostles prayed much. They prayed a lot. As a good example for all of us, to pray, probably more than what we usually do. But this passage of Scripture that we read this morning, in Acts chapter 4, is the first *recorded* prayer of the apostles. And I want us to look at this prayer, to see how the apostles prayed, and perhaps we can be encouraged as well to pray with the apostles.

Verse 23 tells us that "after they were released . . . ." And of course, we want to know who "they" were and what it [was that] happened and what were they held by, so that they were released.

Now the "they" that is in this passage of Scripture refers to Peter and John. Being "released" refers to the fact that they had just been in prison overnight. Now there's a jail right across the street. Well kind of, across two streets.[1] Over here to my left and to your right. And there are some folks that are in that jail. Peter and John had been in jail overnight. They had just been released. What was the occasion of their being imprisoned? Well for those of you that know this story, of course, you're familiar with the fact that Acts chapter 4 verse 23 follows on Acts 4 verse 22, and before. And in order for us to find out what happened to them, of course, we need to read backward through chapter 4 and into chapter 3.

We know that in Acts 2, that the Holy Spirit had been given to the apostles. And those who had received the Holy Spirit had begun to proclaim the gospel. And in fact, the end of Acts chapter 2 tells us that three thousand people responded to Peter's sermon, an invitation to repent. What a wonderful occasion that was, as the early followers of Jesus began to experience his presence in their midst, even though he'd been gone at that time.

In Acts chapter 3, verse 1, it says, one day—we don't know what that day was, or how long it was after the Day of Pentecost meeting, but it probably wasn't too long after, maybe in a few weeks, maybe in a few months—but one day, Acts 3:1 tells us, Peter and John were going up to the temple. And as they passed by the gate "Beautiful"—this is a story that many of you will remember if you know the story of these first apostles—as they passed by the gate "Beautiful," they saw again—I'm sure they've seen him before; they weren't strangers to the temple—and they saw again, this lame man who was sitting there near the temple gate. And of course, if you know the story, this is a good place to be if you're lame. It is a good place to be if you're in a position to rely upon the kindness and the generosity of others. And there he was in his usual location at the gate "Beautiful," collecting alms from the passersby. Why is it a good place? It's a good place because people were walking through those temple gates, most of the time, with their hearts right, most of the time they were there to worship, most of the time they're there to give honor and glory to God. And that's a good place to depend on the generosity of those who are going to be in the presence of God.

1. The Chesapeake City Jail, on 400 Albemarle Drive, is two-blocks over from Great Bridge Presbyterian Church, which is on Cedar Road, the main street that also provided the entry to City of Chesapeake offices.

This man, no doubt, had wanted to go in to the temple and praise and sing with them. But because of his physical condition he could not, and because of his physical condition, also legally, he could not because the law prohibited people of his bodily type to enter into the temple, to enter into the holy of holies. So, he sat outside the temple gates. Day after day, month after month, year after year, and that one day, Peter and John walked up to the temple doors . . . and Peter looks at this man, he'd seen him many times before. He looks him in the eye, and this time says, "Silver and gold I still don't have. You know as a poor fisherman, I still don't have silver and gold today. But guess what I've got today, that I didn't have the last time I came by? In the name of Jesus Christ of Nazareth, rise up and walk." And he took him by the hand, and the Scripture says, this man's legs were strengthened, he jumped out and picked up his mat, he followed Peter and John, finally, into the temple courts, and he began to praise, jumping and leaping and praising God. And that, of course, arouses a stir around the area. Again, there were already three thousand who had come and joined with the new believers. And as a result of the healing of this man, Peter preached another sermon. And by the time the end of that sermon came, and by the time that all of the people were excited about what had happened, the people that had come to the temple gates, looked to see whether or not the man was there like he was many, many times before, and lo and behold he wasn't there, and lo and behold he could hear what was going inside the temple courts, of people praising the Lord. And they walked in and they saw this man, who they had seen sitting there for years and years, and he was standing and jumping and praising God. Oh, things got exciting. And people responded to that. And Acts, the early part of Acts 4, it tells us three thousand people had multiplied practically overnight, 66 percent.[2] We can use about a 66-percent increase after my sermon, Amen? I just gotta go find somebody to heal.

It increased 66 percent from three thousand to five thousand men, not accounting women and children. The authorities, of course, were keeping close tabs on what was going on. These were the same authorities, as you might recall, who just a few weeks ago had kept close tabs on the leader of this gang of twelve. And of course, you know his name was Jesus. These were the same authorities who were concerned that the people were thinking this Jesus was, somehow, what the people had hoped for, the Messiah. These religious authorities were concerned that messiahs

2. Acts 4:4.

might come and rile up the people, somehow get them excited, somehow get them thinking about revolution, somehow get them thinking about overthrowing the Roman government and kicking them out of Judea. And of course, if that happened, then of course the temple structure, the temple authorities, those who were in power, would also lose their places and positions of authority, of prestige, and of financial security. These religious authorities, of course, were very invested in maintaining the status quo. They were concerned about this man, Jesus, and they had found a way to silence him. Now they were concerned, however, that in the wake of Jesus being silenced, there were three thousand people responding to his followers. And there was four thousand people responding to his followers. And there was five thousand people responding to his followers. And these guys are walking around, they're healing lame men at the gates, and they were doing it in the name of Jesus. So, of course, what did they do? Well, they got the guys who were leading the praise and worship session in the temple. And it says they put them in jail overnight. And chapter 4 verse 21, then on the next day they brought them into interrogate them and to find out what they were doing. And of course, Peter and John simply said, "We can only do what the Lord has told us to do. And the only thing that we're doing is we're healing in Jesus' name. And we invite you to receive the salvation that is available only in the name of Jesus." What could they do?

Well, verse 21 of chapter 4 tells us that the religious leaders threaten them again. This wasn't the first time. This certainly wouldn't be the last time. If you follow up the story throughout the rest of the book of Acts, you'll know that the threats kept coming, and the threats would multiply intensely. And the threats would open up into actual persecution and scourgings and floggings and other kinds of physical punishment. But in this case, chapter 4 verse 21, the authorities threaten them, they let them go, finding no way to punish them because of the people. There's five thousand people out there. Who knows what they were doing. Maybe they had gathered outside the gates of the police courthouse. But finding no way to punish them because of the people, for all of them praised God for what had happened. Maybe they had gathered outside the courthouse, they were holding their own prayer meeting. "Praise the Lord! Thank you, Jesus, for healing this man!" And there's that man in there, with the apostles, it tells us in Acts chapter 4. And of course, what could they do? Those religious leaders had seen that man out there for months, and years, and decades. They'd probably given him permission, they gave him a parking permit right outside those gates. They probably put a few alms in his collection plate over the years. But now, of course, there he was. They were praising God. For the man, on whom the sign of healing had been performed, was more than forty years old. That's the context, after Peter and John were released.

They went to their friends and reported with the chief priests and the elders and said to them: "When their friends heard this, they raised their voices to God together, and began to pray." And began to pray. There was a situation, of course, and put yourself in the shoes of these friends. Twenty-four hours ago, they were in the temple courts singing and praising God and celebrating this wonderful achievement of God, this wonderful manifestation of God's power in healing this man, who for years, had been sitting and waiting. Twenty-four hours ago, they were hearing Peter proclaim it and teach and talk about God's . . . , of universal restoration, as his sermon in Acts chapter 3 talks about. Twenty-four hours ago, they were celebrating the greatness of God, and then less than twenty-four hours later they know that their leaders have been thrown in jail. They are no doubt waiting up all night. We know that they had all-night prayer meetings when people, when their leaders had been thrown in jail, according to the rest of the book of Acts. Maybe some of them stayed up all night. Maybe some of them had a prayer meeting. Maybe others of them began to call out to God. When they heard it, they raised their voices to get to God and it says they began to respond in prayer. This response in prayer was not artificial. This response in prayer was not just because of the circumstances. But how do we know that? We know that because we know that the apostles, these early followers of Jesus, had built-in, and had emerged from, a life of prayer. Acts chapter 1 verse 14 tells us this: that all these were constantly devoting themselves to prayer together with certain women. How many of you know that we have got women who are the prayer warriors? Somebody say Amen. The men said Amen in this one. All of these were constantly devoting themselves to prayer, together with certain women, including Mary the mother of Jesus, as well as his brothers.

[Acts] 1 verse 24 says, "Then they prayed and said, 'Lord, you know everyone's heart. Show us which one of these two you have chosen.'" And God heard their prayer by revealing through lots that Matthias must be the one who would be the replacement for the one who had fallen away.

Acts 2 verse 42 says this, that the three thousand "devoted themselves to the apostles' teaching and fellowship, to the breaking of bread and [to] the prayers." We know that these early followers of Jesus the Messiah, as Messiah, devoted themselves constantly to prayer. Their lives were governed by rhythms of prayer. Their thoughts were governed by a continuous devotion in prayer. Their hearts were oriented continuously in prayer to their God. And thus, when this occasion came around and they heard the testimony of James, Peter, and John,[3] and when they heard about what had happened, and when they saw that they were okay, when they heard that the threats were ongoing, they respond according to the ways in which their hearts had already been attuned—which was in prayer.

The apostles show us that the moments of prayer emerge out of lives of prayer. Moments of actual utterances, occasions in which we actually pray are organically emerging out of lives devoted constantly to prayer. And their prayer began in verse 24, "Sovereign Lord, who made the heaven and the earth, the sea, everything in them."

Know now when you and I pray, oftentimes, certainly this is the case for us, we're concerned about what happens in our personal lives. We pray for what happens in our families. We pray for what happens in our job positions. We pray for what happens in the lives of our friends. We pray for what happens in the circumstances in which we experience trials and challenges. We pray for the things that hit us most close to our hearts. But the prayers here are addressed to the God who made the heavens, the earth, the sea, and everything in them. The God who we pray to is a God who is not only concerned for us as individuals, but holds us in the palm of his hands and sees our lives intertwine with the lives of others, who sees our lives intertwined with the lives of the heavens and the earth, the seas and everything in them. The God we pray to is a God who holds us and everything else together in his hands, and he is able to answer our prayer, and he's able to meet our needs. Because our prayers and our needs, although they concern us, are also intertwined with the lives of those of others.

Peter and John, of course, in this case, their well-being was intertwined with how the religious leaders were going to act and respond to their circumstances. Peter and John's future and their health and their flourishing was dependent upon how the three and four and five thousand

---

3. Editor's note: In the rest of the sermon, James is mentioned on occasion alongside Peter and John; obviously, James is absent from the narrative in Acts 3, and it is clear Amos is adding James in inadvertently in light of his bringing Acts 12 (where James's martyrdom is centrally featured) into the discussion.

would conduct themselves in the midst of a very tenuous political and social situation. One wrong move, one bad mistake, and something else could happen. Maybe just like what happened with Jesus a few weeks before. And the fact, we know that a few chapters down the line, that there was maybe a wrong move made, and we know that one of the other apostles lost his life.[4]

Lives of prayer do not necessarily mean that everything we ask and pray for come out exactly the way we hope. But our lives, and the details that surround the intricacies of your life and of my life are bound up with the lives of so many others. And thus it was that when the apostles began to respond in prayer in this situation, in this circumstance, for Peter and John, and for themselves, and the three, four, five thousand, they recognized they couldn't pray, and they didn't pray [to] a God who was only focused upon them. But they recognized that they prayed to and responded, and were responding, to the Lord who was sovereign over all of creation, including the seas and the creatures and everything in them.

Sovereign Lord, who has made the heavens and the earth, the sea and everything in them: it is you who said, by the Holy Spirit, the same Holy Spirit who empowered Jesus, the holy servant referenced twice in this prayer, to go and to do the things that he did, which Luke writes about in volume 1 of his book. The same Holy Spirit who would empower Jesus to teach the apostles. The same Holy Spirit who would have shown Jesus how to teach the apostles to pray. The same Holy Spirit who had been with Jesus as he walked the road to Calvary. That Holy Spirit was given to the apostles. To teach them to pray. To empower them to go and do the works that Jesus did. To heal the sick and declare the good news to the poor. To walk alongside them as they walked with religious leaders and others who were opposed to their lives and their ministry. That Holy Spirit who enabled Jesus to pray in the garden, who had enabled Jesus to forgive the sins of those who had put him on the cross. That Holy Spirit is with the apostles on this occasion, enabling them to pray. And that Holy Spirit is available to you and to me today and tomorrow.

When we're not sure *how* to pray, when we're not sure [*whether*] to pray, when we're not sure *when* to pray, the Holy Spirit was with Jesus, given to the apostles, is available to you and me to pray through us when, where, and if we don't know how. It is you who said by the Holy Spirit, through our ancestor David, your servant, why did the gentiles

4. E.g., James in Acts 12:1.

rage? And the peoples imagine vain things? Here in verses 25 and 26, Luke records that the early followers of Jesus prayed David's prayer. Why do the gentiles rage and the peoples imagine vain things? The kings of the earth took their stand and the rulers gathered together against the Lord and against the Messiah. In this occasion of intense pressure, in this occasion of perhaps confusion and anxiety and despair, in this occasion where they might have just spent the whole last night worrying about James and John and Peter. Worrying about this, the beginning of this movement. Worrying about whether or not things were going to be safe and secure for them tomorrow. And in this tense moment in which they responded instinctively, "Sovereign God, by your Holy Spirit, enable us to pray." And the Holy Spirit brings to mind the prayers of the righteous who had gone on before. As you and I hide the word of God in our hearts, and as you and I abide in rhythms of the life of prayer, when that moment comes forth, when it's time to say the prayer, when it's time to utter the prayer, when it's time to speak the prayer, the words of the saints that have gone on before us will come from within our spirit, as the Spirit of God speaks into our spirit, and enables us to pray. Not just our own prayer, but the prayers of those who have gone on before. And take the prayers of the saints and bring them into our hearts and into our lives, for just this time, for just this moment, and for just this occasion.

David, of course, as we know, was familiar with being persecuted. He had lived it before becoming king on the run. King Saul had been active. He [David] knew about persecution. He knew about the raging of kings against the Lord's anointed. And when he had become king he also had known because he had to lead Israel against wars on the left side and the right side, and on the front side, from the top and the bottom. And he knew about the gentiles who had raged against the people of God, the people of Israel.

Here in Acts chapter 4 we find that the early believers and the early followers of the Messiah instinctively went to the prayers of David in Psalm chapter 2, prayers that he had prayed, reflecting on his personal situation, prayers that he prayed, reflecting on the national situation. And his prayer welled up from within the spirit of these early followers of Jesus. And they began to pray by the power of the Holy Spirit, using the words of their ancestor, using the words of the saints who had gone before them: "Why did the gentiles rage against the Lord and against his Messiah?" Here was a prayer the apostles prayed so intensely, in tune to their personal situation, but yet so [aware] that their well-being is tied in with the well-being of the nation [of Israel], of the pagans, of the gentiles around about them.

And again, you and I pray for our personal situation, for our personal realities. Oftentimes, sometimes, when we pray, even in the congregation corporately, as we pray for [ourselves], let us also realize with the apostles, that we're praying for others. And I think we do a great job here at Great Bridge Presbyterian Church, in terms of a praying for us in relationship to others. We think about the fact that across the street is City Hall, representing all that City Hall represents. Mediating local government in local context. And of course, down about an hour-and-a-half away we have got State Home, in Richmond. And up about three hours away, on a good day, we have the national Home, on Capitol Hill. Think about how our lives are intertwined with all of these things. And how this prayer so appropriately situates the well-being of a vulnerable and fragile community, amidst local, national, and international forces. But it's, after all, the Sovereign Lord who made the heavens and earth, who enables us to pray, and gives us the prayer of those who have gone before us, so we can find ourselves within God and get situated in God's world. For all of what we don't know about how our street, and Main Street, and Wall Street will happen, for all of what we don't know about how our lives are dictated by forces beyond ourselves, but we know that the person to whom we pray is a sovereign God who controls all of these things. Somebody say Amen!

A prayer that teaches us about God's promise, a prayer that allows us to inhabit God's promises in very, very concrete circumstances: after they had called upon the Lord through the prayers of David, they were able to recognize that David's prayers was not just David's prayers, but their prayers. For in this city, verse 27, in fact, both Herod and Pontius Pilate, with the gentiles and the people of Israel, gathered together against the holy servant Jesus whom you anointed. David's prayer was prayed a thousand years ago, twelve hundred years ago [from the time of the apostles]. I know scholars keep debating about when David lived. Doesn't matter. It was a long time ago before they got this prayer. David's prayer was prayed under different circumstances. David's prayer was prayed under different pressures. But on this moment, and on this day, as they gathered together, as they heard the testimony of Peter and James and John. David's prayer became their prayer. David's prayer became an opportunity for them to abide in God's promises. David's prayer became an opportunity for them to live into all that God had for them, in that moment, as a community situated in relationship with those around and about them.

Their Herod and their Pontius Pilate: who is our Herod and our Pontius Pilate today? Maybe our governments are not persecuting us directly. But you know there are many communities, believing communities around the world, for whom that's not the case. And they're struggling with the Herods and Pontius Pilates in their local contexts. And perhaps the Spirit of God now is enabling them to pray through David, through others. And the Scriptures now become, not just the prayers and not just the recordings of prayers of others, but the Psalms, the Lamentations, and the Prophets, and the songs become opportunities for us to pray, for us to lament, for us to sing, and for us to worship. Praying with the apostles, yesterday, then, and now.

Let's close our meditation in just a few moments. I want us to look at the end of this prayer in verse 29. As they were praying, as they were worshiping, as they were calling upon the sovereign God, to say, Lord, turn your face to our situation. And now Lord, look at their threats. And now Lord, look at our circumstances. Look at our condition. Look at our situation. Look at the complexity of the world in which we live and move and have our being. Look at the threats that assail us and decide whether they're political, whether they're economic, whether they're social, whether they're personal. Look Lord God at our fragility. Look Lord God upon our vulnerability. And grant to your servants, to speak your word with all boldness. Grant us, O Lord, in this pressure-filled context, grant us, O Lord, in this moment in which we are assailed by forces larger than what we can handle, the boldness that we need. Grant us, O Lord, the internal fortitude that we need to be faithful in this context and this situation. Grant us, O Lord God, the capacity in our spirit to live out these prayers. Grant us, O Lord, boldness.

A prayer asking that God would hear and touch my transforming, my empowering us from within. A prayer—and I believe this is for you and I today—that as we pray and as we look to God to touch our lives. That God touches us first and foremost *inside*. Grant us Lord God, boldness from within. Grant us Lord God, your boldness. Grant us, Lord God, your touch so that our prayers are not just what we say, but take hold of our hearts and of our lives. Look at their threats. Grant your servants, to speak your word with all boldness, while you stretch out your hand to heal. And signs and wonders would be [done] in the name of your holy servant Jesus. Lord, not only reorient our hearts, not only reorient our perspective, not only reorient our internal dynamics, but Lord, that outward flows your word, empower us to do, to go, to heal. Lord we know that Peter, James, and John got in trouble for healing this man in your name. But give us the internal fortitude to continue to do thy works. Why? Because they were only doing your works, Jesus. Lord, not only change our internal hearts through our prayer, but empower our hands to make a difference in the world. "And when they prayed the place in which they gathered together was shaken. And they were all filled with the Holy Spirit, and spoke the word of God with boldness."

Lord, not only transform our hearts, not only empower our hands to go and do, but Lord empower our lips to declare in thanksgiving and in praise, in anticipation of the great things that you are going to do. Lord, may we begin to speak forth, from our lips, what you do with our hands, and what you accomplish in our hearts. And we pray with the apostles, then and tomorrow, Lord God, we ask, you will continue to teach us. You will continue to empower us. You will continue to pray through us. You will enable us to live the prayers of the saints before us. You will empower us to do the prayers of the saints before us. And you will enable us to speak the prayers of the saints before us. And you will teach us to pray as the apostles prayed. As they prayed, as you taught them to pray, in Jesus' name, Amen.

Tony Richie Reflection—"The Most Significant Activity"

Yong preaches that prayer connects supplicants not only with God but with saints across the ages. Christian prayer has roots in Israel's spontaneous, unaffected petitions to Yahweh for all their hopes and needs (Psalms). Nevertheless, like Christ's "Not my will but thine" its essence isn't asking (for things) but offering (of self). Prayer isn't an appeal to an omnipotent problem solver but approach to the Heavenly Father in utter trust and unfeigned devotion (The Lord's Prayer).

Prayer, though mysterious, is the universal, spiritual language of beings created in God's image connecting us with God who is Spirit. Prayer includes speaking, listening, waiting/tarrying, discerning reflection on Scripture, the Holy Spirit's illumination and leading, solitude, contemplation/mediation, and action. Prayer is experiential and multifaceted. Prayer is about communion (union) with God—being with God, enjoying God's presence—through interpersonal (I-Thou) encounter. Thus prayer is fundamentally a loving relationship. Surrendering, yielding, waiting in the presence of the Beloved, who is ever-present, and fulfills and satisfies the praying lover.

Prayer occurs primarily as a gift and work of the Holy Spirit, without whom real prayer is impossible (Rom 8:26–27). However, Christianity's incarnational/sacramental nature affirms that the human psyche (conscious/unconscious processes) is inextricably present in prayer. Getting to know God better, enhances self-awareness. Casting away inadequate and, perhaps, idolatrous images of God, worshiping the true and living God, we come to know ourselves more fully, more truly, casting away false self-images, becoming authentic human beings, not by ceaseless introspection but by dwelling in the Light, which exposes and overcomes the darkness in our own souls. Affections and dispositions are sanctified. True prayer is transforming.

Fundamentally, prayer involves humble, grateful response to God's loving, saving initiative in Jesus Christ. Paradoxically, it comprises both privilege and duty. Conversation and communion with God is priceless. Maintaining intentional episodes of prayer set in a sustained life of prayer is serious. Thus Karl Barth famously defined all theological work as a form of prayer. Certainly prayer may be the most significant activity of any congregation or individual.

9

God's Servant among the Nations

M A T T H E W   1 2 : 1 5 – 2 1

Fuller Theological Seminary, Pasadena, California,
25 February 2015*

Good morning Fuller. It's good to be here with you this morning. I'm particularly glad that my wife is here, and my daughter Annalisa, who is leaving in three days to Costa Rica, for spring term. I'm going to miss her for four months. I'm glad you're here honey. . . .

All right it's time to get serious. I've so enjoyed chapel this year in terms of following our journey through Matthew, Amen!? And thinking, as well, about the theme of our vocation as we have walked with and through the Gospel of Matthew. And so I've tried to anticipate where Mark and others will be preaching in Matthew, this passage jumped to mind as I was looking through Matthew chapter 12, the passage we read this morning. And you might well guess why this passage came to mind to me as a Pentecostal theologian. I mean, look at what it says right here. When Jesus became aware of this he departed, many crowds followed him, and he cured all of them! Somebody excited!? I think that's what it says, he cured all of them. It makes my Pentecostal heart warm, right?

---

* Mark Labberton, president of Fuller Seminary, was preaching through the Gospel of Matthew for the weekly chapels during the 2013–14 academic year. The section I chose for this week was located between two others that he preached on before and after my sermon.

What better passage to preach out of, from Matthew 12 talking about vocation, discipleship, following the path of Jesus, than this verse: "he cured all of them." But then it says that he ordered them not to make him known. Well that's just contrary to what a Pentecostal preacher like myself would want to do. I might want to broadcast that, I want to organize the crusade, I want to get everybody in, and line them all up, and get them all healed, Amen?! It is okay to say Amen today, okay? It is okay to say Amen today. You won't bother me.

"And this was to fulfill what was spoken through the prophet Isaiah." Now let's get some context for this verse. We didn't read the passage preceding and we're not going to read the passage following. But this is a passage that refers to Jesus healing them all, sandwiched between two healing stories. I mean again, healing all, healing before, healing after, I mean you got healing coming out all over the place here. But what is interesting is that in verse 15, when Jesus became aware of this, of course, then you have to ask about what exactly happened with the prior healing. And then you go back to that prior healing, and this was the man with a withered hand.

How many of you all are excited to praise the Lord that a man with a withered hand no longer has a withered hand? We praise God for healings. The last phrase, however, to that pericope announces how the Pharisees were upset that the man's hand "unwithered" on the Sabbath. And it says, they began to plot against them. And all of a sudden, the healing that we're celebrating, all of a sudden, the miracles and the signs and wonders we're celebrating, turned political. Come on somebody. Why can't we just experience the goodness and the joy and the miracle-working power of God? Why does everything have to become politicized?

And then we read into the next passage after this passage we're talking about. When Jesus delivers a man from the demonic possession that made him blind and mute. And once again, the Pharisees come in after him. And once again, the Pharisees' attempt to undermine his ministry, and Jesus then closes that part of the story by saying, "that when this happens it's not just about the deliverance, it's not just about an exorcism, it's not . . .—and those are all good! Deliverance and exorcism, those are good. We want to pray those in, we want to experience those!—but it's not just about that. It's about the kingdom of God. Now we gotta get political again. Why can't we just leave all that politics aside? And then as I look at this text, and Jesus ordered them not to make him known.

Now you might recall, this is seminary, that Matthew is—whoever Matthew is, the name of the disciple—writing for Jews, to convince them that Jesus is Messiah. And one way he does that is by referring often, and at length, to the text in which [he] establishes the framework for understanding and anticipating and heralding the Messiah, which is the First Testament, the Older Testament. And so Matthew then says he's got to somehow explain this very, very messy and ambiguous phrase that keeps popping up, starting in Mark, but also throughout Matthew, and not as much in Luke, where he ordered them not to make him known. This is what scholars call the "messianic secret." And everybody's got a theory about how this all works. And there's a lot of good—maybe—and not so good as well, explanations for this messianic secret. Now Matthew gives us his version of it. This is his attempt to explain, right? Why Jesus said not to make him known. This is how he explained it. He said, "This is to fulfill what the prophet Isaiah said, 'Here's my servant whom I've chosen, my beloved with whom my soul is well pleased.'" Isaiah 42. "I'll put my Spirit on him." And that's another reason why my Pentecostal heart was drawn to this passage. It's one of those few places in Matthew where the Spirit sort of just pops up. And we'll try to figure out what is all involved. But "I'll put my Spirit on you, and will proclaim justice to the gentiles." And here's verse 19. This is really the key that helps Matthew explain—again, of course, whoever Matthew is—why Jesus ordered them not to make him known. Verse 19: "he will not wrangle or cry aloud nor will anyone hear his voice in the streets."

Matthew finds an Isaianic text that allows him to explain and to understand the so-called messianic secret; why Jesus was not quite about to simply hold a big rally, not quite about, at this point in time, to organize a mass demonstration. He was content to allow the healings to be healings, and to allow their political ramifications to unfold without a demonstration. "He will not wrangle or cry aloud, nor will anyone hear his voice in the streets." This is the longest passage of the Old Testament that Matthew rehearses in the Gospel, of the many, many passages in the Old Testament. It's interesting that he finds this text from out of Isaiah, the forty-second chapter. And to understand further, I think [it is helpful to know] how this text functions, what is happening in Isaiah 42, and again there are lots of theories.

Now I'm just a theologian and I'm trying to do something with the Bible here, okay? So, excuse me for a minute. This gets complicated. I'm a theologian trying to do something with Matthew, who is relying upon Isaiah. It's complicated. And if you go to Isaiah then, depending on which Old Testament theologian you ask, there are like two, three, four, five, six, or seven of them.[1] And they all have something going on here. But Isaiah, and particularly the fortieth [chapter] through the end of that book, refers to the Messiah, [which] means the Anointed One, and that Messiah is anointed precisely to bring about the restoration of Israel. So, most scholars would put this part of Isaiah either during or maybe after the exile, during which time the people of Israel are yearning and longing and hoping and believing God for his messianic visitation. And this restoration of Israel is not going to happen apart from the Spirit of God coming upon God's anointed representative. And that's what part of this text invites us to understand. That here is my servant, this messianic servant, this messianic servant, who doesn't cry out loud, this messianic servant who performs miraculous signs and wonders. But these miraculous signs and wonders are freighted with political significance; the restoration and the renewal of Israel is literally a miracle. It's a sign, it's a wonder, but it's a political sign, it's a political wonder. And the Spirit of the living God comes upon the representative of God to accomplish this miracle of miracles, this healing and restoration of a people.

"Here's my servant whom I've chosen, my beloved, with whom my soul is well pleased. I will put my Spirit upon him." And I get goosebumps. I say "Come on Lord! Bring the Holy Spirit! Bring the Holy Spirit!" Because you know, in my tradition, the more of the Holy Ghost we got, the more healings can take place. The more signs and wonders and miracles can take place.

But then the text reads like this: "I will put my Spirit upon him and he will proclaim justice." Wait a minute here. I thought it meant something like I'll put my Spirit upon him and he went out and healed the sick. But I'll put my Spirit upon him, and he will *proclaim justice.* The man with the withered hand was barred according to a just law, from certain activities in the temple. The person who was demon possessed, who follows after this message, who was not only blind but mute; mute meaning this person had no voice; mute, meaning this person had no capacity for self-representation; mute, meaning this person had no political standing in his community. "And I will put my Spirit upon him, and he will proclaim justice." And all of a sudden I begin to see that the signs and the

---

1. I am here referring, of course, to the common scholarly consensus that there are at least a Deutero- (covering chs. 40–55) and a Trito-Isaiah (chs. 56–66) in addition to Isaiah of Jerusalem.

wonders and the healing, they're all great, but the signs and the wonders and the healings, cannot but be political! Why? Because they announce the coming of the messianic kingdom. The coming of the kingdom that proclaims and acts and instantiates a just order.

"And I'll put my Spirit upon him, and he will proclaim justice" . . . to the gentiles. To the gentiles. I think we understand what that means. Probably 99 percent of us here fit under this category. What would it have meant for the prophet Isaiah to say that the coming Messiah would be anointed by the Spirit to bring justice to the gentiles? If, in fact, this latter part of the book of Isaiah unfolded in or after the exile, then we understand that this was a time in Israel's history, in which its horizons, its borders, if you will, had literally been broken down, expanded, and exploded. Israel had to reconsider itself, not just as the elect of God for God's sake, but as the elect of God for God's sake, which is according the promise of Abraham, for the world. Israel had to come and reconsider its own identity, now in light of this messianic empowerment. So, whereas the earlier prophets in the earlier parts of the Old Testament were judges that came to restore and solidify and lead a tender and vulnerable nation, beset and surrounded by hostile enemies, now in this context, they were already scattered abroad, yearning and longing for the restoration and renewal of Israel. But this restoration and renewal for Israel, for Isaiah, would include all gentiles.

What would Isaiah, and of course his readers and hearers of this prophetic word, have thought about these so-called gentiles? They would have to wrestle deeply with how this messianic deliverance of this messianic renewal would have implications for precisely the people under whom they were in captivity. They had to wrestle precisely with the meaning and the implication of what it meant for this messianic appearance to reconcile, perhaps, how unthinkable that might be. Here we are, if you will, exiled from our home. Messiah is supposed to deliver us and restore us to the land. But instead, justice is going to be proclaimed. That's going to cut across the borders that we might want to re-erect, that's going to cut across, if you will, the identities that we want to re-solidify. And somehow, these gentiles, these Babylonians, these Assyrians, and these whatchamacallits, they are part of God's plan to bring about and proclaim justice.

Isaiah might have had a fairly wide view of the world. Where would his worldview have extended beyond the borders of the immediate exilic surroundings? There's references to Kush, there's references to Ethiopia.

He might've had a quite wide view of this world of the gentiles. But it would not have extended into what we would call today, the sub-Saharan regions of Ethiopia or Cush. It would not have included the Nubians, and it would not have included other civilizations in that time, existing even five hundred years before Jesus. Isaiah would not have known about these people, but I would like to say that as the Spirit of God would've empowered Isaiah's words for that time and that exilic community, I believe that those words would have included those people. Above and beyond how far Isaiah himself could have seen, how far Isaiah himself might have been challenged to believe, God will . . . this messianic minister of God will proclaim justice to the gentiles.

Matthew had drunk this Isaianic "Kool-Aid," if you will. He's caught now into the story he's already cited this text, he can't get himself out of it. As much as he might have wanted to speak a message of comfort to the Jews, he is now embroiled in a global horizon. His message is now caught up and transformed onto a global stage. The hopes that Matthew might have had for the people of Israel are now caught up, so that Jesus now becomes, is identified as saying, "this gospel will be preached to all the nations of the earth." Isaiah's story now has to end with the fact that even though he's writing for the Jews, he's got to say that when Jesus commissions his disciples, he says "Go into all the world and make disciples of every creature," in every Swahili nation.[2] Come on somebody!

Like Luke, he would have realized, yes, it began in Jerusalem and it went on to Judea and he even went into Samaria, I don't like to say that, but it did. But beyond that, it's going to go to the ends of the earth to the gentiles. But how far, really, do you think they saw? Of course, they didn't see Swahili land. Some scholars say that there was enough traffic between the Indus Valley and what we now call Palestine in the first century. There's no hard evidence that it was that kind of traffic. Matthew would not have known of Indus Valley civilizations. He would not have known of the Vedic societies of the second and first millennium before Christ. Matthew would have had no inkling of the gentiles that people like me come from. He would not have known of the Shang Dynasty. He would not have known of the Warring States. Matthew had no clue about the Chou or the Han [regimes]. But as I read this text, and as I hear "go into all the world," I see God already opening a door.

There are horizons toward which you and I have not seen. We have only classified the world in our own ways. But there are gentiles, there are

2. Matt 28:18.

others that escape our categorization, that escape our horizon, that have not entered our imagination, and it is to those gentiles that the Messiah will proclaim justice. And that's what spurred the apostles to go. And they went. And fifteen hundred years later they were still going and trying to figure out who were these gentiles in the so-called New World, a world of Mayans and Aztecs, and they were looking throughout the Scriptures to see where are these gentiles foretold? But yes, they are not Jews, they have gotta be gentiles. And in that case, we have got to realign our theology so we can understand that this Messiah will proclaim justice, even in this land. And we have done a horrible job at it. We have messed it up big time, haven't we? With all good intentions, we have sought to proclaim, enacted, and instantiated this messianic message, and we have brought with it a whole ton of other stuff. Not only in the so-called New World, but [also] in so much of the older worlds. I do ask myself, how do we today recapture, retell, relive faithfully this messianic word, this messianic anointing, this messianic invitation? Messianic simply means, anointed of the Spirit to bring about the healing, the reconciliation, and the justice, to establish God's signs and wonders that proclaim his justice and his kingdom for our world that knows no borders. In Jesus' name, Amen.

[Band softly playing] I'd like us to pray together as we are leaving this place. Everyone put your hands up before the Lord. The God who sent his Son in the power of the Spirit. And then the Son who poured out of that Spirit upon us that we might do the things that the Son did. Straighten out withered hands, deliver the sick and the oppressed, proclaim justice to the gentiles, to the world. If that is our prayer. O Lord, make us servants in the image and footsteps of Jesus, who is our center. Make us do the things he did by your Spirit. Make us establish, herald, and announce the kingdom that he announced in the power of the Spirit. And may there be no hindrance to this good news, that it would go forth from here to the ends of the earth. And all God's people said, Amen.

Tony Richie Reflection—"Crucial Work"

This sermon suggests justice is at the heart of Jesus' messianic mission. Justice is a central theme throughout the Bible and Christian theology. Appreciation for justice runs deep in the Abrahamic faiths (Judaism, Christianity, and Islam) since Abraham's divine election included commitment to "righteousness and justice" (Gen 18:19). Righteousness and justice (ṣĕdāqâ ûmišpāṭ) describe ethical living, particularly equity and fairness, motivated by God's unfailing love (Ps 33:5).

Justice addresses social, economic, moral, political, and legal concerns. Justice is defined as giving someone his/her due or being fair and doing right with respect to properties, opportunities, and rights. Fidelity to the appropriate demands of a particular relationship sums up the biblical ideal of justice. Biblical justice, therefore, focuses on alleviating the plight of widows, orphans, the poor, and the oppressed (Jer 22:15–16).

For Augustine, a successful society is established on justice, without which human sovereignty is impossible, and love, the inner determinate of human life. Atheist philosopher Friedrich Nietzsche argued that there's no ultimate justice, insisting on inevitable ontological injustice due to humans' natural tendency to be unjust. However, Christians accent God's actions for justice in Jesus Christ. Christ's first coming established God's reign in justice. His second coming will perfectly achieve justice. In the meanwhile, Jesus identified the significant triad of "justice, mercy, and faithfulness" (Matt 23:23; cf. Mic 6:8 and Zech 7:9).

Anabaptist traditions exemplify a church standing for a just society. Their efforts to promote religious freedom and their resistance to violence are inspiring and instructive. Tom Finger says that, "increasing interconnections and corresponding tensions emerging among all peoples through globalization . . . make it crucial to work together toward . . . worldwide justice and peace."[3] Amen.

---

3. Finger, A Contemporary Anabaptist Theology, 281.

10

Radical *Ruach*

The Wind and Breath of Ordinary Liberation

EXODUS 15:8–10; 31:3; 35:31

Aloha Foursquare Church, Aloha, Oregon, 27 September 2015*

I failed to mention this morning [in] the first service but you guys do not know how incredibly uniquely blessed you are to have Thomas and Leah as your pastors. Come on somebody! There are on one hand, on one finger of one hand, the number of Foursquare Pentecostal pastors around the country that have a spouse with a PhD. Come on! And you didn't know this, but she is one of the handful of experts on Foursquare Church and Foursquare history.[1] You guys know that? Around the world! Right here, sitting right here. And while she has a PhD, Thomas has his PwT, "putting wife through" her PhD, Amen? Amen. So, you know don't [you]; I mean, yeah, this is a very unique place. Aloha, Oregon. I was driving over here this morning, we stayed at the place in Beaverton last night. And I was asking my wife, I wonder they named their church Aloha Faith Center, maybe some Hawaiian started it, something like that. And then come to find out it's in Aloha, Oregon, well go figure. Praise the Lord, it's just great to be here.

* Rev. Thomas Payne had been preaching through the book of Exodus in a series called "Ordinary Christianity" when I was invited to his congregation.

1. At the time I visited, Leah's PhD thesis (completed at Vanderbilt University) on Aimee Semple McPherson, founder of the Foursquare church, had just been published—*Gender and Pentecostal Revivalism*—and it was shortly thereafter awarded the annual Pneuma Book Award by the Society for Pentecostal Studies.

If you have your Bibles . . . , I'm still a little old fashioned, I've got my Bible here. If you don't, I assume that you got an iPhone or something, feel free to turn it on, scroll down to the book of Exodus with me. I see that you've turned there the last couple weekends already, right? In the book of Exodus, and it's great. . . . And while you're making your way there, can I take another couple of seconds to tell you the real reason why I'm here today? Is that okay? While you're trying to find Exodus . . . , it's right next to Genesis by the way, in case you're still looking.

[Introductory joke] . . . All right I'm glad you laughed at that one, because [it] obviously means you didn't believe me, but that's okay.

Good morning. It's great to be here this morning, great to worship with you. I've entitled our thoughts this morning, "Radical *Ruach*." Have you ever heard that word before? *Ruach*? Try, let it roll out a little bit here, you're going to have to take a deep breath. Breath in a little bit, then go Rrruuaaach. Try it one more time. *Ruach*! Rrrrrrruach. Rrrrrrruach. Rrrrruach. Rrrrruach. Well that's a Hebrew word, by the way, for guess what? Breath, wind, Spirit. Radical *ruach*! I want to talk to us this morning for a few moments about the wind and breath of ordinary liberation. Radical and ordinary *ruach*.

I just met Leah's dad, so she's a pastor's kid. I'm a pastor's kid, I'm a Pentecostal pastor's kid. Grown up [as a] Pentecostal pastor's kid, you know, I heard sermons every week from the book of Acts. Somebody say Amen. For the last ten years as a Pentecostal preacher I've been preaching; 90 percent of my messages come from the book of . . . ? [Audience responds, likely saying "Acts."] So when I asked Pastor Thomas "What are you preaching on these few weeks coming before I come? I would like to be able to sort of connect with you little bit, you know?" He said "I'm preaching from the book of Exodus." I go "X-O what?" I had to re-familiarize myself with the fact that—to find it first of all, it's somewhere back there. And of course, as a Pentecostal preacher I was thinking to myself, How am I going to preach on the Holy Ghost out of the book of Exodus? Hello? Right?

First of all, in the Greek New Testament—which is where the book of Acts is, Amen?—in the Greek, the word for the Spirit or the wind of God is the word *pneuma*. Well [it's] obviously a lot easier to say that right than *ruach*. And the other thing of course is that the book of Exodus is so different. I mean when you turn to the book of Acts, almost from the very beginning, the first chapter: "and you shall be filled with the Holy Spirit," Amen? And you know the last time I read the book of Exodus I fell asleep about the thirteenth chapter or so. And I never got to the Holy Ghost. So, I was a little bit worried about how I can . . . because obviously a Pentecostal preacher has gotta preach on the Holy Ghost, Amen? But I managed to find four references, after I woke up in chapter 14. And aren't you glad [that] I could only find four references? Because I want to preach on all four of them today. Might take me a while, but I think we get you out of here by about two or 3 o'clock. Just hang in there with me.

But I love this theme of the work of God in the ordinary, that I'm hearing. You may not have known, but you got another like five months of Exodus with your pastor here. But I want us to look at these handful of references in the book of Exodus to the divine *ruach*, the divine wind. And I want to start in chapter 31, which is right after chapter 30. The first few verses of Exodus 31, if you got in the Bible, I'm reading out of the New Revised Standard Version: "The LORD spoke to Moses: See, I have called by name Bezalel son of Uri son of Hur, of the tribe of Judah: and I have filled him with divine *ruach*/spirit."

If you, you know, when I think about reading Exodus and Leviticus and Numbers you know, it's kind of like my reading experience of these books, is kind of like you're driving along a long freeway, you know, and you're starting to veer off the road, and every once in a while you'll get one on where, you know, there's little things on the side of the road, to make sure you don't drive off? This verse is one of those little rubber things, just when you're about to doze off,[1] after all the descriptions of all the tents and all that stuff, the other materials in the tabernacle, and then, if you're a good Pentecostal like me, you get one of those wake-you-up events, where there is a reference to him being filled with the divine Spirit. And filled with the divine spirit with ability, intelligence, and knowledge in every kind of craft to devise artistic designs. To work in gold and silver and bronze. Somebody say Amen? Come on Lord, give me that gift. Hello?

To work in gold and silver and bronze and cutting stones for setting and carving wood in every kind of craft. What a marvelously, talented, and gifted person this Bezalel was. The Holy Spirit coming upon him, to enable him to build, if you will, materials for God's tabernacle, for God's temple. One of the challenges, when we try to understand and appreciate the book of Exodus, is that in contrast the book of Acts . . . . The book

---

1. I am referring here, not very clearly, to what is technically called *rumble strips* that are on freeway or highway lanes, designed to keep drowsy drivers from veering off their lane or off the road.

of Acts, you may remember, was about the generation right after Jesus's life, death, and resurrection. And it was probably written within a few decades maybe of when all those events happen. So, the accounts of that story and when it was written were almost about the same time. Unfortunately, the book of Exodus is a little bit more complicated than that. The book of Exodus tells the story of the exodus, which of course is the story of Israel's deliverance, exodus, from Egypt. And you may have known this, but this happened a long time ago, like over three thousand years ago.[2] And depending on which scholars you talk to then, you'll have all kinds of dates. So, let's just settle for a long time ago, over three thousand years ago.

But the traditions that talk about this Exodus, the traditions that were handed down, that bore witness, that repeated these stories were handed out over hundreds of years. And in a few moments we're going to look at one of those songs that was handed down, that purports to be very, very old, from over three thousand years ago. But over the thousands of years then, about two thousand five hundred years ago [from our time], which would have been more than five hundred years after the events of the exodus, there was a time in the history of Judah and Israel in which they attempted to rebuild the tabernacle and the temple. About two thousand five hundred years ago, in that particular context, you would have— this is when the stories were pulled together about when Josiah found the law and they attempted to read and enact the law[3]—they attempted to rebuild and restore the temple. And then after that—that [effort] wasn't very successful—few hundred years later the people of Israel were taken into the exile, and after the exile they were allowed to return to the land. And once again, there were efforts made to rebuild and restore the temple in Jerusalem. And it's in that particular time, about two thousand three hundred years ago [from us], that the [book of] Exodus as we now read it was finally pulled together in the form that we have it today. Now in that particular context, in which the people of Israel were finally reading the story like you and I are reading that today, this story I'm sure played a very important role in the people's responding to God's call to live faithfully in a strange land. To live faithfully in a time in which they felt called to rebuild God's temple, but they found themselves assailed from every

2. To be more accurate, I should have said—not just here but also below, in a few moments, in the next paragraph—"up to three thousand years ago"; maybe this slight exaggeration is due to my taking what is commonly known as "Pentecostal preacher's license"—not that I am recommending it.

3. See 2 Chr 34:8–21.

side, by all sorts of challenges. Here was an occasion, then, of the story in which the divine *ruach* would come upon this individual for these very, very, if you will, specific but yet mundane tasks of being a craftsman.

I want to encourage us today that God has called us, whatever our vocation is: whether we're craftsmen, whether we're artisans, whether we're designers whether we work with stones, maybe more expensive stones, or whether we work with wood, less expensive materials. In our congregation today, there are those of us who are called to all kinds of different vocations. And we may go from Monday to Friday to maybe even a Saturday, attempting to be faithful in these tasks. And this story I think is an encouragement for me, that regardless of where you find yourself, and regardless of how long, maybe, you've been at your particular task . . . I see this person Bezalel, honed in his craft, trained in this craft, faithful in his craft. With the divine *ruach* enabling him to carry out his craft from week-to-week, from day-to-day.

The thirty-fifth chapter of the book of Exodus tells us a little bit more about Bezalel, which I think is very, very helpful and important for us. And this is the last five verses of Exodus 35, starting in verse 30:

> 30Then Moses said to the Israelites: See, the LORD has called by name Bezalel son of Uri son of Hur, of the tribe of Judah; 31he has filled him with divine *ruach*, divine breath [spirit in NRSV], with skill, intelligence, and knowledge in every kind of craft, 32to devise artistic designs, to work in gold, silver, and bronze, 33in cutting stones for setting, and in carving wood, in every kind of craft. 34And he has inspired him to teach, both him and Oholiab son of that fellow [Ahisamach in NRSV], of the tribe of Dan. 35He has filled them with skill to do every kind of work done by an artisan or by a designer or by an embroiderer in blue, purple, and crimson yarns, and in fine linen, or by a weaver—by any sort of artisan or skilled designer.

So not only working with stones, not only working with wood, not only working with crafts, but working with materials, weaving materials, cloth materials, and not only were they inspired and been filled with the divine *ruach*, and divine breath to be able to do that work expertly, but they were enabled by that divine *ruach*, that divine breath, to teach. To pass on their skills, to mentor, to be an apprentice—apprentices [and] apprenticizers—to teach others, to pass on to the next generation the skills and the expertise and the insight and the capacities that had been nurtured.

And each one of us will have opportunity over the course of our vocation, over the course of our day to day, our week to week, our month to month, our year to year, our season to season work, of training somebody else that has come along. And if you're brand new in your job then you're getting introduced to that craft, to that calling, to that vocation, through a mentor. Wouldn't you want to thank the Lord for somebody who was filled with the divine *ruach* to be able to help you to gain the insight and experience and the perspective that you need in order for you to do the job well, Amen? These are mundane tasks we might think, but we see here the book of Exodus that in the time during and after the exile in which the people of Israel found themselves in a strange land, they set themselves still yet to be faithful to their Lord, to rebuild the temple as it could have been rebuilt, given all the constraints, given all of the political and other forces that were aligned against them. They needed faithful laborers. They needed skilled laborers. And the divine wind was there to enable them, to empower them, to do their work. That's why I call this radically, ordinary *ruach*. That is with this, on our Mondays through our Fridays and even into our Saturdays, as we're faithfully attempting to follow God in our vocations, and in our craft, Amen? We need more of this Spirit of God in our lives.

There are two other references, I said that there were four, right? We've seen two of them here. These two that we've just read in 31 and 35 had to do with Bezalel and the divine *ruach* that enabled him to do all the work that he did. The other two references come in Exodus chapter 15. So, if you want to scroll up on your phone or scroll to the left on your Bibles. Exodus chapter 15 is a wonderful hymn, song. And we'll start in verse 1 and you might recognize this song: "Then Moses and the Israelites sang this song to the LORD: 'I will sing to the LORD, for he has triumphed gloriously; horse and rider he has thrown into the sea.'"

How many of you remember singing this song in Sunday School? [Yong humming the song]. You know when I sing, I move people . . . to the exits. So, I'm not going to sing today. But you can here, play that song back in your in ear-balls, yeah. Horse and rider are thrown into the sea.

So, this is the story of the song of Israel, coming out from when they had been delivered by the Lord from Egypt, right? And the Pharaoh and his armies that were behind him. If you remember this story, God had led the people out of Egypt, led them to the Red Sea, there are mountains to the north and south, the Egyptians were behind him, and the sea was ahead of them. And they said "Lord, what are we gonna do? What's going to happen here?" And you know the story, right? That God caused the sea to open up. God put the cloud between the Egyptian army and them, and allowed the people of Israel to pass over. And then lifted up that cloud, and the Egyptians saw the Israelites across the seas, saying "we're going to come and get you." In fact, if you go down to verse 8. Here's where we have the first of the references to the divine *ruach*. Here's how it reads in my New Revised Standard Version.

> 8At the blast of your nostrils the waters piled up, [Yong shares an aside here:]—the wall opened up, right? For Israel!—
> the floods stood up in a heap;
> the deeps congealed in the heart of the sea.
> 9The enemy said, [Yong shared an aside here:]—There's Pharaoh and his armies: "I see you!"—"I will pursue, I will overtake,
> I will divide the spoil, my desire shall have its fill of them.
> I will draw my sword, my hand shall destroy them."

This is the song of Pharaoh, looking ahead across the sea. And he charges forward now that the cloud was lifted up, right? And then, in verse 10, the second reference to the divine *ruach*: You blew with your wind, the sea covered them; they sank like lead in the mighty waters."

Somebody say Amen? Those are the other two references; did you catch them? The divine *ruach*, the divine breath. The divine breath that opened up the oceans to begin with, and then the divine breath that was pulled back and closed it back out over, and allowed the chariots to sink like lead into the ocean or into the sea. It's what I call the extraordinary, if you will, the *spectacular*. Blowing. In fact, the translation says the spectacular *blast* of Yahweh's breath. That's the kind of stuff, right, that we in Pentecostal circles pray for, Amen? We want to see the spectacularity of the Spirit of God. We want to see and hear about the spectacularity of the healings of God. And this kind of story, this kind of song allows us to celebrate that our God is a spectacularly powerful God! Amen? Who can blow the waters apart, dry the land in moments, allow the people to pass through, save his people. And when our enemies come against us, and when we've got big enemies, when we've got strong enemies, we've got powerful enemies, we need a powerful blast of the divine *ruach*, Amen? That's what we need. And this song allows us to celebrate, allows us to recall, remember, that God is a big God. Who is bigger than the problems that we had, who is bigger than armies [that] confront us, who is bigger than the challenges that we might encounter in life. And all of us understand that we encounter many of these.

But I also want us to appreciate, however, that there may be also another rather ordinary reading of Exodus 15. In fact, an extraordinarily, ordinary reading. Or, depending on how you like to frame it, a rather ordinary, extraordinary account. Grammatically, in this text, it is just as good to translate it, "in your breathing, the waters piled up" (in verse 8). And it is just as appropriate in verse 10 to say, "and with your breathing, the sea covered them." Do you like my translation better, or do you like the New Revised Standard Version's translation better? Right? "You blew with your wind, at the blast of your nostrils." Well, that's an appropriate translation. But grammatically it is just as appropriate also to talk of the [breathing of] the breath, of the breath as the wind.

And what's interesting, I think, is that God's, if you will, supernatural salvation is enacted, unfolded, through very, very natural elements. The winds, the seas, the waves. Now some scholars from generations past have attempted to provide what they would call natural explanations. Oh yeah, there's a certain time of the year in which there is a low tide and then there's a high tide. The Israelites must've passed over when it was low tide, and when the Egyptian Pharaoh came across it was high tide. And then, of course, they'll say God drowned the Egyptian pharaohs in six feet of water. Okay. I'm not trying to explain this one way or the other. I'm simply calling attention to the fact that Yahweh, the *ruach* of Yahweh, can produce spectacular results, and that's when we talk about the blast of his nostrils. But the *ruach* of Yahweh also works in the very ordinariness of the winds and the waves and the vocations of our lives.

In fact, the prophet Elijah later on, he would go out and he would look for the storm. And he would look and try to listen for the wind. And then he would sense the still, small voice of the *ruach* of Yahweh, speaking with barely a flutter of the divine breath.[4]

You know, when I think about the fact that you've got this epic extravaganza meeting tonight, I don't know what kind of blast of nostrils is going to unfold tonight.[5] Maybe it's just going to be looking at spreadsheets of the budget. But I want to encourage us, to see the divine *ruach* in the numbers, in the names, in the narrative. I want us to see that God is doing something extraordinary in and through the ordinary.

4. 1 Kgs 19:11–13.

5. I am referring here to the annual business meeting announced before the sermon to which all members and other interested persons were (strongly) encouraged to attend.

My son has been teaching me a lot the last few months. He's moved back in with us. How wonderful that kids that graduate, go off to college, get married, and get to move back in with their parents, Amen!?[6] But he's been teaching me, he's been calling my attention to the fact that in the Christian tradition there is a very, very old history, long history of contemplative practice in which Christian monks and nuns would center themselves through the Holy Spirit by observing the divine *ruach* in their breath. We sang a song earlier today, right? That calls attention to that: "It's your breath in our lungs, and we pour out our praise to only you, O Lord."[7] And when we sing that song it's not about whether or not it's a blast of Yahweh's nostrils, or the gentleness of his breath. There's no duality there between, "it's your breath" and "it's our praise . . . ." But somehow in this very ordinariness of our praise is the extraordinariness of Yahweh's breath. Yahweh's *ruach* enabling, and every breath you and I take is participation in that extraordinarily ordinary presence of the living God in our midst.

I don't know where you're at today. Maybe you need to find new vocational inspiration in your craft, in the mundaneness of your work, in the day-to-dayness of your responsibilities. I encourage you if that's where you're at that, don't discount the *ruach* Yahweh, in the very rhythms of your life from day to day. Maybe you need the spectacularity of the divine *ruach* that can be characterized as a blast. Maybe you need that wind of the divine Spirit to blow through your office and turn the papers upside down—somebody say Amen? Maybe you need a divine influx of funds in your business, somebody say Amen? Maybe you need something that spectacular, and if that's the case, God does that too! The Spirit of God works that way as well! Maybe you just need to be centered. Maybe you're a homemaker. Appreciated our sister sharing this morning, right? Maybe you're just talking to your neighbor, and something we do in the very mundaneness of life. Let's not underestimate; the divine *ruach* is there. In our breath. In our praise. In our computing. In our conversation. In

6. Aizaiah and his wife Neddy joined us in our Pasadena home during the summer of 2015, while they were in transition from their pastoral work at New Life Church in Renton, Washington (see above, the introduction to sermon 4) to what he is now doing (working in higher education and completing his PhD in practical theology at Claremont School of Theology; the "deal" was that our kids would bring us grandchildren—Neddy was seven-plus months pregnant when they moved—and we welcomed Serenity Joy into our home a few weeks later!

7. From the chorus, "Great Are You Lord," which was sung before the sermon; see also https://www.youtube.com/watch?v=uHzow-HG4iU.

our diaper changing. We're changing diapers, well my wife is changing diapers for our granddaughter.[8] I'm giving her back to my wife when that time has come. [Laughs.] But whatever it might be, the divine *ruach* is there for us. Let us pray.

Tony Richie Reflection—"Expect the Spirit"

Amos Yong's sermon proclaims that the Holy Spirit is present and active in the entire range of human living and working. The concept of vocation (*vocatio*: calling, summons) has a rich history in Christian thought and practice. Luther challenged existing ideas of his day that calling applied exclusively to religious orders or institutions specified by the church (e.g., marriage). Luther argued from 1 Corinthians 7:17–24 that divine calling includes secular, even mundane, activities and occupations. Such vocations provide opportunities for God's self-revelation in disguise, so to speak. Calvin agreed, explaining that these callings are God's provision for the stability of the common life and to counter rebellion. "Commoners" and laity could be just as sure as nobility or clergy that they were living out God's calling with dignity and integrity.

The Genesis creation account indicates work is an inherent element of human being (2:15). The fall brought toil into work but did not remove humanity's vocational calling (3:17). Therefore, Dorothy Sayers insists, "work is the natural exercise and function of man—the creature who is made in the image of his Creator" ("Why Work?"). Indeed, Jesus described his own redemptive activity as "work" in partnership with the Father (John 4:34; 5:17). Shouldn't we expect the Spirit's involvement in our workday? What about the rest of our day?

John Wesley's famous—and final!—sermon at Oxford ("Scriptural Christianity") insisted the Spirit-filled life is normative for all Christians. However, he distinguished between the Spirit's "ordinary" and "extraordinary" gifts. While affirming extraordinary gifts—prophecy, healing, speaking in tongues, and so on—Wesley emphasized ordinary gifts, the fruit of the Spirit: love, joy, peace, etc. (Gal 5:22–24). Clearly, "righteousness, peace, and joy" (Rom 14:17) consistently exhibited throughout the course of ordinary daily life is the most dramatic sign of the Holy Spirit's presence and activity. The "Spirit-filled life" means all our life is filled with the Spirit.

8. Although Serenity lived in our home during the first year of her life (with her parents), I don't think I have changed her diaper more than once, ever (thanks Alma!).

11

Mission in Translation

A C T S 2

Presbyterian Church of the Master, Mission Viejo,
California, 4 October 2015*

For our second[1] New Testament Scripture reading this morning, I'm
reading from Acts chapter 2, verses 1 through 13.

> When the day of Pentecost had come, they were all together in
> one place. [2]And suddenly from heaven there came a sound like
> the rush of a violent wind, and it filled the entire house where they
> were sitting. [3]Divided tongues, as of fire, appeared among them,
> and a tongue rested on each of them. [4]All of them were filled with
> the Holy Spirit and began to speak in other languages, as the Spirit
> gave them ability. [5]Now there were devout Jews from every nation
> under heaven living in Jerusalem. [6]And at this sound the crowd
> gathered and was bewildered, because each one heard them

---

* The occasion was Presbyterian Church of the Master's annual missions service,
and the associate pastor who oversaw the mission efforts of the church, Daryl Ellis,
suggested I make the connections between my Pentecostal perspective and issues related to multiculturalism in Southern California and of the so-called "reverse mission"
phenomenon; the title for my message, then, ought to make sense in light of how I
open up Acts 2.

1. A section from Acts 1 was first reading before I came up to preach, although I
am now uncertain which verses specifically.

speaking in the native language of each. [7]Amazed and astonished, they asked, "Are not all these who are speaking Galileans? [8]And how is it that we hear, each of us, in our own native language? [9]Parthians, Medes, Elamites, and residents of Mesopotamia, Judea and Cappadocia, Pontus and Asia, [10]Phrygia and Pamphylia, Egypt and the parts of Libya belonging to Cyrene, and visitors from Rome, both Jews and proselytes, [11]Cretans and Arabs—in our own languages we hear them speaking about God's deeds of power." [12]All were amazed and perplexed, saying to one another, "What does this mean?" [13]But others sneered and said, "They are filled with new wine" (NRSV).

May the Lord add his blessing to the word.

Good morning Church of the Master. It's good to be here with you . . . Thanks to Pastor Darrel and Pastor Jackson for the invitation.[1] . . .

I want to take a few moments this morning to talk about "Mission in Translation." "Mission in Translation." Mission is an activity of translation. It's an activity of translation across space and time. If you think about the message of the gospel, as it gets handed over from generation to generation, to our children and those who are far off, Peter says, at the end of chapter 2 in Acts, when he's preaching the Day of Pentecost sermon. Mission is . . . happens in translation across space and time. Mission happens as an act of translation. We see missionaries going out, doing the work, the deed, the preaching, the building, the translation of the gospel across time and space and across languages and cultures. I want to take a few moments this morning to talk about three aspects of mission in translation. I want to look at that through our two Scripture readings this morning, in the first chapter and the second chapter of the book of Acts.

The first aspect of translation I want to look at is a translation from restoration to renewal. We saw that in Acts chapter 1, when the disciples were once again sitting at the feet of Jesus. And if you remember the disciples, they spent three years getting an undergraduate degree in mission. Somebody same Amen. So, now I'm a Pentecostal preacher, I'm going to need a little help this morning. So, when I lift up my hand, give me a good old "Amen." The more Amens I get, the faster I go, and the faster we finish. [Laughter.] Alright, that brought them forth. [Laughter!]

So, the disciples had spent three years getting their undergraduate degree in missions. In fact, Acts chapter 1, as we read this morning, tells us that Jesus, after he rose from the dead, spent another forty days,

---

1. Referring to Rev. Daryl Ellis and to senior pastor Jackson Clelland.

another semester, with the disciples in class. And of course, he, it says, he shared with them many convincing proofs, but more important than anything else, he talked about the kingdom of God, if you remember that, in Acts 1:5.

Boy, those disciples, they had now gotten a whole undergraduate degree in missions, and they had got another graduate seminar in missions. They were ready for mission, weren't they? And of course, he says, "Go and wait in the Upper Room and pray for the Holy Spirit. John baptized in water, but I'm going to send the Spirit upon you." And of course, their question, they were so eager by now, they had readied themselves for three years and one semester to go forth and do mission. And they wanted to know, "Lord, is this the time when you will restore the kingdom to Israel?" Isn't that an interesting question? And if you think about the original context of the disciples, they were still thinking about the fact that God promised deliverance of Israel from all of Israel's oppressors. God had promised to restore the covenant to Israel. God had promised to restore the land to Israel. But they still found themselves under Roman rule and Roman occupation. Can you imagine that after a whole undergraduate degree in mission and another graduate seminar on mission, that they were still anticipating that the beginning of mission would be that God would restore the kingdom to Israel?

And isn't that the case with this us, oftentimes? You know, when we go on mission, as sincere as our hearts are, we're still focused on the restoration of, if you will, our version of the kingdom. We still want God to accomplish God's kingdom, sort of, on our terms, in our way, in our space, and our time, according to our political circumstances. We're like the disciples, we've all got undergraduate degrees in mission, we've all got even graduate degrees, and seminars in mission. But yet still, as sincere as our hearts are, I think we're oftentimes like the disciples. We're still so focused upon, if you will, God kingdom, but manifested in our terms, in our perspective, according to our preferences, our values.

And of course, the Lord Jesus was quite amazing—his transition, this translation from restoration of our kingdom, to renewal—and of course, his answer, if you look at his answer carefully, he doesn't really answer the question. The disciples wanted to know: "Is this the time, Lord? After all our studies, after all our tuition dollars, I mean, is this the time?" You can tell I'm a seminary professor, right? I'm thinking about tuition dollars already. "Is this the time when the kingdom would be restored, O Lord?" And of course, the Lord doesn't really answer the question. He just says, "You know what, you will receive power after the Holy Spirit comes upon you." The Lord doesn't say "*Now* is the time"; the Lord just says, "It's not for you to know what time it is." The Lord doesn't just abuse them. I mean, after three years and one graduate seminar in mission, they're a little dense. He says don't worry about it. Not for you to worry about the time, but you will receive power after the Holy Spirit comes upon you and you will be my witnesses.

"You might be thinking about the restoration of kingdoms, real kingdoms. I'm gonna be talking about the renewal of your spirit. I'm gonna be talking [about], be giving you, the Spirit that renews you for the mission. And that will correctly empower you to bear witness. That will correctly enable you to tell of me to the world around you. That will empower you." So the Lord moves them, if you will, from restoration of the image in their own understanding, to renewal in the Holy Spirit. Somebody say Amen.

In the second translation, I want to focus on "from Jerusalem to the ends of the earth": "And you will receive power after the Spirit comes upon you, and you shall be my witnesses in Jerusalem, in Judea, in Samaria, and to the end of the earth." I mean, here are just fishermen, local merchants in the Galilean world, rather uneducated. I mean, yes, they did have a college degree,[2] but they hadn't done any sort of studying abroad at that time yet. And God had promised them, "this translation, this empowerment of the Spirit, this ability to bear witness in my Spirit will carry you from Jerusalem to Judea to Samaria to the ends of the earth. And you know, that's the story of the book of Acts, isn't it?

The story of the book Acts demonstrates the capacity of this renewal of the Spirit to carry forward these fairly uneducated, these unrecognized, socially marginalized individuals. Carry them forward from Jerusalem to Judea to Samaria to the ends of the earth. And God brought about incredible acts of translation in their lives. God brought people to them and enabled them to carry forth the gospel to, if you will, the ends of the earth. It's a marvelous and incredible thing that . . . this is what I call the ideal of mission, right? That it continues to go on, and pass beyond, and get translated beyond border after border after border. I mean, for them to get even from Jerusalem and Judea into Samaria was a major miracle of incredible proportions. Jerusalem Jews didn't go into Samaria.

2. I am playing off the contemporary analogy that one could complete an undergraduate degree in three years of full time study; the disciples had their three years with Jesus.

And isn't it interesting that God had to bring alongside this ragtag bunch of disciples; another student that had graduated from another school, he was Greek-speaking. His name was Philip, as you know. God brings about a Greek-speaking missionary to join up with the apostles. And then from this experience of empowerment by the Spirit, this Greek-speaking person is the one that takes the gospel into Samaria; the place that the Jews were a little bit shy about going into. So God just brings about some help. How many of us need help this morning? We want to carry the gospel to the ends of the earth. We want to go, I don't know where our Samarias are. Here in Mission Viejo, is that Laguna Niguel? Is that Laguna Beach? Where are our Samarias? Where are those places, maybe it's Hollywood? That is, sort of, right around the corner, if you will. But we want the gospel to go there. We want to share it with our neighbors. We want to take it into that Samaria, but we oftentimes lack the perspective, the vision, the imagination. Maybe the language. And God brings alongside of us his capacity, his people empowered by that same Spirit to bear witness to the gospel in the language of the Samaritans. And even to the ends of the earth. Isn't that an amazing accomplishment of God, through the Holy Spirit?

I am a direct product of mission to the ends of the earth. As, somehow, missionaries arrived in Malaysia in the 1950s, and my parents came to know Christ through these missionaries. And now the ends of the earth, the Malaysians, have come to California. And that brings me to my third translation. It's not just from Jerusalem to the ends of the earth, but it's from the rest of the world to us. The rest of the world to us. Isn't it interesting that the ideal of mission is that it goes to the ends of the earth. And of course, God brings it about miraculously somehow. I mean, even if it takes shipwrecks of people like St. Paul, he's going to get them to the ends of the earth; to Rome. But that's such a far-out ideal for most of us. Most of us are "Jerusalemites," we're "just-right-here-ites." Maybe we do commute a few hours a day, I don't know. But we're more or less, sort of "localites."

So, the reality is, that God not only sends some, maybe a few of us to the ends of the earth. But God brings the ends of the earth here. And that's what happened on the Day of Pentecost, wasn't it? Yeah, it was these disciples, these 120 in the upper room. You know, they were just longing for the restoration of Israel. They got instead, the renewal of the Holy Spirit. They had visions and dreams of going to the ends of earth, although they had no idea how they were gonna do it. They didn't speak the languages, they hadn't got cross-cultural training, they just loved Jesus. And God said, "I'm going to bring some help. The reality is, I'm going to bring the ends of the earth to you." And it just so happened, they're in Jerusalem on that Day of Pentecost. The rest of the earth, the rest of the world was somehow gathered in Jerusalem. And that's what Luke tells us in Acts chapter 2, and that's what we read, isn't it? That as they were just worshipping God in the language that God had given them, that people from around the Mediterranean world were listening to the disciples extolling and lifting up God's wondrous deeds of power. The reality is that God will enable us. God will maybe take a few of us to the ends of the earth. But you know what? Most of us don't have to worry about going very far. Our neighbors from the ends of the earth are right here in Mission Viejo. Somebody say Amen.

Our neighbors right here are looking to hear the witness of the Holy Spirit through your life. And you may be asking yourself, "I'm not quite sure I speak Punjab.[3] I'm not quite sure I speak whatever it is, the language that my neighbors speak here in my neighborhood. Farsi. I'm not sure that I even know what to do." And yes, it's not gonna be easy. But one way in which it happens, is that they began to break bread together. They began to share meals together. And that even wasn't easy. I mean there were Hebrews and Greek widows that they were sort of arguing about.[4] I mean, you get a bunch of widows together, see what happens.

So, it's not easy. But the opportunity is here. And the opportunity invites you and me to open up our hearts once again, and to ask the Lord and say, "Lord of the harvest, Lord who sent the Spirit the first time, and Lord who continues to send the Spirit, invite us to live into that Spirit. May you give us, may you give me, in our church, in our community, in our workspace, in our home, our neighborhoods; may you give us the capacity to bear witness by the power of the Holy Spirit in the languages, in the perspectives, in the accounts of others. May you give us, O Lord, that language. Come Holy Spirit, once again. May there be a new Pentecost that can enable the translation of mission, above and beyond our own visions of what that kingdom looks like, above and beyond the comfort zone of our own, if you will, neighborhood and localities, but yet, at the same time, so deeply embedded within this amazing world that is this city, that is this region, that it is this place called Southern California,

3. Editor's note: technically, it is Punjabi.
4. See Acts 6:1.

upon whom the ends of the earth have descended. Now, O Lord, bring new Pentecost."

Let's pray: Holy Spirit, we open up our hearts, we open up our hands, we open up, O Lord God, our souls, once again to you. And we ask that you pour out your Spirit afresh in our lives, in our church, in our congregation, in our workspaces, in our schools, in our neighborhoods. O Lord Jesus, sometimes each one of us, we don't feel like we have a witness, a testimony. Holy Spirit, give us that witness, that testimony. In Jesus' name, Amen.

[Host leader takes over, and gets them to respond to the word of God through a profession of the Apostles Creed, followed by Communion.]

Tony Richie Reflection—"Going Glocal"

Amos Yong preaches that the kingdom of God is so much larger and grander and so far beyond human biases and presuppositions that only the power of Pentecost can bring it to us. Perceptions of the shape and scope of God's kingdom (*basileia*) are determinative for Christian mission. Wolfhart Pannenberg suggests God's reign is essentially eschatological. It exists presently as proleptic anticipation or foretaste awaiting full and final confirmation at the consummation. This "now, not yet" status suggests a present, albeit partial, participation in the future, in the *eschaton* (Heb 6:5). Present signs of the kingdom inspire confident, hopeful witness of Jesus. C. S. Song insists God's reign counters racism and nationalism or any form of oppressive regimes or economic systems with all-encompassing inclusiveness, crossing all boundaries. Cultural, ethnic, national, economic, caste or class, or even religious, and any other societal barriers are subsumed and transcended in Christ (Luke 14:15–24).

Historically persistent provincialism has plagued the church. Assumptions arising out of excessive narrowness of interests and views representing one's own immediate context apart from awareness or serious considerations of others are both scandalous and disastrous. Contemporary globalization, or the increasing interaction of people through the growth of the international flow of money, ideas, and culture, has contributed to advanced awareness of others. However, there's concomitant retreat into radical separatism, either literally or, more often, ideologically. Such exclusivist attitudes are completely incompatible with "the gospel of the kingdom" (Matt 24:14).

Recently a new term has been coined combining the words global and local. "Glocal" aptly describes the multifaceted nature of Christianity. The kingdom of God is *both* universal *and* local. It reaches out to everyone everywhere while respecting their "who" and their "where." God's reign reflects God's own magnanimous love for the world (John 3:16), and directs Christians to love after the same pattern of generosity and nobility—that is, with inclusivity and impartiality (Jas 2:8–9).

12

The Life in the Spirit
and the Life of the Mind

LUKE 10:25-29

Foursquare National Education Symposium, Life Pacific
College, San Dimas, California, 1 March 2016*

Thanks Steve. Getting embarrassed here.[1] I love Foursquare so much because you guys are the only ones that invite me to do anything. The Assemblies of God never asks me to do anything[2]—and I've still got their card in my wallet somewhere. . . . I left it in the car I think. It's just great to be able to be with you.

Thank you Lord, for being with us tonight. Thank you, Lord, for being with us, not just tonight, but today. These days. This week. These moments. Father, thank you for these people that are here, that represent

---

* I was invited by Dan Hedges in his role as chair of the Foursquare Educational Task Force; this meeting was attended by Foursquare leadership, educators, and pastors committed to the educational work of that church. Life Pacific College, the venue of this conference, is the flagship—even the only accredited—undergraduate college for the Foursquare denomination or group of churches.

1. I was introduced by Steve Overman (to whom this book is dedicated, in part), who was very generous with his commendations.

2. Hyperbolic and exaggerated! Effective, however, in the Foursquare context, given that the latter has always been seen as the much smaller "little brother" compared to the much larger Assemblies of God (with whom I retain credentials).

Foursquare across this country. And Lord, we're here because you've called us to this work; this church; this community. And you've called us, Lord God, to labor in this vineyard for its future, which is what education is all about. And we're humbled, O God, that you've called *us* to this task. That you've laid upon us the responsibility for our children and our children's children. We're humbled, O God, that we get to attempt to discern what your Spirit is doing and, perhaps, will do. We're humbled by the fact that we are called to pursue after that working of your Spirit. To the best that we can discern. Lord, for the future of the Foursquare. For the future of the church. Even as we say, O come Lord Jesus, we pray. Lord I thank you for the brothers and sisters in this room, who have this call, a call that we're not able on our own to carry out. So, we are here, O God, availing ourselves in your presence of your Spirit. We thank you for being here. Take, O God, our meager efforts and do your work with it. In the name of Jesus we pray, Amen.

Well I'm just thrilled that . . . I'm really honored to be amongst this group of national educators, Foursquare educators. Thank you, Dan, for the invitation and the team that didn't overrule him on this. I'm not sure how Foursquare works around here. [Laughter.]

I want to spend a few moments tonight talking a little about what I'm calling, "The Life in the Spirit and the Life of the Mind." Or maybe the title and the slide is the "Life of the Mind and Life in the Spirit." Isn't that our opportunity, and our challenge? Isn't that true? For us in the Foursquare, and as an Assemblies guy, I see every one of you as collaborators in this most important task, and one of the deepest challenges that I think we face as Foursquare, Assemblies, as people of the Spirit, as Pentecostals. Because I think that, by and large, one of the reasons why this is such an important venture for all of us is that historically—and we continue to live into this legacy, we continue to wrestle and battle with this legacy—that the life of the mind and the life of the Spirit have been seen, or understood to have been, at odds. So, rather than the "Life of the Mind and the Life of the Spirit" or "Life in the Spirit and the Life of the Mind," it's something like the "Life of the Mind versus the Life in the Spirit" or "The Life in the Spirit against the Life of the Mind." And I think there are a number of reasons for that. I want to take a few moments to unpack that.

Mark Noll, you might remember him, about twenty years ago published a book called *The Scandal of the Evangelical Mind.*[3] How many of

3. Noll, *The Scandal of the Evangelical Mind*. Note that in the next few moments,

you have looked that? A few of us here. *The Scandal of the Evangelical Mind*. Well, one positive way to take Mark Noll's *Scandal of the Evangelical Mind* is to actually say: at least there *was* an evangelical mind of which he could identify as scandal. [Laughter.] Because nobody would have bought a book, in 1996, called *The Scandal of the Pentecostal Mind*. They wouldn't have known what it was referring to, right? There would have been no such thing like the Pentecostal mind to have been scandalized.

The evangelicals—at least up to 1996, when the book first came out—had been at least wresting with the idea about Christian higher education for decades, right? And of course, Noll, in his analysis, identifies what the problem . . . what the scandal was. The scandal, of course, was a pietism with a burning heart and an unfortunately cold head—one of the scandals, or contributory [factors] to the scandal, that Mark Noll was talking about.

A second contributory stream toward this scandal of the evangelical mind is what he called the dispensational orientation toward the world, right? If we really are convinced that the world is going to end tomorrow, [contrary to this sensibility] universities are designed to take care of the world after tomorrow. Somebody say Amen. And if the world is going to end tomorrow, we're wasting our time, aren't we? Right? So, that was the second problem. You've got this pietism, this hot heart and cold head, oriented toward the end.

And then of course a third thing was the part of the scandal, what we would call Pentecostalism. That was part of Noll's diagnosis of the scandal. Part of the reason why, I think, and we're of course Pietists. I mean, in some respects it was three strikes on us. I'm not sure how dispensationalism is doing in the Foursquare, but it's still pretty hot in the AG. You go parse that one out yourself, alright?

And of course, I mean, you go back a hundred years. Our movements came out of a period of time in American history, American higher education, American church, in which our options for collaboration and options for alliances were few. And so, we hitched ourselves to those who held on to the word, because it was from the word that we felt the invitation came to live life in the Spirit. And the path we chose took us, if you will, *away from* the education which was associated with criticism, skepticism, questioning, right? Rather than building faith, [such was]

I mention the publication of the book as 1996 instead of 1994, when it was originally published. My discussion in the next few paragraphs focuses on Noll's reading of Pentecostalism vis-à-vis dispensationalism and fundamentalism in ch. 5 of his book.

undermining faith, at least in the way in which that dichotomy got played out in the early twentieth century. That particular contest, of course, was simply, if you will, another chapter in the last couple hundred years of modernity. So, the modern world, the Enlightenment, had already divided, if you will, the spirit from the body, the spirit from nature, the spirit from creation, the spirit from the human realm, and we, of course, we're gonna be people of the Spirit! We simply had to inhabit, in that framework, the other side of the divide, right? Which put us against the body. Against the mind. Against nature, if you will.

And of course, modernity's wrestling with these issues was also a result from and part of two thousand years. Alfred North Whitehead, a philosopher in the early twentieth century, said that all of the history of philosophy is a series of footnotes to . . . know what he said? Plato.[4] And of course, Plato was the one who had initially introduced the vision between the real and the ideal [on the one hand], as opposed to the nominal and the material [on the other]. And so, we've seen, if you will, centuries and centuries of this bifurcation.

And here we come, in the early twentieth century, and boy we were getting blessed by a visitation of the Spirit. But we only had this bifurcated construct to work with. It was either the Spirit or no Spirit. And guess what? We were going to go with the Holy Ghost, no matter what else anybody else said, right? Of course, one of the really, fundamentally interesting things about it was that our going with the Holy Ghost meant also our going with the image of God, with the created, material, fleshly creation, the dust of the earth, right? Because the Holy Ghost came upon fleshly tongues. The Holy Ghost came upon squirming bodies. The Holy Ghost came upon broken bodies. The Holy Ghost, in other words, met us right here. Not like up here [pointing to our heads], right? But we didn't have the categories. We didn't have the conceptual framework. We didn't have the language. And so, if we're forced to choose between the Holy Ghost and other ghosts we're going to go with the Holy Ghost, Amen? But that simply meant that we went our own way. We went our own way with the fundamentalists. Of course, with the Holy Ghost—the fundamentalists came with the word and without the Holy Ghost, right? But that took us away from this path of nurturing the life of the mind, which was seen to be part of nature, materiality, the human condition. We didn't have options to find a third way. Instinctively, we embodied that third

4. See Whitehead, *Process and Reality*, 39.

way, but we didn't have the language and the capacities to articulate it. We embodied that third way because the Spirit had come upon flesh already. That's what the Bible said, right?

And we were embodying the third way, but we didn't have a way to articulate it, except in our tongues. And the interpretations weren't quite connecting. The interpretations weren't quite able to generate this third way, in these early 10s . . . , 20s, 30s, and so on, here we found ourselves on the other side of the "versus." We'll take the Spirit, you can have the mind. Somebody say Amen. Ha ha! Right? I mean if it's between the mind and the Spirit, come on somebody? Better go with the Holy Ghost! And that's what we did. We didn't have models, exemplars, possibilities to carve out this middle way.

Well, you know, growing up Pentecostal, all the big questions in life can be understood, can be answered, by going to the book of Acts. Somebody say Amen. Just follow the apostles, man, follow the apostles. Well, we're going to a little bit, something of that type. But I want to look at Luke. He's one of the apostles. Or maybe, at least he was an author, with regard to these apostles. He hung out with them. Luke is, I mean, we know that Luke authored the book of Acts Amen? And so, if there is ever a theologian of the Holy Ghost, it's Saint Luke isn't it, right? And of course, the whole apostolic narrative, the Acts narrative is . . . I mean the Presbyterians and the Baptists call it the Acts of the *Apostles*. We call it the Acts of the *Holy Ghost*, right? The Acts story is the Acts of the Holy Spirit.

I want to look at a passage in Luke today, and I think you realize that, of course, Luke's Gospel account is also the acts of the Holy Ghost. Because Luke, more than anyone of the other apostles, more than any of the other Gospels, tells the story of Jesus as the story of the Holy Ghost. The story of the man who was anointed by the Spirit to do the works that he did, right? And Jesus comes in the synagogue in Luke 4, and he pulls the scroll off from the shelf, and he opens up to the prophet Isaiah, and he says, "The Spirit of the Lord is upon me, and has anointed me." And the rest of the Gospel is about the Spirit-anointed Jesus' ministry.

So, we can read the entirety of the Gospel of Luke, in that sense, as a presentation of the Spirit-anointed Messiah. I want to look at Luke 10 today, tonight, for a few minutes with you. The story of the Good Samaritan. And actually, the beginning part before that. And of course, the context of that narrative that we'll be looking at in just a moment is the mission of the seventy and the seventy-two. Now that's Luke's theme, isn't it? The acts of the Holy Ghost is the mission of the kingdom. Jesus sends them out in the Gospels, and then the Holy Ghost sends them out in Acts. The work of the Spirit is about the work of the kingdom. And that's the context within which this story unfolds. And we see the Spirit in Mission. And we the Spirit in prayer, in Luke 11. So, I want to look with you, very, very quickly at a few verses in Luke 10. I want to start reading verses 25 to 30:

> 25Just then a lawyer stood up to test Jesus. "Teacher," he said, "what must I do to inherit eternal life?" 26He said to him, "What is written in the law? What do you read there?" 27He answered, "You shall love the Lord your God with all your heart, and with all your soul, and with all your strength, and with all your mind; and your neighbor as yourself." 28And he said to him, "You have given the right answer; do this, and you will live." 29But wanting to justify himself, he asked Jesus, "And who is my neighbor?" 30Jesus replied, "A man was going down from Jerusalem to Jericho, and fell into the hands of robbers, who stripped him, beat him, and went away, leaving him half dead (NRSV).

Let's stop right there. I want to invite you tonight, for these next few moments, to live with me into this narrative. Into this space, in which the life of the Spirit and the life of the mind come together. I want us to live into this Lukan space, this Luke, the PhD, or MD, or whatever the D's he got back in the day. But who was also the theologian of the Holy Ghost. I want us to live into this, step into this Lukan space, into this narrative to inhabit, if you will, Luke's account of a life full of the Spirit, but yet one that loves the Lord our God with all our minds.

The lawyer asked Jesus, in Luke 10, "What must I do to inherit eternal life?" And Jesus said, "What is written in the law? What do you read there?" He answered, "You shall love the Lord your God with all your heart, with all your soul, and all your strength and with all your mind." Heart, soul, and strength come from Deuteronomy, okay? We can attempt to do a kind of Synoptic analysis here. Mind appears in all the Synoptic Gospels. If we take Markan priority, that's fine. Mark wrote to a Greco-Roman audience. Mind adds on to soul, heart, and strength. Why? Because it fits a Greco-Roman and Hellenistic anthropology. How do we understand the nature of what it means to be fully human?

For the Hebrews, it was the "gut," the heart. "Thou shall love the lord your God with all your heart, soul, and strength," called attention to Hebrew anthropology. But if you step into a Greco-Roman-Hellenistic world, now it's not just heart, soul, and strength, but *mind*. So, whether it's Markan priority or whether it's Lukan priority or whether they were drawing from separate traditions, it doesn't matter. We're articulating a theological anthropology that is holistic. And the Gospels accounts recognize it, and preserve it. "Thou shall love the Lord your God with all your heart . . . ," in other words, thou shall simply love the Lord your God with *all* that you are. And *all* that we are, as creatures of dust, includes our *minds*. Now that's a no-brainer, pun intended.

But it's interesting when we're forced to choose, right? It has been between the Spirit and the mind. And in this case, there is no choice that's required of us.

Notice that in this case, the context [involves] an attorney, a lawyer. Also, somebody trained, intellectually, legally. There has been intellectual process of education for the legal profession. And he wants to know, "Teacher, what must I do to inherit eternal life?" The other Gospels would say very, very clearly . . . . There's one account that uses "Lord," and another one talks about the religious leaders. Both of those other accounts, Matthew and Mark's, say that they were trying to trap him. We may get a sense of that here in Luke. We may, in the broader context of a number of other Lukan passages, but in this immediate passage it's not up front and center. Rather, we get, almost, a genuine question. And boy, there is no more important question than this one, is there? C'mon somebody! What in the world must we do to get eternal life? Right? And of course, Jesus says . . . unfolds "The Four Spiritual Laws," right? [Laughter.[5]]

Isn't it amazing that this most profoundest, this most important, this most weightiest of all questions, involves this most deepest of commitments? That is not apart from, but can only be *with* the *mind*. That this most momentous of occasions, the one part of the examination, and the test that you better not fail, involves not just the heart and the gut and the strength and the soul, but it calls forth as much intellectual "mind-muster" as you can generate. Here is where, if you will, your mind is most fully on trial, not when it's most fully on hold. Here is where we're called to strive into the deepest and the toughest and the most dissonant of spaces. Because the call, the answer, involves engagement of that which oftentimes is . . . "my mind hurts, let me just go to sleep for a while . . . I

---

5. Created by Campus Crusade for Christ founder Dr. Bill Bright, "The Four Spiritual Laws" is the title of an outreach booklet widely used in evangelical (and Pentecostal) circles to help laypersons lead others to a "born again" experience of conversion to Christ.

wanna check out." Yeah. I mean, I thought Jesus might have given some other answer.

"What shall I do to inherit eternal life?" Jesus answered to him, next, "What is written in the law? What do you read there?" This is peculiar to Luke; Luke, compared with the other Synoptics. This passage appears in the other Synoptics, but differently. Isn't it incredibly amazing that in this particular instance in which this most profound of charismatic theologians, Luke, his account involves precisely the kind of Socratic method that we wouldn't have expected from a Spirit-filled evangelist? Because Jesus's answer is two other questions. C'mon somebody!

"Lord what must I do to be saved?" "Repent and be baptized and be filled with the Holy Ghost and . . . ,"[6] right? But Jesus says [instead], "What's written in the law? What do you read there?" Of course, he's talking to a lawyer. A lawyer who knows the law, so he counters the question with a question. He could have left it there. But he counters the question in a way that presses precisely the question of where life of the Spirit and life of the mind ought to meet. "What is in the law? What do you read there?" You know what kind of question that is? That's a hermeneutical question. Yeah, yeah, yeah, I wasn't speaking in tongues. [Laughter.] That's an interpretive question. That means that the answer is not obvious. That means that we might have to step into this word, we might have to step into this space of the word of God. And we might have to stay there for a while. Not sleep there for a while. Wrestle with hermeneutics; interpretation; argument; debate. Wrestle with the implications of these words.

And the rabbis give us incredibly powerful images, where they would sit around these tables and they would argue Torah, for years and years and years. Then of course, we want to go out and save the world, we don't have time to argue Torah.

"What is written in the law? What do you read there?" What are the interpretive, hermeneutical, methodological, and interdisciplinary tools that you might bring to your reading of the word? Jesus is inviting the lawyer into a dialogue. A conversation. A journey. Inviting him to live into this space of the question and maybe not just one answer, but a number of possible answers. How do you read what is happening in the law? How do you understand? What's your perspective on the law?

---

6. Which is a paraphrase of an answer to another, similar, question in Acts 2:37–38.

Boy, I mean, wouldn't it have just been easier for Jesus to give him the answer, right? Holy Ghost, give me the answer, give me the answer. And maybe the Holy Ghost says, "Learn hermeneutics." No, that was definitely not the Holy Ghost. [Laughter.] "What do you read there?"

And of course, we know that the story then unfolds with the Good Samaritan's story. A man was going down from Jerusalem to Jericho and fell into the hands of robbers who stripped him and beat him. And went away leaving him half dead. I'm not going to read verses 31 and following. Because the point for me isn't the fullness of the Samaritan's story, but the point is how the Samaritan story invites us to live into this space with the Spirit and the mind come together?

Luke is the only one [of the Synoptic Gospels] that has a Samaritan story. Matthew doesn't have it. Mark doesn't have it. In fact, the only time that the Samaritan, or Samaria, ever appears in Matthew—it doesn't appear in Mark—is when it says that the disciples told Jesus not to go into Samaria. And the times that Samaria and the Samaritans appear in John are all bad. Jesus has a demon, like the Samaritans![7] In fact, it's interesting that the Samaritans appear only in Luke, right?[8] Ten lepers. Remember that? It's not in the other Synoptics; it's not in John. And then we have this Good Samaritan—what in the world is he doing here?

I'm tempted to speculate that Luke, in all of his education, knew something about the struggle to pursue the life of the mind. But we'll come to it in a second. His was not an abstract, speculative life of the mind. But it was, I think, still deeply a life of the mind. And I'd like to invite us to think about this account of the Good Samaritan, as illuminating precisely what happens when the mind is engaged. The mind engages itself when it encounters something that is new, unexpected, unanticipated, and [when what it encounters] cuts against the grain of everything we assumed, presumed, or believe in.

When you're riding your bicycle, you don't need to think about it. Most of the time, when you're driving, you don't need to think about it. You get in your car, you're habituated, and you somehow get to where you need to go. The only time you need to think about, when you're driving, is when you don't know where you're going. But [usually] you're not thinking about driving, you're thinking about how to get where you need to

7. John 8:48.

8. Again, I must be thinking here relative to the Synoptic Gospels, although the context might be a bit confusing since I also referred to the Fourth Gospel in the preceding sentence.

go. You don't need to think about things that you're comfortable in, that you are habituated to do. We don't need to engage the life of the mind, when we're in autopilot. But the mind, and its engagement, is imperative when we are confronted by a situation or a set of circumstances, or a set of unexpected developments in our lives. And the Jews had just gone their merry little way, and the Samaritans had gone their merry little way, and the twain were not going to meet, because they had their mountain to worship in, and they had their temple to worship in,[9] and they talked bad about each other. And that's just the way it was.

Here's a Jewish lawyer, trying to figure out how to get eternal life, right? And of course, we know that Jesus's story was that the Samaritan showed how to live eternally. Jesus is calling the lawyer deeply, to challenge, to critique, to interrogate his assumptions about God's ways. And there's no more powerful way to do that than to simply state, "You know what, you want to know about eternal life? Well I'll tell you about eternal life. And it's [about] the folks that you didn't think were going to get eternal life; that's how eternal life works." Huh? Right? That's how the story is unfolding. The one who doesn't love their neighbor. He's the one who shows eternal life unfolding. He's the one who challenges the lawyer and the Jews and the people of God from out of their assumptions about their election, and the covenant, and faithfulness to Yahweh. Yahweh's faithfulness. Because now, all of a sudden, the story of Yahweh's faithfulness and eternal covenant featured some different actors in their midst.

Now, I think that Luke is also, of course, setting up the story that's going to unfold in the Acts of the Holy Ghost, isn't he? Jesus tells the story of the Good Samaritan for Luke, and that's important. Why? Because. It's important because the apostles still didn't get it, right? They weren't going to go to Samaria when things got rough, they were going to hole back up in Jerusalem![10] But it took the folks that had been out and about, the Hellenistic Jews, from around the Mediterranean, who were already used beyond the road, already used to thinking about God being at work in diverse places that the home folks would not have considered. And they latched upon the fact that, you know, Jesus said something about Samaritans. Maybe we ought to go there.

The Samaritan challenges and the Samaritan turns upside down the worldview of the lawyer and of the Jew. That's what we call intellectual

9. See John 4:20–21.

10. Acts 8:1.

challenge, and maybe [an occasion for intellectual] conversion. The challenge to interrogate deeply one's convictions. Here is what I really believe [about] the way things are. And all of a sudden, we're confronted with an anomaly, we're confronted with a story, we're confronted with what appears to be a reality that doesn't match up to that [assumption]. Now we've got a couple of choices right here. We can dig our heels in. Or we can start asking questions. In other words, what? We can start interpreting. We can start questioning. We can start reading and re-reading, and reading and re-reading, and arguing. And say, "Wait! Now how does that happen? How does this happen? What about this? What about this?"

Nobody said intellectual conversion was gonna be like Pauline conversion: getting knocked off our horse one day, and wake up and all of a sudden we have a new worldview. No, intellectual conversion is called four years of Life Pacific College. Come on, somebody say Amen! And by the way, four years of Life Pacific College is supposed to launch us on a lifetime of intellectual conversion, right? Cause after four years . . . unless you guys at Life do something different than most of the other schools around the country, you don't encounter everything that you're going to encounter for the rest of your life in four years, right? What do you do? You have to learn. Get the tools that you need. To ask questions properly. To do what? To read. And by reading what? Not just texts, although texts are important. Somebody say Amen! But discernment is about reading life. Life in the Spirit. Discernment is about reading reality. It's about reading people. It's about reading circumstances. It's about trying to read the Acts of the Holy Ghost.

This was a challenge. The challenge of the conversion of the mind. He could not have loved the Lord his God with all of his mind, unless he was ready to *change* his mind. Cause otherwise, he's still loving the Lord his God with his own thoughts. Not the thoughts of God. And Luke . . . boy I tell you, this Samaritan story is consistent, isn't it? We encounter at every turn what Luke in Acts 17 says, that "these people go around the world, and they keep turning the world upside down."[11] What does that mean?

Things keep happening in their lives that don't measure up with the ways in which we think the world is supposed to go. Rich are not important. Poor is better in Luke. First, eh, not so good. *Last*, that's pretty good . . . in Luke. The able body, well that's okay. But the poor, the blind, and

11. Acts 17:6b.

the lame, well that's pretty darned good . . . in Luke. The clean, uh. Un-clean? Yeah! Get some lepers going around here . . . in Luke. Males, uh. *Females*! On menservants? Yeah, but *maidservants*! On the older guys, eh, the guys who are supposed to be up in the gates, running the show, eh. But on the young! They're supposed to be just told what to do? [No,] they're going to get the visions, right? The aristocrats, the landowners, eh, well they're supposed to sell their stuff. What we really want are *doulous* [slaves or servants]: fleshly, stanky, *doulous*, full of the Holy Ghost. That's the nature of the kingdom.

[So I am] sitting over here, [saying,] "I got PhD, I got good practice, I got the role at the gate, I'm used to answering this question from people about eternal life," right? And Jesus says, "Come on. How do you read this?" Gotta start converting. Gotta start changing your mind. Gotta start opening up to the possibility that my ways are not your ways. And one time changing of mind, is just the first step. The rest of your life is gonna involve—this is now Paul—the renewing of the mind.[12]

Only two last points, where I want to connect what I called the con-version of the mind and the conversion of the heart. "What is written in the law? What do you read there?" The lawyer had a good answer. "You shall love the Lord your God." Wow, he got the words right. You shall love the Lord your God with your heart, with all your soul, with all of your strength, with all your mind. And your neighbor as yourself. I've got these highlighted up here, in bold, because they're all one sentence. There's one verb that runs all the way through this sentence. You shall love the Lord your God and your neighbor as yourself. You shall love the Lord your God with all that you are, all that you are, and you shall love your neighbor. That one act of loving, encompasses both God and neighbor. We don't love God one way, according to Luke, and then our neighbor another way, according to Luke. But we shall love God and neighbor, and in that case, both with *all* that we are. Our heart. Our mind. Our gut. Our soul. And our intellect.

Boy, I never thought I'd be talking about a platonic way of loving, right? But that's the call. That the intellectual conversion toward God is incomplete without the conversion toward our neighbor, and therefore, that the life of the mind includes, and is interdependent with, the conver-sion of the heart. So, for Luke, therefore, there is no separation between either love of God and love of neighbor, or between the intellectual

12. Rom 12:1–2.

response and the gut response. They're all part of our seamless and holistic embeddedness in this world, in which the Spirit is poured out not up there, but upon us fleshly people, who interact with other fleshly people. And probably more times than not, fleshly in the fleshly [carnal] sense, as opposed to in the non-fleshly [merely mortal] sense.

In other words, *orthodoxa*, related to thinking things through, proper conversion of our thinking, of our minds, taking captive our own mentalities: *orthodoxa* and *orthopathos* are completely intertwined. Right thinking and right loving. Right feeling, right hoping, right yearning. That's the affective gut of who we are. That right pathos, that right passion, is not exclusive of right thinking, as most of us have been taught to live out, right?

One of my theologian friends, just a few years ago, said "Yeah, whenever I go to my church on Sunday mornings, I have to purposely park my brains at the door." Why? From his standpoint, otherwise, he'll be criticizing the pastor the whole sermon. Well, unfortunately, you know, I think we can all feel the pains sometimes there, right? But I think that this Lukan narrative invites us to see that right passions involves fully engaging the world with our minds, and not parking our minds somewhere else in order for us to *feel* the Holy Ghost.

Last point I want to make. "You shall love the Lord your God with all your heart, with all your soul, with all your strength, with all your mind, and your neighbor as yourself." And he said to him, "You've given the right answer, do this, and you will live."

I've just said that *orthodoxa* and *orthopathos*, right feeling, right loving, right passions, are interconnected with right thinking. I want to close with this. That *orthodoxa* and *orthopathos* is intertwined with orthopraxis—right doing. You've given the orthodox answer, now do some orthopraxis. Go do something about it. Go love your neighbor with all your heart, your passion, your gut, and your head, and your hands. That's the call. And notice, we can't love our neighbor with our hands, well we could, but we can't fully love our neighbor *and* God without converting in all of these domains. Otherwise, it's partial loving, isn't it? Well we might be really good with loving God with our hands, really, really good at being passionate, but if our minds park back there somewhere, guess what? It's not holistic, is it? It's still a conversion that's in process. And the call of the Spirit, I believe, is for us to live fully into this. With all that we are—guts, heads, hands, hearts—go and do likewise. Go do some *orthopraxis*.

I want to close with a couple of thoughts about life of the mind and the life in the Spirit. I think that's our opportunity and our challenge, as those, these educators. I'm sorry I haven't given you, you know, the ten steps to convincing people to invest money for their children and our colleges and our cemeteries, I mean our seminaries. I mean, you know, to just try to sell our programs is difficult enough, right? But I think it's in part because we haven't found, yet, good models for how we can live fully into this call, this vocation.

I want to invite us to ask ourselves tonight, and maybe tomorrow: can the Foursquare, can we the Foursquare, lead the way in thinking about the role of the Spirit in Christian higher education? So, one of the books I'm working on with a colleague at Regent University is entitled "The Renewing of the Christian University." Subtitled, "The Holy Spirit and Christian Higher Education."[13] How do we think about the role of the Spirit in what we do in education? Foursquare traditioning. What does that mean? It means, as I opened up this evening, and what you and I are doing, is that we are wanting to equip our brothers, our sisters, our colleagues, our friends . . . , what [for]? For the future. Education is always about an investment in the future. That's what we can also say is traditioning. How do we get from where we were to where God is calling us to? That's our future. That's God's future. That's the reign of God. The reign of God that is coming and yet the reign of God is [among you]—Luke said this, Jesus said this in Luke 20:17, or 17:20, right?[14] The kingdom of God is in your midst! In the last days, I will pour out my Spirit upon all flesh. The kingdom of God is at hand. We're already inhabiting the Spirit's last days. And it seems to be going on for a long time! But that simply calls us to increased faithfulness in the task of traditioning. Increased attentiveness and diligence and commitment toward the future. Our future. Our children's future. And God's future.

Come Holy Spirit. Renew our minds. In the name of Jesus, Amen.

[Host speaks, then leader invites Yong to pray for them; he prays, actually begins by praying in tongues, then prays for them.]

13. New working title: Yong and Coulter, *Finding the Holy Spirit at a Christian University.*

14. Actually: Luke 17:21b.

Tony Richie Reflection—"Apostolic Succession"

This sermon makes a lively case for Pentecostals' participation in intellectual development. Pentecostalism is heir to general populist tendencies in America, influenced in part (after McCarthyism) by evangelicalism and revivalism, toward anti-intellectualism. Further, a keen sense of eschatological urgency has lent itself more readily to evangelism than education. But some intellectual suspicion is healthy. Historically, Western intellectual and philosophical resources were recruited to justify colonialism, racism, and sexism. Nevertheless, Pentecostals aren't unaware that lack of knowledge is a destructive force (Hos 4:6).

Theological education integrates *theologia* and *educare*. *Theologia* involves practical *habitus* (salvation-oriented knowledge) and cognitive *habitus* (scientific discipline). Both prescribe theology as a lifelong habit or way of being in the world. *Educare* involves *paideia* or "culturing" in *arête* (virtue of excellence). Combining *theologia* and *educare* result in Christian culturing and spiritual formation. Notably, "seminary" derives from a root meaning to "seed plants." Ideally, theologically educated individuals are equipped to spread piety, civility, and learning throughout the land.

Tension often exists between pursuit of scholarly knowledge and focus on ministerial tasks. Emphasis on scholarship to the diminishment of pastoral/practical ministry can result in perceived irrelevance for performance of ministry. Focus on performance of pastoral/practical ministry apart from scholarship can result in theological inconsistencies and vulnerabilities. Either way, divorce occurs between church and academy.

Rightly done, theological education serves a wide public of church, nation, and academy. Serving the church public concerns clergy education through the theological task of formation. Serving the national public requires a public voice seeking to influence the moral conscience of society. Serving the academy contributes to the advancement of pure knowledge. At its best, higher education is training in intellectual virtue, has inherent sociality, and exists for the common good. Thus the teaching vocation ably embodies ancient "apostolic succession" dogma through its intergenerational transmission of sound theological instruction (2 Tim 2:2).

13

Following Jesus in the Power of the Spirit

LUKE 4:14-21

First Evangelical Church, Glendale, California, 24 April 2016*

Thank you, Pastor Tan. It's an honor and privilege for me to be here. First of all, I thank the Lord for your friendship. You reached out to me when I first got here. Hallelujah, *Gloria Dios*! I thank the Lord for your friendship. You had a ministry here at Fuller for all these years. And also, here at FEC in Glendale. I'm honored and privileged to be able to share this morning's worship with you and the congregation.

* When I arrived at Fuller Seminary in the summer of 2014, I was greeted almost immediately by Professor Siang Yang Tan of the School of Psychology and invited out to lunch at Kopitiam, a local Malaysian restaurant. We have been having lunches every few months since. Prof. Tan is not only a widely authored academic in his field but also pastor of First Evangelical Church in Glendale. He invited me to be the speaker for the weeklong summer retreat for the church in June 2016, and this service in April of that year was supposed to introduce me initially to the congregation. My retreat messages, on the theme "Adventures with Jesus: Moving in the Spirit" (at California Baptist University, Riverside, California, 1–4 July 2016) were titled, individually:
  1. *"Jesus' Preaching: Forgiveness in the Spirit"* (Luke 7:36–50)
  2. *"Jesus' Exorcising: Deliverance in the Spirit"* (Luke 8:26–39)
  3. *"Jesus' Touching: Curing and Healing in the Spirit"* (Luke 18:35–43)
  4. *"Jesus' Freeing: Liberation and Resurrection in the Spirit"* (Luke 7:11–17)
  5. *"Jesus' Saving: Jubilee in the Spirit"* (Luke 19:1–10)
  In anticipation of these five sermons, I opted to introduce the overarching frame of Jesus as Spirit-empowered Messiah in the message transcribed here.

162

Good morning to everyone. . . . It's good to be here this morning. Now you might use . . . , in fact, one your deacons mentioned that you don't use your New International Version as much, I invite you to pick that up if you like. Or pick up your iPhone and go to the Gospel of Luke the fourth chapter of the Gospel of Luke the fourth chapter. I'm going to read from the New International Version, in case you're also going to be following me and that would be on page 727 in your Bible. It's right after page 726 if you get lost. Luke chapter 4. I'm going to start in verse 14, and we're going to go to verse 21. Luke chapter 4:14 to 21.

> Jesus returned to Galilee in the power of the Spirit, and news about him spread through the whole countryside. He taught in the synagogues, and everyone praised him. He went to Nazareth, where he had been brought up, and on the Sabbath day he went into the synagogue, as was his custom. And he stood up to read. The scroll of the prophet Isaiah was handed to him. Unrolling it, he found the place where it was written: "The Spirit of the Lord is on me, because he has anointed me to preach good news to the poor. He has sent me to proclaim freedom for the prisoners and recovery of sight for the blind, to release the oppressed, to proclaim the year of the Lord's favor." Then he rolled up the scroll, gave it back to the attendant and sat down. The eyes of everyone in the synagogue was fastened on him, and he began by saying to them, "Today this Scripture is fulfilled in your hearing."

Bow with me in prayer. We thank you Lord for your presence that has already graced our day. From the first breath we took, when we woke up this morning, the breath of your Spirit given to us. This beautiful day, on this drive in to church, Lord, for our time of worship in which you nurtured our souls. For the time in communion, in which you nurtured our bodies. And now, O Lord God, our hearts are open, and our minds are alert. Come Holy Spirit, in these next few moments and give us your living word. In the name of Jesus. And all God's people said? Amen.

Our title for our thoughts this morning is "Adventures with Jesus in the Power of the Spirit." My heart was very much warmed. I know from talking to your pastor that his heart is also with Jesus and the Spirit-filled life. But my heart was also warmed as I heard the testimonies that a few of you shared. One line that stood out and jumped out and I wrote down: "We have learned so much about how the Holy Spirit has led us." Do you remember that? That witness that was given by the brother over there as he shared about what was happening. "We have learned so much about how the Holy Spirit has led us." Pastor Tan mentioned that I'm from the Assemblies of God. I'm a second-generation Assemblies of God pastor's kid. Second-generation Pentecostal preacher's kid. And second-generation Pentecostal preacher. And so, of course, when we think about the work of the Spirit, we always think about the book of the Holy Spirit, which is the book that in some of our Bibles is called the Acts of the Holy Spirit, Amen? The Acts of the Holy Spirit. Some of our other titles are the Acts of the Apostles. And we often go to these Acts of the Apostles or these Acts of the Holy Spirit in order to discern again and again, and to be taught again and again, about the person and the work of the Spirit. But how many of us know that the person who wrote the Acts of the Holy Spirit, also wrote another book that is part of our New Testament? The author of the book the Acts of the Apostles also wrote the Gospel of Luke. Luke, I want to invite you to consider with me today, and hopefully I'll do well enough so you'll sign up to come for the retreat in a few weeks. Lord help me!

Luke, I want to invite us think about today, is the theologian of the Holy Ghost in the New Testament. The theologian and author of the Holy Spirit; and he writes about the acts of the Holy Spirit in the book of Acts. But he gives us before . . . the twenty-eight chapters of the book of Acts, he gives us twenty-four chapters preceding that story, the Acts of the Holy Spirit. And the preceding story is the acts of the Holy Spirit also, but focused in the life and ministry of Jesus.

The Gospel of Luke gives us the story of Jesus, the one who was empowered and filled with the Holy Spirit. Then the Acts of the Holy Spirit tell us about that same Holy Spirit who empowers and fills the disciples, the followers of Jesus, to now go and do the things that Jesus did. Now I want us to look this morning at this passage in Luke 4, in order for us to get a sense for what it means for Luke to have set forth and write about the disciples being sent forth in the power of the Spirit, and for them to be simply following in the footsteps of Jesus, the Spirit-empowered Messiah.

Luke tells us in Luke chapter 4 verse 14 that Jesus returned to Galilee in the power of the Spirit. Matthew doesn't tell us that, Mark doesn't tell us that, John doesn't tell us that. But here is, as you know, as we read through this passage in Luke 4, this is the beginning of Jesus' public ministry. The last verse that we read, "Today this Scripture is fulfilled in your hearing," opens up then to us the rest of the Gospel of Luke in which Jesus goes out and does what he does, as the one full of the Spirit. And the one who is full of the Spirit, it says, returns to Galilee in the power of the Spirit. So, we obviously know that there's something, there is a background story.

If you remember your stories of Jesus, that you've learned over the years, at Christmas time, we know Jesus was a Galilean. We know Jesus was from a little town of Nazareth, in Galilee. We know Jesus had been born and raised in Galilee and in Nazareth. And here we find Luke telling us that Jesus returned to Galilee in the power of the Holy Spirit. This is not the first time that Luke tells us about the power of the Holy Spirit in this gospel. We're only three chapters into this story of Jesus, and we know that Jesus himself comes because his mother was overshadowed by the Holy Spirit. Remember that reference in Luke chapter 1: "How shall I be of child? I know not a man, I'm not married." "Oh, the Holy Spirit will overshadow you. The Holy Spirit will come upon you, and you shall be with child. And you shall call his name Jesus, for he will save his people from their sins."[1] And Mary goes up into the hill country, three months pregnant, and she hears and she knows that she's got an older aunt who is not supposed to be pregnant, but she's heard that she's six months pregnant. You know the story here. And that's Elizabeth. And this young, vulnerable, frail girl, Mary, could not have been more than in her young teens, finding herself with child and not understanding how to handle this, even though she been given a word from God. While she knows that she can find wisdom and comfort and encouragement from one who is just a few months ahead of her, in terms of carrying a child, but many decades ahead of her in terms of wisdom and maturity. And she goes to her aunt Elizabeth. And Luke tells us that when Mary knocked on her door, remember that story? And when Mary said "Hello, is anybody home?" And all of a sudden the Holy Spirit came, it was like the Holy Spirit who had overshadowed Mary, through the sound and the knock and the voice, zapped Elizabeth! And Elizabeth feels this six-month-old child in her womb jump for joy. And Elizabeth becomes the first one filled with the Holy Spirit![2] Not one of the twelve disciples. Not one of the established leaders of the church. Not even the husband, Zechariah. But this old, forgotten, ashamed, barren-until-six-months-ago woman, she gets filled with the Holy Spirit and she begins to prophesy over her niece, this vulnerable teenage niece. And she says, "Blessed are you!" Exactly the words that Mary needs in her spirit. The words after the three months

1. Luke 1:34–35, paraphrased; but, to be accurate, the clause, "you are to name him Jesus, for he will save his people from their sins," comes from Matthew 1:21b.

2. Luke 1:41b.

of, I'm told, morning sickness. I don't know too much about it personally, but after three months of morning sickness, after three months of
questioning, after three months of wondering whether the word was going to be carried forward, she knocks on the door: "Are you home?" The
Holy Spirit descends upon Elizabeth and she begins to prophesy a word
of blessing upon Mary. And the Spirit who had hovered now upon Mary
and that helped conceive this child in her begins to fill her again, and
Mary begins to sing her song before God. The three months of silence,
three months of questions, three months of worries, and Mary with Jesus
in her tummy begins to sing forth a marvelous song before God.

Jesus was born, we know the story about Jesus going and getting
lost from his parents' perspective, right? And we know how they took
three days to discover that here he was at the age of twelve full of the
Spirit about his Father's business. But we're not told too much else about
[his childhood] other than that he grew in spirit and wisdom.³ And we're
told in chapter 3 of Luke, that the Spirit comes upon Jesus in the Jordan,
as John is baptizing him. And the voice comes from heaven says "This is
my child, whom I am well pleased, hear him."⁴ And then at the beginning
of chapter 4 verse 1, if you still have page 727 open for you, Jesus comes
baptized and full of the Spirit from the Jordan. And it says that "full of
the Holy Spirit, [he] returned from the Jordan," verse 1 chapter 4, "and
was led by the Spirit in the desert," where for forty days he was tempted
by the devil.

So, you've got this highlight of Jesus' life in the Jordan, the baptism
with John. Jesus receives the Spirit again, the one conceived of the Spirit,
nurtured by the Spirit, cultivated in the Spirit, receives the Spirit again,
and he's led full of the Spirit into the desert. Now I don't know about
you, but when I get full of the Spirit I want to go do great things for God.
Preach the gospel around the world; I don't want to go into the desert.
But he's led full of the Spirit into the desert. And in the desert, he is confronted with his needs. In the desert, he is confronted with the seductions
of the world. In the desert, he is confronted with shortcuts, the possibility of shortcuts, to achieve God's purposes. And it's in those moments
of need, it's in those moments of temptation, it's in those moments of

3. Luke 2:52 says actually: "Jesus increased in wisdom and in years, and in divine
and human favor" (NRSV).

4. Correction: Luke 3:22 records the voice from heaven saying, "You are my Son,
the Beloved; with you I am well pleased"; the imperative, "hear him," derives not from
Jesus' baptism but from his transfiguration (see Matt 17:5 and Luke 9:35).

questioning that Jesus overcomes by the power of the Holy Spirit in his life. And it's in that context that he then, through the desert experience, full of the Spirit, through those questions, and through those moments of challenges, returns to Galilee in the power of the Holy Spirit.

How many of you know that the power of the Holy Spirit, the work of the Holy Spirit, has a history, has a life history. We often think about the Holy Spirit as simply coming down, moment by moment. I want to introduce us to the fact, that Jesus returns to Galilee in the power of the Spirit. But Jesus returns to Galilee in the power of the Spirit because he already had been shaped by life in the Spirit. Life in the Spirit, life in the Spirit that has its prominent, if you will, spectacular moments, like the baptism. But life in the Spirit that works nevertheless, even in the silent moments. Again, we have glimpses in these first thirty years of Jesus's life where we see the Spirit manifest and present and here, if you will. But we also know that Jesus grew in the Spirit and in wisdom over the years. What's your life in the Spirit?

I can think about my own life in the Spirit as having incredible high-lights. My born-again experience when I was six years old. My Pentecostal experience when I was twelve years old. Been blessed with a wonderful wife when I was twenty-two, when we got married. Three years later, we were blessed with our son. Powerful moments in which God transforms us. I graduated my PhD in 1998. Experienced a fresh revitalization and call on my life. But that, if you will, highlight could only have happened with twelve years of school before that, Amen?[5]

And we often don't recognize the journey as part of the life-history of the Spirit. We often only focus on these highlights, on the special occasions, on the knock on the door, of the prophecy that came forth, on the baptism in the Jordan, and all of those are important. And every one of us has the testimony of when those highlights happened. But those highlights are part of a larger life-story, somebody say Amen. Those high-lights are part of a larger life story in which the Holy Spirit is nurturing, is birthing, is nourishing, and is causing to grow in our hearts, and in our lives. Sometimes in ways that we can't observe, sometimes in ways that we can't even articulate. Sometimes through the desert experience, when we had the needs of hunger, when we have the temptations to stop pursuing the call. Sometimes when we are tempted to take shortcuts in our lives, in our work, in our commitments, in our ministry. All of those

5. Technically, thirteen-and-a-half years: four years undergraduate and nine-and-a-half (1989) in graduate school.

are part of the moments in which the Spirit is present, and oftentimes it's when we feel like the Spirit is perhaps farthest away, that perhaps that's when the Spirit is closest to us.

And Jesus returned to Galilee in the power of the Spirit. Jesus comes back to bring it full-circle, in the power of the Spirit. What's our life-story as we think about Jesus's life in the Spirit? The Scripture goes on to tell us that he went to Nazareth where he had been brought up. And on the Sabbath day he went into the synagogue as was his custom. He stood up to read and the scroll of the prophet Isaiah was handed to him. Unrolling it, he found the place where it was written. This wasn't exactly like scrolling through our cell phones. The way in which Jesus handles the scroll tells us that he had spent much of his time, perhaps over the preceding thirty years, studying these scrolls. He knew where to look, he knew where to go to, to identify the text, "the Spirit of the Lord is upon me." Jesus returns to Galilee in the power of the Spirit because he had spent years studying the promises of God in the Scriptures. And Jesus didn't just make up his calling. Jesus, in studying the promises of God in the Scriptures, we can say, began to hear the call of God on his life. In studying the promises of God in this Scripture, Jesus began to imagine the call of God on his life. This wasn't something that Jesus made up, but Jesus began to see that he was part of what God had prepared to do long before he had come around.

I want to take just a few moments to talk about the prophet Isaiah, because I think this is such an important way for us to understand how the Spirit works. The Spirit has a life-history, a life-story. Each one of us can evaluate and attempt to discern those high points and those silent moments of the Spirit. But each one of our life-histories is embedded within a bigger story, a bigger history. Jesus says fullness in the Spirit was embedded within a larger vision. It was a vision that this prophet Isaiah told and wrote about hundreds of years before Jesus came around. There's probably two prophets in the Old Testament that are, if you will, . . . I mean, part of what it means to be a prophet is to be inspired by the Spirit, Amen? But there are two prophets of the Old Testament that talked a lot about the Spirit, and they talk a lot about the Spirit in two very distinct ways.

Did you know, for instance, that Jeremiah the prophet says not one word about God's Spirit? Not one word. So, he wasn't one of those.

Ezekiel the prophet says a lot about the Spirit. But when Ezekiel talks about the Spirit, the Spirit is kinda like a Star Trek machine, transporting him here and there, lifting him up among strange-looking creatures with wheels, yeah? Star Trek! You know, that is where a lot of the Star Trek imagination comes from, the book of Ezekiel. And go back and read the book of Ezekiel, you'll see that God's Spirit is all about, like, automatic transport in and through strange transport vehicles. Okay. There's a lot of Spirit in Ezekiel.

But Isaiah also talks a lot about the Spirit. You know, Isaiah was a prophet who lived in the eighth century before Jesus. And there's lots of different theories. I mean Isaiah is the longest prophetic book in the Old Testament.[6] There are sixty-six chapters. And I don't know, if I were you, I kind of nod off after about the fourth chapter, Amen? But if you look at Isaiah's sixty-six chapters, and there's a lot of different theories about it. Isaiah prophesied in the eighth century when the Assyrians were threatening Israel. The Assyrians were ready to wipe out the Israelites. Hezekiah, one of the kings of Israel, in Jerusalem, was surrounded by Assyrians.[7] You might remember the story from the Old Testament. And Hezekiah was praying, "God can you extend my life somehow," remember that story? And one day, during that siege, they woke up and they looked out over the walls and the Assyrians had been slaughtered or had ran away. That was the Assyrian threat. But that Assyrian threat and the minimizing of it gave Israel reprieve for only a few decades. The Babylonians came in soon after, and about 115 years later there were two waves of exiles that the Babylonians took away. Some people say that if you read the gospel of Isaiah, that it starts in the eighth century and then there's parts of it that's in the exilic period when they were taken away to Babylon, and then there's a third part of Isaiah, they say, that records how after the exile, they come back to Israel. We don't need to worry today about attempting to date these texts. But I do think it's important that these texts found meaning, even if Isaiah had given all these prophecies. They found meaning and they were received and preserved by the people of Israel, precisely in and through the exile. And what happened after that? It was in Isaiah 61, a text in which most scholars understand as having been given new meaning in this after-the-exile period. And in this after-the-exile period it's difficult for you and me to understand what happened at this point so long ago, right? But let me give you an analogy of a much more recent set of historical events, in order for us to appreciate what this post-exilic period means.

6. Thanks to Robin Parry for reminding me that while Isaiah has the most chapters of any prophetic book in the Old Testament, Jeremiah has over 7,000 more words.

7. In Isaiah, the story of Hezekiah unfolds over chapters 36–39.

I'm from Malaysia. I was ten years old when my parents moved to California. And I've only been able to go back and visit Malaysia a few times in the last forty years. And of course, each time I go back and visit I understand a little bit more about my history. I remember more about it, but I also realize that every visit I go back it's different from when I left four years ago. When I, before I left, when I was ten years old we learned English in public school. I remember Malaysia was a British colony and by the early 1970s, it was still the English standard of education, so when I went to public school I learned Malay and I learned English. The year after I left, they stopped teaching English and everything had to be done in Malay. That's one way in which things have changed. Other [changes include] ways in which the Malaysian government has changed drastically over the last forty years, in other words, new governments, new rules, new laws, new relationships.

I think, for instance, about the fact that in Stockton, California, where my parents landed in the mid-1970s, there were large populations of Laotians and Cambodians and Vietnamese who were part of, who were refugees from the Southeast Asian wars, of the late '60s and early 1970s. And I've recently met Vietnamese students at Fuller and other places who now say that when they go back to Vietnam, when they go back to Cambodia after forty years, it's not the way it used to be forty years ago. There are different governments, there are different social systems, and there are different factions, in terms of tribal arguments now that have taken place in that context. And that's one of the things that happened during the exile.

The exile resulted in Israel being taken off to Babylon for seventy years, not forty in my case: seventy years. And after seventy years the Israelites went back, were restored to their land, but they found that the Babylonian government had allowed for intermarriages. The Babylon government had allowed for different tribal groups to emerge and take control of these regions. And now it was, you know, the people that were in exile, saying "Lord when are you going to restore us to Israel?" And when it finally got restored, it wasn't [to the] promised land that they thought it was. Things had changed after seventy years, and it is in that context that [the Isaianic] prophet continued to speak of the Messiah. [The Isaianic] prophet said that "the Spirit of the Lord is upon me because he's anointed me to preach good news to the poor, proclaim freedom for the prisoners, recovery of sight to the blind, to release the oppressed, to proclaim the year of the Lord's favor."[8] You see that was the original message of the prophet Isaiah. To a people that were yearning for home and would come home to find it was not the home that they had left. A people that were yearning for security. A people that were yearning for freedom from the oppression of the Babylonian government, only to find that now that they were back home, they were now being oppressed by other factions. If you remember the story of Ezra-Nehemiah: Ezra-Nehemiah tell us about the struggles that the people of Israel had after they had been restored to the land, and they tried to build the wall and they tried to build the temple and they kept getting resistance, and kick-back and push-back from all sides; that was the state of the postexilic period.

Isaiah the prophet, throughout the sixty-six chapters of Isaiah, tells about the Messiah, a shoot shall come from the stock of Jesse, a branch shall grow out of his roots, the Spirit of the Lord shall rest upon him, the Spirit of wisdom and understanding, the Spirit of counsel and might, the Spirit of knowledge and fear of the Lord.[9] A Spirit from on high will be poured out upon the people and then the wilderness. Imagine going back to Southeast Asia today and thinking about the wilderness. And then the wilderness becomes a fruitful field. And the fruitful field is deemed a forest.[10] Here is my servant whom I uphold, my chosen in whom my soul delights, and I put my Spirit on him and he will bring forth justice to the nations.[11] This Spirit-anointed prophet in the book of Isaiah will bring forth justice to the nations; will hear the cry of the people taken into exile, restored to a land, that land, that they could not recognize as home, restored to a land in which there were all kinds of infighting all around. This is the messianic servant, the one who's promised [to] Israel to lead them by the power of the Spirit. To proclaim the year of the Lord's favor in the day of vengeance of our God. To comfort all who mourn. Jesus comes into Nazareth, opens up this scroll, and he identifies not just the personal story of the Spirit but the national and transnational story of the Spirit. The bigger story of the Spirit's redemptive work, and Jesus identifies his call as a call to live into that story. I want to encourage us this morning as we bring this to a close.

8. Isa 61:1–2.

9. Isa 11:1–3.

10. Isa 32:15.

11. Isa 42:1; see also sermon 9 above, on Matthew 12, citing from Isaiah 42.

What is the bigger story of the Spirit into which your story fits? What is the bigger story of the Spirit's redemptive work, to which your story contributes? What is the bigger story of God's redemptive work in the world, which the Spirit's work in your life and in my life has prepared us to participate in? Jesus answers the call. He answers the call by identifying the bigger story that existed, that was spoken of by the prophets hundreds of years ago. And he identifies the fact that today, he said, this Scripture is fulfilled in your hearing.

You know, this passage in Luke, and I will close with this, is Luke's table of contents to the rest of this gospel. In the rest of this gospel, Jesus preaches good news the poor. He opens the eyes of the blind. He releases those oppressed variously. And he proclaims the year of God's justice, God's peace, God's shalom. Jesus responds to the story of God, by the power of the Spirit. That's Luke's account of Jesus. And the powerful thing about the Acts of the Holy Spirit and the Acts of the Apostles, is that the apostles could now receive the same Holy Spirit and begin to step into God's story, God's redemptive work.

Lord Jesus, as we close our time, fill us once again with the Holy Spirit given to Jesus and that Jesus pours out upon our lives. Empower us to do the works of Jesus the Messiah. Take our life-stories and make them a part of your bigger story, your gospel story. In Jesus' name.

[Applause; host leader transitions to a closing hymn, followed by a closing prayer by someone else, and finally Doxology.]

Tony Richie Reflection—"Life's Ultimate Meaning"

This homily challenges believers to see the story of Christ, and their own stories, as part of the larger story of God's purposes accomplished in the Holy Spirit. In the fourth century BCE Aristotelian philosophy proposed that goal-directedness or purposefulness is an irreducible and objective feature of the natural world. Contemporary philosophers and scientists still debate the appropriateness or usefulness of teleological categories for discussing modern philosophy and science. Christian teleology affirms that the universe and everything in it has a cause and a purpose because God created it. The biblical story of creation, redemption, and consummation sets the framework for God's purposeful goal (*telos*). Everything exists for God (Rom 11:36) through Jesus Christ (1 Cor 8:6; Col 1:16).

The active role of the Holy Spirit in the cosmic purpose is critical (Gen 1:2; Ps 104:30; Rev 5:6).

Spirit Christology interprets the messianic mission of Jesus Christ with an emphasis on the prominent role of the Holy Spirit (Luke 4:16–21; Acts 10:38). Robust Trinitarian Spirit Christology brings welcome pneumatological enrichment for evangelical Christology. It further clarifies the *imitatio Christi* (John 13:15; Phil 2:5; 1 Pet 2:21). Believers live out God's purpose or *telos* in Christ by the same Spirit who anointed Jesus of Nazareth.

Hollis Gause (*Living in the Spirit*) suggested that the Christian life is essentially a journey (*via salutis*) of symbiotic redemptive experiences in Christ in the Holy Spirit.[12] The exodus of Israel and their entry into the promised land, along with the missiological itineraries of Jesus and the apostles, are paradigmatic for Christian identity, missiology, spirituality, and theology. Life's ultimate meaning and purpose, its divine *telos*, is discoverable—and enjoyable—as co-travelers in Jesus Christ and the Holy Spirit.

12. Gause, *Living in the Spirit*.

14

Life After a Knockout

The Holy Spirit on the Rocky Road

ACTS 7:54—8:1

The Barn, Springfield, Missouri, 25 September 2016*

All right, good morning! It's great to be here. Been to Springfield a few times before. I want to thank Pastor Dan for opening up this opportunity to share with you. I think about all the incredible Assemblies of God churches here in Springfield, Missouri. And my first opportunity to preach in Springfield was in a barn! Come on somebody, hallelujah! Praise the Lord! God is good. Praise the Lord for his presence, Amen? . . .

Now I've been told pastor is working through a series of messages called . . . what is it called again? [Response:] "Life Lessons from the School of Hard Knocks." You guys realized that, right? You have been walking through. What? That's a tough series, brother. Life lessons from the school of hard knocks. So, . . . what else am I gonna preach on, but a

---

* I was in Springfield, Missouri for a Science and Faith conference organized by Evangel University (Assemblies of God), and was invited to preach at a new, avant-garde service organized for college students by Evangel Temple Assembly of God Church and held in, and called, The Barn, a building and meeting space separate from the main auditorium. The hip-pastor of this college-age group, Daniel Morrison (also a PhD student in New Testament, writing on the Apocalypse, at McMaster Divinity College), was in the middle of a series he called "Life Lessons from the School of Hard Knocks," to which theme I adapted.

Pentecostal sermon! Somebody say Amen! And if you have your Bibles, or if you want to turn on your cell phones, I am just going to go to, of course, the book of Acts. But I'm not [going] to be in Acts 2 today! Somebody say thank you Jesus! Heard too many of those messages over the years, Amen?

We will start in Acts chapter 7, the book of Acts chapter 7, and I'm going to read from the New Revised Standard Version, starting in verse 54. Acts 7:54 to the first verse of Acts chapter 8. You guys might remember this part of the story. It's after Stephen has given a very brilliant and eloquent and dynamic and Spirit-filled message; verse 54:

> 54When they heard these things, they became enraged and ground their teeth at Stephen. 55But filled with the Holy Spirit, he gazed into heaven and saw the glory of God and Jesus standing at the right hand of God. 56"Look," he said, "I see the heavens opened and the Son of Man standing at the right hand of God!" 57But they covered their ears, and with a loud shout all rushed together against him. 58Then they dragged him out of the city and began to stone him; and the witnesses laid their coats at the feet of a young man named Saul. 59While they were stoning Stephen, he prayed, "Lord Jesus, receive my spirit." 60Then he knelt down and cried out in a loud voice, "Lord, do not hold this sin against them." When he had said this, he died. [Ch. 8] 1 And Saul approved of their killing him.

Holy Spirit, may the words of my mouth and the meditation of our hearts be acceptable in your sight. In Jesus' name, Amen.

So, I've entitled our reflections this morning, "Life After a Knock-Out: The Holy Spirit on the Rocky Road." Life lessons from the school of hard knocks. Life after a knockout. I want to start by pausing for just a few moments, before the big knockout. And as you might well guess, by looking at the passage that we're focused on this morning, I want to look at the last few moments of Stephen's life before his knockout; for just a few moments here at the start. Times when life is most difficult. Times when life is precarious, if you will. And maybe there are a number of us here, I understand this is the younger crowd of ETA,[1] Amen? So, it may, except for maybe a couple of older geezers like brother Doug over here . . . [laughter[2]], except for brother Doug, you know; he might've actually

---

1. Reference here is to Evangel Temple Assembly, the "mother" congregation of this group.

2. Referring here to Douglas Olena, a friend and in attendance there in The Barn,

lived through, perhaps, . . . I mean, he's still here; he might have lived through some of those precarious moments in life. But those moments in life when, if you will, the punches are coming hard. In Stephen's case, those moments in life where the rocks were coming hard, if you will. Right before the knockout. Those moments in life where, if you will, to use a boxing metaphor, there is bopping and there's weaving but there's hurt. And there's a sense in which I don't know how long I can keep avoiding the knockout. I'm not sure how long I can stay at the precipice of this cliff. I'm not sure how long I can continue to stand in these circumstances. Some of us might [know] what it feels like in this moment before the big knockout.

And of course, in these moments we have Stephen, the pentecostal! Amen? Filled with the Holy Ghost! Filled with the Holy Spirit! You know, I'm not used to thinking of those moments right before getting knocked out as being moments full of the Holy Ghost. I'm used to thinking about those moments when things are bad and getting worse, in every moment . . . , I'm used to thinking about those moments when God has, sort of, left me in trial . . . , I'm used to thinking about those moments right when I'm being hit back and forth by the enemy as a time in which God is testing my faith and has withdrawn his presence. But Stephen was filled with the Holy Spirit. And he gazed, in verse 55, into heaven and saw the glory of God and Jesus standing at the right hand of God. My, my! You know, those moments when I'm being pummeled by life-circumstances, and those moments when I'm being the victim, if you will, of unjust treatment, those moments when I'm being accused by my enemies, I'm all too consumed with the darts that are coming at me; I'm all too consumed with the worries of life; I'm all too consumed with the challenges; I'm being confronted.

And Stephen, as he is going down, as he is going down, as he is going down, he looks up, and he puts and fastens his eyes on the right hand of the Father and he sees Jesus. And he makes eye-contact with Jesus! Somebody say Amen. That's a call for us, who are feeling pummeled. That's the voice from heaven that says, "Nevertheless, I've gotcha! I'm looking right at you. You might feel like you're surrounded. You might feel that the stones are coming hard, and they're coming fast, and it hurts. But I got you. I'm looking right at you. You might not see me, but if you would turn your eyes. If you turn your eyes."

also Professor of Logic and Philosophy—with a doctoral thesis on Foucault—at Global University (of the Assemblies of God), based there in Springfield, Missouri.

Stephen had, for his, who knows, not too long of a life yet in Jesus—I mean, we're not quite sure what the chronology is here in the book of Acts, in terms of when Stephen comes into the faith, when Stephen gets, if you will, instructed by the apostles, when he gets appointed as one of the deacons, when he starts preaching, who knows? It might've been a few years. But you can tell from his message that he had begun to fasten his eyes upon Jesus. Somebody say Amen! He had begun to learn to look up to the throne. He'd begun to learn to look up at the right hand of the Father. And here it was, it didn't matter that the rocks are coming hard and strong and fast and big. It didn't matter that he could feel it here and here and here and here and here! He looks up and fastens his eyes upon the Lord, who is his rock and his salvation. Amen!

Well, I wish I could say that he lasted another round. Come on somebody! I wish it would have ended, if you will, you know, the angels coming down from heaven, fending off the rocks, right? I mean it could have. Daniel was in the Lion's den. Shadrach, Meshach, and Abednego were thrown into the fiery furnace; they came out smelling like perfume or cologne or whatever it was. Why couldn't the angels of God, as Stephen was fastening his eyes upon Jesus, have begun to ward off those rocks? So, that the mob would have gotten tired, picking up stones, or they would have run out of stones! Come on somebody! See that's why this message is called life after a knockout. After a knockout. For all the fullness of the Holy Ghost, for all the looking into the eyes of Jesus, the story doesn't end like the testimonies that you and I want to tell. Hello? It doesn't end like classical Pentecostal testimony, unfortunately. The bell rings. The final stone hits its mark. And the knockout is complete. Is there life after a knockout?

You and I might say to ourselves, you know, for some of us that final tragedy, that deep blow that follows months and months and maybe years and years of prayer and fasting and believing and exercising faith and keeping our eyes on Jesus, we might say, "I'm not sure, if that happens, what life would look like."

I want to invite us for the next few moments to adopt another perspective. And ask some other questions about life after a knockout. I want to ask us to think, for example, about whether or not we might actually be part of somebody else's knockout. I want us to think about whether or not there is life for us, if somebody else were to have suffered a knockout. I believe that this passage invites us, however difficult this journey might be, to begin to understand this question. What would it have been like to have been part of the mob that was going to come out of that battle victorious? What would it have been like to be a part of that group of people who felt that they were doing the work of God? Who felt that they were themselves, if you will, following out the mandate that God given them? Who felt that they were on God's side of things?

Verse 54 says, "when they heard these things they became enraged." They became enraged. Can you feel the rage? I was gonna say, can you feel the burn?[3] But no, not the good place to ask about that question, here in Springfield, Missouri. [Laughter.] Can you feel the rage? Can you feel the rage? They became enraged, and they ground their teeth at Stephen. Oh, I mean this is the heat of the battle. This is when you feel like the enemy's coming at you strong, you're gonna double up on the armor, you're gonna double up on the word, you're gonna double up on the belt of truth, you're gonna get the breastplate warmed up, you're gonna get going, you're gonna respond. Somebody say Amen. They were feeling the rage. Grinding their teeth.

Verse 57, "when they further heard Stephen's words, they covered their ears and with a loud shout." You know sometimes, we might be part of a mob, but maybe it's too noisy, maybe there's too much going on, and maybe we can't quite hear everything quite right. Maybe life circumstances are too busy. We might be part of a mob, but we might not even know it because things are just too crowded in our lives. And things are just too hectic in our lives. And we get caught up in life and the mob is knocking somebody out, and we're being carried along by the, if you will, circumstances of life. And particularly when they rushed together against him and they dragged him out of the city and began to stone him, you know sometimes the knockout is taking place in the suburbs. Or sometimes a knockout is taking place in the inner cities. Or sometimes, simply, the knockout is taking place in the city next to us, and it's just far enough away, and we might just not realize, if you will, if we might be part of the mob. We might not realize, if you will, when somebody else is suffering a knockout. Somebody else is battling life-circumstances, but we are too busy, our ears are full of noise and sound, or screams that are coming

3. September 2016 when this sermon was given was a few weeks before the 2016 American presidential elections; the Democratic contender, who lost the nomination to Hilary Clinton (who lost the election), was Bernie Sanders, and part of the enthusiasm for his message was carried by the phrase, "feel the Bern," chanted widely during the Democratic primaries and even ongoing at Sanders public appearances—so I was playing on words in this case.

from yonder . . . around the hills are barely getting to us. And we're not able to hear the cry of those who are being knocked out.

I don't want to get political here. I only got five more minutes anyway. I'm going to get political. No, I'm just kidding. By the way, I'm Asian American. Hello? As an Asian American, and I'm listening to "Black Lives Matter." And my Asian American friends and my Asian American community, we have all the privileges of majority culture. And sometimes I hear in the Asian American community: "If those black brothers and sisters would just work as hard as we did . . . ." We've drowned ourselves out with our own voice. We will not be able to hear the pain and the cry that's been coming from around the corner. We're too busy wrapped up in our own story, in own battles, in our own concerns, and our own anxieties, and our own fears. And the mob is going on and we're part of that mob and don't even understand it.

Lots happening in the world that we're complicit in and not even aware of. But then there's a deeper level maybe of awareness, isn't there? "They dragged him out of the city," verse 58, "and began to stone him and the witnesses laid their coats at the feet of a young man named Saul." Let's get a little closer to home here. Maybe it's not happening around the corner, but maybe it's right here in our neighborhood. Maybe we're the Saul, and we're holding the clothes. We might not be picking up the stones, but we're holding the clothes of those that do. Comes and gets a little closer to home. We can't claim now that life is too busy. We can't claim that we didn't really hear or understand. We can't claim that we were a little confused and we don't know what the real circumstances were. We're right there! We're in the scene of the crime. We're still innocent? We're not picking up the stones. We're not throwing anything. We're just kinda of observing and keeping the peace.

Well, Saul does get off that easy, does he? Because in chapter 8 verse 1, he may not have been picking up the stones. You and I may not have been actively at work, but you know what? Sometimes even when we're "innocent bystanders," we are approving of the mob. We are approving of the mob. We're going through life. We have decisions to make.

You know I'm married to a Mexican American, fifth generation, five generations in Texas then they moved up to Eastern Washington. And my Mexican-American in-laws and sister-in-laws and brother-in-laws in Eastern Washington are very Republican. Somebody say Amen. Come on, somebody say Amen! Nothing wrong with Mexican Americans being Republican. Somebody say Amen. [Laughter.] But this has been a hard few months for my Mexican-American Republican in-laws. Somebody say Amen. Can I just say that this has been a hard few months for all Republicans. Somebody say Amen. Or can I just say that this has been a hard few months for all of us. Somebody say Amen. But of course, the Mexican-American community is really struggling, particularly if you're Republican, right? You wanna vote Republican, you wanna support the Republican ticket. But you've got compadres and comadres. Come on! And we're not just talking about them sixty, seventy, eighty years old.[4]

I mean, things are complicated, right? And how do Mexican-American, whether Republican or not, believers, exercise your responsibility as citizens with the vote, on the one hand, but yet at the same time, exercise their responsibility as Mexican Americans, and their compassion as believers in Jesus, for what are complicated and complex lives; not numbers, not labels, not documented or undocumented issues, but lives, relationships, compadres, comadres, and brothers and sisters in their community. And it's not easy to approve, in the background, and not assume that one is already implicated in the process. Is there life after a knockout?

For those of us who have been too busy drowned out in our own selfishness, for those of us who feel like we're really innocent, we haven't really done anything, or even for those of us who may have in our hearts affirmed and approved of somebody else suffering a knockout in their life-circumstance, in their hopes, in their aspirations, in their longing and yearning, and in their prayers and their crying out to God, we have affirmed and approved, if you will, when they have been on the receiving end of a knockout: hard questions for us to think about when we think about the knockouts of life. But I want to start bringing us to a close here, brother. That the Lord will help me. If the Lord will help me.

Stephen knelt down. I want to come back in our closing moments to Stephen. Stephen knelt down, and cried out in a loud voice, "Lord, do not hold this sin against them." Hmm. But you and I are the Sauls [who are] innocent. We've been standing in the background and we haven't been doing anything. But we have been approving. And the declaration of the gospel is loud and clear, when Stephen says "Lord, do not hold this sin against them." Stephen is now living out the gospel at the final bell. He

---

4. Remember again the broader national context of this time, deep into the campaign season for the 2016 presidency; Republican nominee (and now president) Donald Trump ran on a platform that included erection of a border wall to keep out undocumented Mexican immigrants from the USA. For further reflections post-election, see Yong, "American Political Theology in a Post-al Age."

is going down for the count, and he is not coming back! This is not just preaching, not just words, he is living the good news. And the good news is "Lord, do not hold this against them." They are forgiven.

Whoever you forgive, will be forgiven. Amen? But forgiveness does not necessarily mean there are no consequences. Now, somebody say Amen. Let me repeat myself. Forgiveness does not necessarily mean there are no consequences.

I don't know what Paul was thinking about as he's standing aloof, watching the clothes, approving in his heart. And he hears the loud shout, right? That's what it says. Stephen shouted out, mustering up all he could, as he was going down for the count. As if he wanted the person way in the back of the canyon to hear the forgiveness. "Lord forgive *them!*" I don't know what Saul was thinking. Saul was forgiven. But life after Stephen's knockout, for Saul, meant that he had to live out the consequences of his implicit [support of] and complicit[y] in Stephen's knockout. You know I see that in the book of Acts—how many of you know—that Saul in [and for] the rest of his life is going to suffer knockdown after knockdown after knockdown, after knockdown, after knockdown?

Chapter 9 he's on his horse. Come on somebody! Life lessons in the school of hard knocks. Boom! Remember that story [of Saul getting knocked down]?[5] The book of Acts? You all know your Bible, right? The book of Acts, chapter 13, no 14 sorry. He's in Lystra. You see the same thing he was approving of happened to him. He got stoned and was left for dead.[6] They assumed he was gone. This was going to be knockout. But somehow, God said no, no, no, the consequences are not complete. Hello? I gotta hurry up. I'm just half way through the conclusion right now. He gets up somehow, right? He goes into Philippi and he gets beaten and thrown into the Philippian jail.[7] He goes into Jerusalem in Acts 21, and it says the crowd tried to kill him.[8] He goes on a ship to get to Rome, and guess what? Everybody else gets knocked down because of that guy. They're all struggling in the ocean, in the Mediterranean Sea, swimming for their lives; he survives that.[9] He comes on the isle of Malta, and guess

5. Actually Acts 9:4 says only that Saul "fell to the ground," and nothing about a horse.

6. Acts 14:19–20.

7. Acts 16:22–24.

8. Acts 21:27–31.

9. Acts 27:13–44.

what? Boom![10] I mean, "When are these consequences gonna stop Lord? I already said I was sorry. He said he forgave me. That should've been it!" Somebody say Amen.

Knockdown after knockdown after knockdown. And of course, yeah, he ends his life locked up. That's seven times, by the way, that I've just recounted of Saul and Paul and his knockdowns. Living out life after a knockout that he was complicit in, that he supported, that he cheered on in his spirit, that he was forgiven for, but for which the consequences of his life's journey would continue to allow him to hear that call, that declaration, the good news.

You know, I'm going to go outside of Acts for a couple moments in 2 Corinthians chapter 11, starting in verse 23. This is Saul himself, Paul now, talking:

> [23]Are they ministers of Christ? I am talking like a madman— I am a better one: with far greater labors, far more imprison- ments, with countless floggings, and often near death. [24]Five times I have received from the Jews the forty lashes minus one. [Yong's aside]—This is like overkill, isn't it Lord?—[25]Three times I was beaten with rods. Once I received a stoning. Three times I was shipwrecked; for a night and a day I was adrift at sea; [26]on frequent journeys, in danger from rivers, danger from bandits, danger from my own people, danger from Gentiles, danger in the city, danger in the wilderness, danger at sea, danger from false brothers and sisters; [27]in toil and hardship, through many a sleepless night, hungry and thirsty, often without food, cold and naked. [Yong aside]—You thought life was tough, right?— [28]And, besides other things, I am under daily pressure because of my anxiety for all the churches. [29]Who is weak, and I am not weak? Who is made to stumble, and I am not indignant?[11]

You know, I wonder if that declaration of forgiveness was God's in- vitation to Saul to now begin to receive the stones that were cast to get [and kill] Stephen. The stones that did Stephen under would now be felt by the one who held the clothes of the mob. The one who would approve in his heart that this was the right thing, he would now live out the rest of his life, if you will, within the sound of Stephen's declaration, "Lord, do not hold this sin against them." And Saul experiences at that moment the liberation, if you will, from his fear of the knockout. Saul experiences at

---

10. I did not mention here explicitly that he was attacked by a viper; Acts 28:3.

11. 2 Cor 11:23–29, NRSV.

that moment, the invitation of the Lord to now embark on the journey that led to Stephen's own, if you will, battle.

I want to close with this. Stephen said "Lord Jesus" in verse 59, "receive my spirit." Those last words in which he said, "Lord, receive my spirit," right before he said "Father, forgive them for they know not what they do." That was Jesus, I guess. Sorry, I added a couple of words there. Sometimes I get a little confused. But, here was Stephen releasing his spirit, releasing his spirit that was full of the Holy Spirit, we're told earlier in the same passage. Receiving, releasing his spirit to Jesus, carried by the Holy Spirit, and in that moment, he shouts out, "Lord, forgive them!" And the Holy Ghost moves from that center point, where all the rocks were coming in, and moves over the crowd and touches a bystander—poor guy. And the Holy Ghost lands on this bystander. He didn't know it yet. He was going to get on that horse. He was still gonna ride and carry out what he believed was the God-appointed mission begun with Stephen. But the release of Stephen's spirit at that knockout released the Holy Ghost in Saul. I mean, not directly; the text doesn't quite say that. But guess what happens after that knockout? This life is over, but the gospel goes because of that event, that sequence of unfortunate and tragic events into its [next] destination, which is Samaria.

The apostles couldn't be gotten into Samaria on their own terms. But you needed the Holy Ghost through a tragic—from our perspective, in some respects, unnecessary—sequence of unfortunate events. We needed a tragic knockout, and the gospel went from Jerusalem and Judea into Samaria. And the gospel then went from that fellow who was standing in the back, approving of what had happened, to the ends of the earth.

I'm not sure that this is an encouraging message. I'm not here to make us feel good about life's knockouts. This isn't, if you will, a message that we can easily embrace. Because it is difficult, I want to suggest, to embrace one's own martyrdom. You don't survive in the other side to see what God does with it. But you can only trust, can't you? And you can trust that the Holy Ghost is up to something, even in the midst, and through, life's knockouts.

Tony Richie Reflection—"Even If"

The preceding faces the reality of suffering among the faithful, finding solace and strength through trusting God's superlative benevolence,

purpose, and wisdom. The book of Job dramatically portrays the suffering of the righteous. It doesn't attempt to answer all our questions but
it encourages us to hope in God anyway. Job's faithfulness in suffering
established an exceptional reputation for righteousness (Ezek 14:14, 20).
There's assurance about the final outcome for those who similarly perse-
vere (Jas 5:11).

Alvin Plantinga, described as "America's leading orthodox Protestant philosopher of God" (*Time*), advanced a brilliant freewill argument
for the existence of evil in a world created by an omnipotent and omnibe-
nevolent God. But Plantinga readily admits that evil is beyond human
comprehension. Yet faith prevails. Corrie ten Boom (*The Hiding Place*),
who endured unimaginable atrocities in a Nazi concentration camp,
spent the rest of her long life speaking and writing about her Christian
faith and facilitating healing and reconciliation. She said, "In darkness
God's truth shines most clear."

Polycarp, Perpetua, and a long list of martyrs, beginning with Stephen and, eventually, including Paul, and continuing today, have given
their lives for Christ. Origen, tortured so severely he eventually died from
injuries, refused to recant. The reality of suffering doesn't annul the reality of faith. Rather, believers overcome suffering, and even death, through
the efficacy of Christ's own suffering and death (Rev 12:11). Bart Millard
(MercyMe), during a child's chronic illness, wrote "Even If" based on the
young Hebrews' reply to Nebuchadnezzar (Dan 3:18). The chorus goes:

> I know You're able and I know You can
> Save through the fire with Your mighty hand
> But even if you don't
> My hope is you alone[12]

---

12. Millard, *I Can Only Imagine*, 155.

15

The Powers at Home and Within, and the Powerful Reign of the Holy Spirit

MARK 3:19B-35

Landeskirchliche Gemeinschaft *jahu*, Biel, Switzerland, 25 June 2016*

GOOD MORNING TO YOU. It is such a joy to be here and to worship the Lord with you here in Biel, Switzerland. As a Pentecostal minister who is from California, Biel is like on the other side of the world. But that's okay because the book of Acts says that we shall receive power and be witnesses to the ends of the earth.

But like Paul, when he got to the ends of the earth in Rome, he found believers. And so, my wife and I are very excited to be amongst believers this morning. And Paul, if you remember, had to go along, and he had to ask people if they had heard of the Holy Spirit. But we can tell

---

* Landeskirchliche Gemeinschaft jahu can be translated loosely as The Jahu Christian Community Church. Thanks to Rev. Dr. Walter Dürr for the invitation to preach to this congregation after "Come Holy Spirit: Global and Cosmic Yearnings," Annual Study Days plenary lectures, hosted by the Studienzentrum für Glaube und Gesellschaft [The Study Center for Faith and Society] at the University of Fribourg, Switzerland, 19–21 June 2017 (one of my talks has since been published as "The Spirit Poured Out: A (Pentecostal) Perspective after Pentecost"). Dr. Dürr also translated the sermon into Swiss.

this morning that we don't have to ask that question: we can feel the Holy Spirit in your hearts.

And what a wonderful week it was to think a bit about the Holy Spirit, that we feel in our hearts. And we've already heard many of the testimonies about the study days. And one of the highlights for me and my wife was to go to the cathedral service on Tuesday. And we got there a little bit late, and we—it was filled up—we had to stand at the back. And our sister here shared her seat with us. And we were enjoying the service, and all of a sudden there was Hillsong songs! And we knew that the renewal had come to Switzerland, Amen! [Laughter.] What a wonderful thing it is, for your pastor to, for the Lord to give him in his heart the desire to have this kind of meeting [to organize this conference] and event. And so, I know that all of you are thankful for Pastor Kristoff and Pastor Walter, Amen? [Cheering.]

The text that was given from the lectionary is from Mark chapter 3. I have a title for the next few moments, "The Powers at Home and Within, and the Powerful Reign of the Holy Spirit." This is, as you might remember, a difficult passage. But as a Pentecostal who read about the Holy Spirit in this passage, I could not say no about preaching on it. But how do you explain a passage that Christians have struggled to understand for two thousand years? So maybe I won't quite fully explain everything in the next thirty minutes. But as I sat and worshipped with you this morning, I felt that there was something significant about this text for us today.

One of the things that the Lord impressed upon my heart as I reread and meditated upon this text is the first verse, when it says in the English version, "Then Jesus went home." One of the other translations, "Then Jesus went into his house." Or it could mean that Jesus went into *a house*, in his home area.

I was wondering, for instance, that many of us, many of you, have spent some of these last few days at the study days, and you have enjoyed and been refreshed by the Holy Spirit. But now, in some senses, you have come home to Biel.

And I began to think that this—the fact that Jesus went home—is significant for our reflection this morning. This very difficult passage unfolds in this *home* of Jesus. These very difficult sayings happened within this home area of Jesus. Sometimes some of the most challenging circumstances in our lives occur at home.

Now, in the broader context of Mark, Jesus has already gone out and about. Jesus is introduced, early in Mark, as the one who preaches that the gospel of the kingdom is at hand. Just in the first two chapters, Jesus has gone into the synagogue to heal people. In the first two chapters, Jesus touches and heals bodies on the Sabbath day. Lepers are cleansed. Those who are paralyzed get up. The man with the withered hand is straightened out. Jesus is not only preaching about the kingdom, but he is working the signs that the kingdom is present. Do you say Amen to that? That is a good way for a Pentecostal preacher. [Laughter.]

Jesus had already been doing the miracles of the kingdom of God, about in the country, and now he had gone into his home area. Perhaps now he had even gone into his home. Perhaps he'd gone into his house, and interestingly, his family then heard that he had come back. And his family began to attempt to try to calm him down, because then, verse 21, it says the people were saying that he has gone out of his mind: "How could such things come from Nazareth?" they were wondering. What was the significance of this healing man with powers to touch people's lives? What does it mean that the kingdom of God is at hand? In those days, they might have thought that the kingdom of God referred to the deliverance of Israel from the Romans. And what does it mean, instead, that Jesus is touching bodies? What does it mean, instead, that Jesus is casting out demons from those who are afflicted? And they were trying to understand the connection between the message and the actions of Jesus.

And here's where some people were wondering, "What kind of spirit inhabits this Jesus?" They thought they had recognized this as the quiet young man that grew up in the neighborhood. Maybe they had done carpentry work with him. Maybe they had learned together in school when they were younger. But now, all of a sudden, it seems that Jesus has emerged as a preacher of this coming kingdom. And all of a sudden, Jesus is doing powerful deeds that are changing the communities, and they were kind of wondering, "What has got into him?"

And that's where these sayings unfold, about [how] the kingdom divided against itself cannot stand. And that's where we have this saying, about a people being forgiven for their sins, about whatever blasphemies they utter: but whoever blasphemes against the Holy Spirit cannot be forgiven because he is guilty of an eternal sin. And this has puzzled many, many exegetes for a long time.

Mark's text says, in verse 30, "for they said, he has an unclean spirit." The most straightforward reading is that those who say that the works of Jesus are of an unclean spirit are those who are committing the unforgivable sin. In other words, those who cannot recognize that Jesus's healing is a healing of God. Either they *cannot* recognize it, or they *will not* recognize it. Somehow, they are choosing to ignore that God is present in our midst. Somehow, instead, they're saying that this is of another spirit, an evil spirit. Those who say that Jesus's words and works are of the evil spirit are the ones who are blaspheming against the Holy Spirit.

But interestingly, verse 31, "Then his mother and his brothers came; and standing outside." Now this is a very interesting comment that Mark makes. Because, first of all, if Jesus was in his own home, it is interesting that his family is now outside. In other words, some who had believed had come into Jesus's home. Some who believed had come into [his home] to receive his ministry and his presence, but his mother and his brothers were outside. Maybe they had questions themselves. Maybe they thought, like some of the people, that he was out of his mind. Possibly not Mary, the mother, but maybe some of the brothers and cousins [and extended family]. Even though we can imagine that Mary herself had some questions; Luke says, she kept things in her heart and wondered about these things.[1]

But how many of us realize that sometimes it is at *home* that things are most difficult? Like, for Jesus, he was welcomed everywhere, it seems, except in his home country. And verse 21 says his family tried to restrain him. Maybe they tried to say, "Don't go into the house to hold a Bible study." And then he still goes in that house, and the people followed him to hear it. And outside, all of the doubters and the skeptics were buzzing around. And maybe putting pressure on the family, they found themselves outside, and they were wondering, "What do we do? Do we go to support the son? What do we do here?"

When my mother was a new believer, she had converted from being raised in a Buddhist home. Her father was very against her becoming a Christian. And he would not allow her to go to church. And he would not allow her to read the Bible, or even to pray outside of the altars of where they had the family Buddha and the other items. Here was a case in which literally, it was at home where the struggles were the most intense. And here was my mother, a fifteen-, sixteen-, seventeen-year-old girl, on the one hand, wanting to respond to Jesus, but on the other hand, having to honor her parents. And she struggled with that for a number of years. Now she will give the testimony, that after a few years, God also turned her parents' heart[s] to Jesus.

---

1. Luke 2:19.

But sometimes, we might find that our parents, our family members, are standing outside. They may not fully understand what God has called you and I to, and we find themselves outside, metaphorically, of our call. It's difficult to understand what God is doing and what God is saying in our lives. And sometimes, for us, it's difficult to be obedient to the Lord because of these circumstances. Maybe it's our immediate family members that don't understand. But maybe it's just our home that we had been raised in. Maybe it's just the community that thought that they knew who we were, but now don't understand that we are attempting to serve Jesus. Maybe it's like those who just thought that Jesus was a carpenter, to wake up one morning to find that he was preaching about some gospel of the kingdom.

And how many of us have found that God is turning out hearts and lives? Perhaps the Lord is renewing our spirit. Perhaps the Lord is emboldening our speech. Perhaps you are being led to step out in faith, and to pray for somebody. But maybe you're also not quite sure whether or not you should take that big step. Because you wonder what your home community might think of you, if you start to get, maybe, too spiritual. You might think that they might say, "Has she gone out of her mind?" Sometimes following Jesus requires us to take that big step, [to be] bold. And it might be easier, sometimes, if we were to go from Biel, maybe, to go to Fribourg.[2] Maybe most of the Fribourgans won't recognize us, and then we can be a bit more bold in this alien territory, that Catholic territory, Amen! [Laughter.] But at home, it's a little bit, maybe, more difficult sometimes.

This passage also invites us to go even deeper than our *home* territory. Because, as we can see in this text, the struggle is not just about home in terms of geography. But the struggle, I believe, is about home in terms of what makes up our inner reality. It's about what goes on in our minds, as is indicated in the text. It is what goes on deep in our spirit as indicated in this text. Sometimes the deepest struggles are in our heads and in our hearts. Sometimes the deepest works of the Spirit happen right here in our heads and in our hearts. And sometimes those are the most powerful struggles that are within us.

How many of us realize, sometimes, that we wrestle deeply, and go over and over again in our mind about following the Lord? Sometimes it might be unbelief, like the people that chose not to believe in the works

2. About a forty-five minute drive, so not quite next door.

of Jesus. But sometimes it may just be, just be questions, and we wrestle deep within our spirit about how to follow Jesus. The powers at home and the powers in our home. Our struggling with family and our struggling with ourselves. Our saying, "Lord, we want the Holy Spirit's work *in* our lives," but we struggle sometimes to fully receive that work. We struggle, sometimes, about whether or not to step out in faith. The deepest obstacles are truly spiritual and within.

The people said, "It's because he has an unclean spirit." They named it as a spiritual problem. But they misdiagnosed the spiritual. And I believe it's the case with us oftentimes as well. We realize that we have a spiritual need. We realize we need more of the *Holy* Spirit. But oftentimes we may not recognize and not be able to receive that Holy Spirit. We have doubts, internally, and they are exacerbated by our context, by our home. And these doubts build on one another, and it turns out, sometimes, that they paralyze us.

You see, it's interesting that Jesus had just gotten done, before coming into this context, healing a paralytic. We might not be paralyzed in the sense of being in a wheelchair. But we might be paralyzed in our spirit because we cannot allow the freedom of the Lord to move us into the next realm. And notice how the crowd was sitting around him, and they said to him, in verse 32: "Your mother and your brothers and sisters are outside asking for you." Can you imagine the intense, if you will, spiritual warfare going on if we were in a similar situation? On the one hand, feeling like we're right in the center of God's will, but on the other hand, doubting voices, questions, even perhaps from those whom we know and love that are around us.

As an Asian American, if my mothers and brothers and sisters are outside, and they're asking for me, I get up and go outside. It's called honoring your parents in my culture. But I'm talking about that even deeper wrestling in our spirit. When the voices are coming back and forth.

But Jesus replied, "Who are my mother and my brothers?" And looking at those around him he said, "Here are my mother and brothers. Whoever does the will of God, is my brother and sister and mother."

I was very, very touched to have been, and we're blessed to have been able to experience, the [water] baptisms that we had earlier today. And I believe if I understood the translator right, when you asked the first parent, "Why do you want to baptize your child?" the answer, according to what I heard was that: "We are thankful to the Lord, and receive and recognize this child as a gift from the Lord." Now that's a very powerful confession, I believe. Because there are many, many different ways to receive children. Certainly, one can be thankful for children, but one might not recognize children as gifts from the Lord. And in some circumstances, you might well know of some parents who, because of challenging circumstances, do not see their children as gifts from the Lord. I've got another testimony about that as well.

My parents are Pentecostal ministers. And when I was nine years old, they had my younger brother Mark, who had Down syndrome. And I remember the first two years of [his] life, my parents kept asking the Lord, "Why was Mark born to them?" And I remember the members of the church coming to our house, and all of us were praying that God would heal Mark. All of us were praying that his tongue would go back into his mouth. They were praying that his toes would close up. In other words, they wanted God to take away all of the symptoms of what made him look different. At that point in our lives, it was very, very difficult for us to recognize Mark as a gift of the Lord. And it took many, many years for my parents and for me to begin to see that this *was God's gift to our family*.[3]

Sometimes circumstances in our home make it difficult for us to recognize God's work in our midst. From a naturalistic point of view, Mark could just have been an accident of nature. In other words, don't underestimate the power of this confession that recognizes our children as gifts from the Lord. I believe there might even be a parallel with this difficult text and what I've just said.

Because remember, they were saying that either Jesus had an unclean spirit (those who were the doubters) or Jesus had the Holy Spirit (those who were the believers). And it's very, very possible, I believe, that when we're confronted with what might appear to be normal circumstances, we have these two choices.

Is Mark the result of the devil at work in our lives? Or can we understand Mark as a result of God's working in our lives? Are children just a financial liability? Or are they a gift from the Lord? Is this of some strange spirit? Or is this of the Holy Spirit? And you and I might wrestle in our minds: how do we name this reality in our midst?

But I want to suggest that those who brought their children to be baptized show us the way. It is not just about naming the [name] of the Lord, but it is about *doing* the will of the Lord. Amen? It's about bringing

---

3. The introductory chapter to my book, *The Bible, Disability, and the Church*, provides an updated testimony of our transformative journey as a family with Mark.

the children to be baptized. It is not just declaring in our heads that these children are from God, but it's about bringing them into the community to be raised in the Lord's presence. If we are struggling with questions, believe me, I know as a theologian, sometimes there are no answers you can figure out. But the answer may not be in our thinking about it, but in doing the will of the Lord: stepping out in faith, in the community of faith, and saying, "Lord, I don't have all the answers, I don't have all of it figured out, but I want to be faithful, I want to be open to your Holy Spirit. I realize I have my doubts. I realize that our family is divided on these issues. But I'm going to step out in faith." Whoever does the will of God is part of the family of God.

In closing, I would like to say a prayer with us this morning. I want to pray that the powers at home and within would be freed by the power of the Holy Spirit. Can I ask you to stand with me for a moment? Let us open our hearts continuously to the Lord in these moments.

Lord Jesus, we thank you for sending your Holy Spirit. Send your Holy Spirit into our hearts. Renew and transform our minds. Help us to do the will of the Father. Send your Holy Spirit into our homes. Send your Holy Spirit into our families. Bring your peace and your mind into these spaces. Help us to do your will as a family. Send your Holy Spirit into our community in view. Send your peace and your joy into this community through us. Enable us to do your will in this community. Come Holy Spirit. In the name of Jesus. Amen.

Tony Richie Reflection—"With Gentleness and Respect"

This final sermon accents the complexities of familial relationships with potentially oppositional faith identities. From the opening chapters of Genesis onward family is a consistent focus of Scripture. However, very soon (chapter 4!) violent conflict occurred between siblings arising out of conflicting views on pleasing God. The first act of violence in the Bible involved a family's "interfaith" conflict and led to fratricide! Later, Jesus, warning of familial strife because of faith in him, challenged disciples to all-surpassing loyalty (Matt 10:34–37). Tragically, contemporary interreligious violence between descendants of two brothers, Isaac and Ishmael (Jews, Christians, and Muslims), exemplifies an ancient-but-persistent trend.

Reinhold Niebuhr once observed that "religious diversity remains potentially the most basic source of conflict."[4] Yet Christians are enjoined to pursue peace with everyone (Heb 12:14). How to approach that daunting task? Authoritarian domination of other religions leads to resentment and resistance. Secularist relegation of religions to irrelevance is ineffective and offensive. Only a religious solution to this religious problem is realistic and workable. By firm commitment to mutual engagement in humility and charity people of faith and goodwill can cooperate together. Real relationship-building along with spiritual discernment in interactions with religious others through dialogue is essential.

Where is Christian witness? It's the witness of presence. Embodying Christ's presence to others can be most effective. Of course, the witness of presence invites alert readiness and appropriate responsiveness to religious others for opportune occasions of more explicit sharing. As the apostle puts it, we bear witness of Christ our Lord "with gentleness and respect" (1 Pet 3:15 NIV).

---

4. Niebuhr, *The Children of Light and the Children of Darkness*, 125.

Epilogue

Whereas the prologue sought to situate the broader personal and scholarly context for comprehending the preceding collection of sermons, this epilogue hopes to sketch the contours of apostolic preaching for the present time. If the sermons illustrate apostolic preaching descriptively, then the following generalizes toward a normative pentecostal and Christian theology of preaching. This is because *pentecostal* in this context, consistent with the modalities manifest in the pages in this book, is understood less in terms of the contemporary Pentecostal movement than of the apostolic experience launched by the Day of Pentecost outpouring of the Spirit on all flesh for the purposes of bearing witness to the ends of the earth and the ends of time. If the *that* of the scriptural narrative is presumed to provide the template for the *this* of the present Christian life,[1] Pentecostal or otherwise, then the thesis to be argued here is that apostolic preaching is not just to be discovered and uncovered in the pages of Scripture but to be performatively engaged in our contemporary proclamation and inhabitation of the biblical gospel or kerygma. Our reflections now hence distill the essentials of the apostolic kerygma (the *that*) that casts a two-thousand-year shadow over proclamation of the gospel today (the *this*) as it pertains to the opportunities and challenges for present Christian discipleship (the *who, where*, and *when*) in the third global millennium.

---

1. I explicate more about pentecostal hermeneutics as "this-is-that" in my essays: "The 'Baptist Vision' of James William McClendon, Jr.," reprinted in Yong, *The Dialogical Spirit*, ch. 4; and "Reading Scripture and Nature," reprinted in *The Hermeneutical Spirit*, ch. 12. In this book, however, "this-is-that" is treated homiletically rather than only hermeneutically, and this presumption expressed in the sermons above is now explicated as part and parcel of apostolic preaching transmuted for the present time.

The *Kerygmatic* Spirit

What then is apostolic preaching? First and foremost, apostolic preaching is about the *kerygma*, the gospel. What then is the gospel? I suggest that the apostolic gospel can be understood along three trajectories: that having to do with Jesus the Christ, that having to do with the reign of God that Jesus proclaimed, and that having to do with the God of Jesus Christ. If I were to highlight the main thematic contents of the apostolic kerygma, I would say that these summarize in general what the messages in the main body of this book is about.

First, apostolic preaching is about Jesus Christ. The twelve apostles preached Jesus, and we, preaching in their wake, do—or should—also. We preach what they preached: Jesus Christ. In preaching Jesus Christ, then, we proclaim the man from Nazareth as the anointed Messiah. Jesus is the Christ, which means nothing less than the Anointed One, the Messiah, as one who was filled with the Holy Spirit. St. Luke summarizes, from his account of Peter's preaching to Cornelius's household, the center of the apostolic message in this way: "God anointed Jesus of Nazareth with the Holy Spirit and with power; how he went about doing good and healing all who were oppressed by the devil, for God was with him" (Acts 10:38). In other words, the apostolic kerygma has an implicitly trinitarian shape: Jesus as messianically anointed by the Holy Spirit.

Here of course, we understand *trinitarian* surely within the tradition of post-Nicene orthodoxy, although for our purposes, what grounds the kerygmatic proclamation is less the deliverances and conceptualizations of the fourth-century confessions than the apostolic writings and their reception of the Hebrew canon. This is not to minimize the achievements of the Nicene-Constantinopolitan Creed, but to recognize the contextual character of its authoritativeness in relationship to the scriptural bedrock of the apostolic message. This means in part that Nicene trinitarianism helps us further comprehend the apostolic kerygma but also that the apostolic documents are norming norms for our own ongoing reception of the full range of Christian traditions.[2] If "the word of God is living and active" (Heb 4:12a) then it will always need to be understood in relationship to tradition in its dynamic character, hence the apostolic message of Jesus as the Christ is also the norm for our own proclamation of the gospel today.

2. I clarify further the relationship of Scripture and tradition in my *Spirit-Word-Community*, esp. ch. 8.

Yet simultaneously, if the apostolic message focuses on Jesus the Christ, then according to the apostolic writings, specifically the Gospels about Jesus Christ, his message was on and about ἡ βασιλεία τοῦ θεοῦ (*he basileia tou theou*): the kingdom of God or the reign of God, which was coming.[3] This is evident throughout the Gospel narratives, so we are not surprised to hear Luke's summary in this second book put in these terms: "After his suffering he [Jesus] presented himself alive to them by many convincing proofs, appearing to them over the course of forty days and *speaking about the kingdom of God*" (Acts 1:3, italics added). In effect, then, Jesus' own proclamation was consistently about the coming divine rule, and it is clear that his followers thereafter also grasped that this Messiah from Nazareth embodied this reign of God in his own life and deeds, not least in his death and subsequent resurrection.

There is a sense, then, that the apostolic preaching is about *both* Jesus *and* the rule of God, about the Jesus who came and is expected to come again on the one side, and about the divine reign manifest in his life and message and that is also yet coming on the other side. This is what it means to live and preach "in the last days" (Acts 2:17a), as Luke records Peter's explication about the Pentecost event drawn from the authoritative scriptural sources available to him (cf. Joel 2:28). On the one hand, as with St. Paul, we have "decided to know nothing among you except Jesus Christ, and him crucified" (1 Cor 2:2); on the other hand, precisely by preaching Jesus, we also proclaim the kerygma he announced: that in his life and ministry the rule and reign of God has appeared initially among human creatures, and this is what we ought to work toward, anticipate, and welcome also. To preach about the divine rule, however, is also to preach about life in the Spirit, about life in Christ made possible through the Holy Spirit, so that apostolic proclamation is about the reign of God but entered by and through the Spirit.[4]

Yet if the apostolic preaching reiterates Jesus' own proclamation about the divine reign, then the apostolic kerygma then and now also announces the God of Jesus Christ, the God who sent Jesus and seeks to reconcile all creation to Godself through Jesus. This is the *Abba* or Father that Jesus prayed to and related to, and upon whom he relied to be faithful to the covenantal promises of ancient Israel. In that respect, the God of the apostolic kerygma is the God of Israel as well, whose nature

---

3. I prefer *reign of God* since it does not carry the patriarchal, kyriarchical, and hierarchical connotations of kings and kingdoms.

4. See Cho, *Spirit and Kingdom in the Writings of Luke and Paul.*

and character are unfolded also across the pages of the First Testament. Apostolic preaching might have been launched on the Day of Pentecost by the power of the Holy Spirit, but this message is about Jesus the Christ, his message of the divine reign, and the God whose rule is on its way to restore Israel, redeem humanity, and renew all creation.

From this perspective, then, the apostolic kerygma is fully trinitarian, involving Father, Son, and Holy Spirit, all the qualifications regarding trinitarianism above brought forward here as well. The difference might be that our own apostolic configuration is pentecostally initiated via the last days or eschatological outpouring of the Spirit "on all flesh" (Acts 2:17b), leading back through the messianic figure from Nazareth, and then to the Father, so that we might map the trinitarian relations in terms of Spirit-Son-Father.[5] Alternatively, according to the apostolic message, we might also have movement traced from Son to Father to Spirit since Peter also proclaimed, as recorded by Luke: "Being therefore exalted at the right hand of God, and having received from the Father the promise of the Holy Spirit, he has poured out this that you both see and hear" (Acts 2:33). The point is that apostolic trinitarianism is, again, not reducible to Nicene constructs, but effectively precedes the reception of tradition in their various contexts.

The Kerygmatic *Spirit*

The preceding focused on clarifying the nature of the kerygma proclaimed in the apostolic context. In this section, however, we shift to explore how the kerygma is received in the contemporary horizon of proclamation.[6] What is the *Spirit* in and through which the apostolic preaching is mediated to any present moment? Preaching in the apostolic and all subsequent contexts perennially happens by the Holy Spirit, and is "for your children, and for all who are far away, everyone whom the Lord our God calls to him" (Acts 2:39). Hence, Spirit-filled preaching brings the kerygma of the apostolic message to life for any new context of hearers. In the next few paragraphs I explicate this dynamic of Spirit-empowered

5. As I did in my book, *Spirit-Word-Community*; see also Oliverio, Jr., "An Interpretive Review Essay on Amos Yong's *Spirit-Word-Community*."

6. As should be obvious in the sermons above, but just so that we are clear also here, I presume something like the Gadamerian fusion-of-horizons through which the past is received in the present anticipating the future; see Thiselton, *The Two Horizons*.

proclamation of the apostolic message at the intellectual, affective, and practical levels.

Apostolic preaching has content, obviously, as the preceding section summarized. Yet it's not just *what* we present but *how* we present such with apostolic conviction. So, if sermons ought to move listeners to reflection, then we ought to prompt consideration and deliberation. This does not necessarily mean that we must always have answers, particularly when dealing with difficult matters. However, it does mean that we ought to help our listeners grapple with the apostolic kerygma even if the questions have not been quite resolved. This involves not undermining faith but presenting pathways for inquiry.

For instance, I often provide background to texts I am expositing by drawing upon the scholarly consensus, or by at least acknowledging the scholarly disputes and questions. This is done in a way not to prompt skepticism about the issues but to alert contemporary listeners to unresolved elements related to scholarship on the text. The goal, however, is not to introduce intellectual paralysis but to acknowledge that, "now we see in a mirror, dimly, but then we will see face to face. Now I know only in part; then I will know fully, even as I have been fully known" (1 Cor 13:12). Yet simultaneously, this enables honesty in recognizing our limitations even as it encourages open-ended and ongoing inquiry. The point is that we ought not to shy away from the intellectual challenges that the kerygma poses, whether in terms of how we understand such or how that might impinge on our lives. Spirit-inspired apostolic preaching is robustly intellectual, not otherwise.

Apostolic preaching is also, however, not merely intellectual, if by that we mean abstracted via the rational and cognitive aspects of our beings. Truth be told, human cognition is now recognized as not only rational and intellectual but embodied: emotional, affective, and perceptual.[7] Hence, we engage each other, even kerygmatically and homiletically, via *both* head *and* heart: rationally and affectively, reasonably and emotionally. Any appeal to the mind must thereby be accompanied by connection to the inner dimensions of our souls, and vice versa: any call to the depths of our hearts cannot merely remain emotional but ought to be processable rationally and intellectually. Heads and hearts, in other words, are distinctly and inseparably the goal and target of kerygmatic preaching.

7. E.g., Lakoff and Johnson, *Philosophy in the Flesh.*

The workings of the Spirit are to inspire not just intellectual conversion but also affective transformation: of our hearts, desires, hopes, and loves.[8]

Hence apostolic proclamation ought to be modulated as a sonic event.[9] Sonicity is felt and embodied experience. Preaching as oral performance is enacted audially and heard by listeners. What is heard, then, is not mere content but emotions, gestures, and movement. We have made the sermons transcribed in this book available precisely in order to allow for audio and visual analysis. Is *what* is said commensurate with *how* such is communicated? Some of the sermons are in video format, which allows for multiple modes of analysis, but most are available only in audio, in which case, analysts will need to discern vocal modulation in relationship to content delivery. In any case, since preaching is directed toward persons rather than merely brains, kerygmatic affectiveness must operate dually, reaching minds and touching hearts. Spirit-empowered apostolic proclamation is profoundly affective, not otherwise.

Beyond heads and hearts, however, there is also the domain of *hands*: what we ought to do given what the apostolic kerygma entails. Thus, there is the so-what or behavioral dimension: conversion of minds and transformation of hearts leads to doing of hands and walking of feet (or wheeling of chairs, as the case might be). The form of Pentecostal preaching, situated within the revivalist traditions, oftentimes therefore concluded with an altar call: respond to the message by turning your lives over to Jesus the Christ. In coming to the front, one chooses to now act differently. In apostolic parlance, "Repent, and be baptized every one of you in the name of Jesus Christ so that your sins may be forgiven; and you will receive the gift of the Holy Spirit" (Acts 2:38), and this in performed and enacted by lifting up one's hand, opening up one's palms, in order to be appropriately postured to receive the divine gifts, call, and vocation.

A few of the sermons transcribed involved an altar call, even if such might not have included movement to the front of the meeting space. Yet in general, the greater the intellectual intensity of the sermon the more time people must be given to process its implications. This may not therefore lend itself to immediate decisions, but must thereby extend space for ongoing deliberation, even long after dismissal, so that the effects of the kerygmatic call might unfold in their own time. In any case, it is not only

8. For further consideration of the affections as a central domain of the Spirit's work in human lives, see Yong and Coulter, eds., *The Spirit, the Affections, and the Christian Tradition.*

9. As I explicate in greater depth in my essay, "Proclamation and the Third Article."

that apostolic preaching ought to result in a decision to do something, but ought to motivate ongoing discipleship, in other words, a faithful way of life and living. From that perspective, while crisis moments of deciding and choosing matter—their import ought never be underestimated[10]—yet kerygmatic proclamation ought to also orient our habits and dispositions in the direction of the gospel, normed according to the coming divine reign. Spirit-empowered apostolic preaching is thereby fundamentally practical and performative, inviting embodied responses.[11]

Kerygmatic content that does not engage the heads, hearts, and hands of listeners from every generation will be ineffective in bringing about the divine rule that Jesus proclaimed and died for. Apostolic preaching therefore has to be orthodox theologically, orthopathic interpersonally, and orthopraxic communicatively (or perlocutionarily). The Spirit of apostolic proclamation can never choose between right ideas, right feelings, and right behaviors: each of these are the contemporary horizon that either mediates or inhibits reception of the gospel in every context.[12] Spirit-filled kerygmatic preaching connects the apostolic message about Jesus, the reign of God, and the God of Israel to contemporary hearts, minds, and lives.

Apostolic Preaching for the Third-Millennium Global Context

It is now time to bring our considerations to summation. I have here sought to connect the kerygmatic message proclaimed by the apostles with effective kerygmatic preaching in the power of the Spirit. What, however, is the broader contemporary context for apostolic proclamation in the twenty-first century? In other words, how are human listeners—heads, hearts, and all in all their fullness—situated in their engaging with the apostolic word? Asking this question invites further reflection, however brief, about the ecclesial, social/global, and academic contexts of the contemporary horizon. These aspects of pentecostal preaching ought to

10. For more on the crucial role of crisis conversions, see my *The Spirit Poured Out on All Flesh*, esp. §2.3.3.

11. On the interconnections between belief and practice, see my essay, "Poured Out on All Flesh"; cf. *Hospitality and the Other*, ch. 2.

12. For more on orthodoxy-orthopathy-orthopraxy, see my *Spirit of Love*, esp. ch. 5; cf. also the newly published dissertation of my former doctoral student, Trementozzi, *Salvation in the Flesh*.

be observable in the transcriptions across this volume; here, I seek to put theoretical flesh to the homiletic trails charted above.

Contemporary preaching unfolds most often, although not only, in churches. There are many church types, part of dynamic ecclesial traditions. Cognition of where we are located and awareness of the ecclesial stream within which we are wading and navigating enables more relevant and appropriate rhetoric and discursive engagement with the audience, this should go without saying. On the other hand, in an increasingly post-denominational era and in a time when independent churches are waxing vigorously, people have less and less memory or knowledge about ecclesial rootedness. In these fluid contexts, one does what one can about inviting reconsideration of church traditions even while we seek to connect to the apostolic kerygma via these (not always clearly identifiable) genealogies.

Yet, while mindful of the distinctive traits that mark these ecclesial developments and while being careful to connect to them, it is the nature of apostolic preaching to link us to the one, holy, and catholic tradition grounded in the scriptural kerygma.[13] From this perspective, all apostolic proclamation is enabled by the Spirit of the living Word and all apostolic preaching renews the New Testament witness for the present moment. Hence it is not that ecclesiality in all of its differentiated traditions is unimportant, but that each is and provides a distinctive and particular modality of engagement with the apostolic message. This might need to be named in various contexts of contemporary preaching but it might also simply need to be inhabited by the preacher in ways that also invite listeners to be opened up to the otherwise unnamed traditions that nourish their souls. In other words, the apostolic preacher today is mindfully informed by, albeit not slavishly wedded to, ecclesial traditions as enabled by the "fellowship of the Spirit" (2 Cor 13:13) that is also the body of Christ.

Ecclesial audiences are also socially and historically located: *in*, even if not *of*, the world. Hence, apostolic preaching engages congregations not just as those *within* the faith but also as those *living out* the faith in the world. Apostolic preaching therefore cannot avoid the public, the political, the economic, the social, and the historical realities of the contemporary horizon, even as apostolic proclamation also has to engage the global, cultural, and religious dimensions of the contemporary world. This is not

13. See Yong, *Spirit Poured Out*, §3.2; for more on my ecclesiology, see Yong, *Renewing Christian Theology*, ch. 7.

to allow these present concerns to constrain the apostolic kerygma but to ensure that the apostolic witness addresses the principalities and powers of any present age. Yet the Spirit poured out on all flesh, even to the ends of the earth (Acts 1:8), means that there are no spheres or domains of the human undertaking that are cordoned off from the Spirit's presence and activity. Apostolic preaching thus relates the Spirit of Jesus and divine reign to the various realms of human endeavor.[14]

Yet not all apostolic preaching occurs within churches of ecclesial structures. Paul preached at the Areopagus and sometimes Christian proclamation unfolds within the various quarters of the public square. I'm not referring necessarily to street-preaching, even as that is not my recommended or preferred context for apostolic evangelism,[15] but I am referring to other public occasions, even, for instance, wedding and funerals, or opportunities to address non-ecclesial audiences as one who is a minister of the gospel. In other words, being mindful of these contexts, apostolic preaching ought to be attentive to their distinctive opportunities and alert to possible pitfalls. It is not about not wishing to be scandalous per se, but about allowing the gospel to be heard and then for whatever scandal that may arise to be related the apostolic kerygma, not be due to its messenger.

Last but not least, what about preaching in academic contexts? As one who is by vocation a professional theologian, many homiletical occasions are situated within institutions of higher learning predominantly but not exhaustively in Christian colleges and universities, and also in seminary and other theological educational contexts. At one level, these are ecclesially related in some fundamental respects, more so if these are denominationally affiliated institutions of theological education that are training ministers for their churches. In a growing number of cases in which divinity schools are situated in increasingly otherwise secular universities, however, as well as in other related circumstances, the ecclesiality of these locations are more convoluted. Apostolic proclamation in these liminal spaces occurs in some respects in, but in other respects outside of, unambiguously ecclesial environments.

Within this more academic domain, one treads a fine line between assuming theology is the so-called queen of the sciences and one that sees theology as one discipline among others, perhaps even a marginalized

---

14. See, for instance, my *In the Days of Caesar.*

15. E.g., Yong, "Apostolic Evangelism in the Postcolony."

one at that.[16] Such contexts maximize the importance of threading the via media between apostolic confidence and humility, between the possibility of theology contributing an intervention into the broader scholarly and academic conversations on the one hand and the reality that theology is just as much capable of dialogical learning and engagement with the many voices on the other hand.[17] Apostolic preaching focused on the kerygma of Jesus Christ and the coming reign of the God of Israel can surely say something that the academy would want, even need, to hear; otherwise there is no point for kerygmatic proclamation in this space. Yet the apostolic word in this context resounds amidst many other words: what ought the Spirit-filled preacher resonate with and what ought he or she yet resist? Discernment of which is which can only be charismatically and pneumatically achieved. This is both the promise and the challenge for the kerygmatic spirit.

16. Yong and Coulter, *Finding the Holy Spirit at a Christian University*, grapple with these issues.

17. As I try to exemplify and model in my *The Dialogical Spirit*.

Afterword

Tony Richie

Although I had heard Amos Yong teach and make various academic and theological presentations many times, I well remember the first time I heard him preach a sermon in a congregational setting: at my home church in Knoxville, Tennessee, New Harvest Church of God. He and his family were traveling through our area and, as we also do when near their home, they stayed over with us. I took a "step of faith" and did something most pastors don't usually do: I invited a preacher that I hadn't heard previously! And I was pleasantly surprised. Great scholars don't always make good preachers. However, Amos Yong is certainly an exception. My southern, rural, working-class Pentecostal congregation took to him immediately, and responded well to God's word as he proclaimed it, "by the Holy Spirit sent from heaven" (1 Pet 1:12).

Frankly, I found the instant rapport between my congregation and Yong a bit remarkable since he is not at all a "stereotypical" Pentecostal preacher in terms of a dramatic style of delivery. Although pleasant, even entertaining, to hear, the true power of his preaching lay in the content. I will say more about theological content in a moment. For now, I observe that New Harvest is an exceptionally Bible-centered congregation and we heard the word through his preaching in a delightful fashion. He has since preached for us several times, and I've discovered that our initial delight was to be no exception.

To give an example not included in this volume, Yong once preached an Easter sermon at New Harvest on "Resurrection Life for the Perplexed, Terrified, and Unintelligible" from Luke 24:1–12.[1] It was a great message

---

1. "Resurrection Life for the Perplexed, Terrified, and Unintelligible" (Luke 24:1–12), Easter Sunrise Service, New Harvest Church of God, Knoxville, Tennessee, 24 March 2008 (see Appendix).

for a number of reasons.[2] I'll name just a few for relevant observations. First, it was patently obvious that he had spent time with the text. His understanding of the Emmaus Road encounter between Christ and his unknowing disciples showed that he had dug in deep, far beyond common superficial exegesis. Second, his use of the medium of narrative to communicate the text to his listeners was quite effective. He drew our congregation into the story until it literally felt like *our* story. Third, his ability to make practical applications for the lives of Christians in the pew coupled with his willingness to weave his own life-journey and testimony into the sermon gave listeners a solid takeaway and sense of personal investment. Finally, but most notably, we experienced what I now know as Amos Yong's classic creativity in communicating—or perhaps better still, "translating"—complex biblical and theological insights into palatable homiletic and hortatory language. I came away from that Easter Sunday sermon with *both* reaffirmation of Christ's resurrection as taught by the historic church throughout the ages *and* fresh realization that the risen Christ often appears unawares in unexpected places in an unpredictable form to unsuspecting people.

As a preaching pastor and scholar/theologian myself, one of the features of Amos Yong's preaching method and style that stands out to me most is that his sermons tend to be astute people-oriented explications of rather complex theological themes. When an opportunity arose to work with Amos Yong and Josh Samuel on *The Kerygmatic Spirit* I immediately conceived an idea of advocating for an underlying link between homiletics and systematics that I find so evident in Yong's sermons. Further, I suggest that this method and style may be very helpful for pastors and their congregations. In the present volume Josh Samuel well discusses more detailed and technical aspects of Yong's preaching technique and style, so there's no need for me to delve into that discussion. More what I desire to discuss is how thinking theologically about the Bible and the issues it raises can translate into good preaching in the pastoral context.

In the history of Christian thought theology has been described as "the queen of the sciences." However, it is probably appropriate to describe biblical scholarship as "king" of Pentecostal scholarship. This preeminent valuation is to be expected, and applauded, given Pentecostals' high valuation of biblical inspiration and authority. Yet if biblical

---

2. Traditionally, Pentecostals often prefer "message" to "sermon" as an indicator of its origin from another, that is, from God's Spirit. However, "sermon" and even "homily" have become more widely used in recent years.

scholarship helps us understand what the Bible says, and Christian theology helps us understand what it means, then it is preaching that makes it all accessible and applicable for people in the pews. And that's what Amos Yong's preaching does well.

Therefore, in this Afterword I build on my end-of-chapter reflections on each sermon. I tie together prominently recurring themes and highlight major features of the process for understanding Amos Yong as preacher/theologian and accessing his thought in a manner specifically viable for the church as well as the academy. Admittedly, I'm resourcing my deep and longstanding collaboration with Yong as lecturer, preacher, and writer. I further draw on my own long experience (almost forty years as of the time of writing) as a pastor/scholar and, as noted, particularly on my firsthand encounters with Yong's distinctive preaching style in his several preaching appointments at my local congregation (in addition to sermonic material in this volume). In a word, I suggest this homiletical presentation of Yong's theological approach to kerygmatic/apostolic preaching holds rich potential as a medium, and perhaps as a kind of a touchstone, not only for enhanced engagement between scholars and clergy but also for concrete applications of maturing Pentecostal thought at general levels of Christian faith and life for laity.

There is one specific objective I wish to prioritize: the relationship between advanced theology and effective preaching. Out of that conversation I'll further explore two specific ways in which theology is helpful for preaching. The first, and most obvious, is that sound theology undergirds good preaching. Please pardon the use of an example from my own homiltetical and theological journey. My non-academic homiletical and theological beginnings were heavily steeped in dispensationalism via the popularity within evangelical and Pentecostal Christianity of such writers as C. I. Scofield and Finis Dake. Among other things, dispensationalist theology rigidly compartmentalizes huge segments of Scripture as directly applicable only to limited periods (or dispensations) of time. Many find it attractive because of its facile harmonization of major historical and eschatological components of Scripture.

However, dispensationalism espouses cessationism, or the doctrine that certain spiritual gifts—especially speaking in tongues, prophecy, healing, miracles, etc.—ceased after the New Testament or apostolic era. Cessationism is directly counter to continuationism, the view of Pentecostals and Charismatics that spiritual gifts (*charismata*) continue to function in contemporary churches. Of course, as a Pentecostal pastor, I preach that Spirit-baptism and spiritual gifts continue to be active today. For years I struggled to synthesize these disparate viewpoints. It was only after receiving formal theological training that I realized their ultimate incompatibility.[3] Contrary to dispensationalism, a theologically consistent Pentecostal hermeneutic affirms the overall unity of Scripture and, while acknowledging diversity, emphasizes intertextuality. That remarkable realization significantly transformed my theology and my preaching, not only on prophetic or eschatological themes but on many others as well.

Second, and perhaps less obvious to many, but something that Yong ably exemplifies, is that theology is a rich reservoir for preaching. It is this attribute, sort of in reverse, to which my end-of-chapter reflections point. For the most part, my reflections simply draw out theological themes already present in Yong's sermons. Admittedly, I develop and expand on these themes in my own way. I do this extension partly for the pure joy of doing theology, but mainly for an objective of demonstrating potential directions his homilies can be legitimately taken theologically.

As a pastor, my intent is to invite preachers, especially pastors but other preachers as well, to reverse that process, so to speak. In other words, I'm persuaded that preachers who study theology well enough to articulate it precisely and then to translate it well into hortatory proclamation and application—or in other words, into good preaching for people in the pews—attain to a caliber of preaching otherwise unlikely. Theology isn't just for theologians! Theology is for preachers and for the congregations they serve. And this fact is quite evident in this collection of Amos Yong sermons.

Let's think together about some of the profound themes in this volume of Yong's sermons. Their range, to name a few, includes the Trinity, Christology, pneumatology, ecclesiology, eschatology, soteriology, and anthropology. They also address ethical and political theology, theodicy, inclusivity, universality, marginalization, hermeneutics, intellectual development, and ecumenism and pluralism, as well as charismology, prayer, and evangelism, along with other aspects of ecclesial mission. Yet Yong translates these (and other) complex, profound theological themes into preaching that is understandable, practical, and applicable—and, often, even entertaining—for his hearers (and readers). Most of all, this is biblical preaching made more effective by theological expertise.

---

3. Yong explicates this incompatibility in his *In the Days of Caesar*, §8.1.

Even the title of the present volume is suggestive: *The Kerygmatic Spirit: Apostolic Preaching in the 21st Century*. *The Kerygmatic Spirit* suggests theological themes. *Apostolic Preaching* suggests biblical focus. *Preaching in the 21st Century* relates contemporary and pastoral concerns. I wouldn't be surprised if perusing these sermons helps preachers become better theologians and theologians become better preachers. More precisely, it could aid preachers and theologians in the task of theological preaching.

Of course, I heartily affirm that ultimately the Bible itself is the inexhaustible and indispensable resource for pastors and other preachers. As an adjunct professor of theology at Pentecostal Theological Seminary I often attend chapel services on campus. I'm always especially amazed by how our biblical scholars surprise and stimulate us with the word of God. Lee Roy Martin, a professor of Old Testament, is a great example.[4] In the autumn of 2015 I heard him preach a message from Psalm 73:17 on our encounter with God in worship as setting all of life's ups and downs in context and giving perspective for the life of faith and a walk of closeness with the Lord. At that moment nothing could have been more relevant, more uplifting for me. Obviously, preaching the Bible is incomparable.

Further, I'm well aware of Barth's advice that preachers hold a Bible in one hand and a newspaper (or today, a blog!) in the other. I agree. As preachers we are called to help our congregations frame current events, happenings, and trends according to God's word. A few years ago New York University did a study of the New Harvest Church of God.[5] Among other things, it involved a representative from NYU coming to our church and doing Q&A with the congregation without my presence. Later I was told that one key question was about our approach to pastoral leadership. It essentially inquired as to whether the pastor has the authority to dictate the civil policies and practices of the congregation. The congregation answered that Pastor Tony's preaching and teaching helps us be informed about current issues from a biblical and doctrinal perspective but we make our own decisions prayerfully based on our commitments and values. Of course current events and issues provide material for preaching.

4. See also Martin, ed., *Toward a Pentecostal Theology of Preaching*, and Martin and Williams, eds., *Spirit-Filled Preaching in the 21st Century*.

5. It was part of a larger and extensive study conducted by, David Elcott, Taub Professor of Practice in Public Service and Leadership at New York University, Wagner, from 2013–15, on "The Religion and Civics Project"; see https://wagner.nyu.edu/leadership/religionandcivics.

What about testimony? In some of my written work, I've utilized the practice of testimony for everything from transformative congregational involvement in worship to ecumenical and interreligious dialogue.[6] However, a lot of great preaching is quite autobiographical (or testimonial). Given the incarnational nature of Christianity, that is entirely appropriate. Inevitably each preacher, intentionally or not, draws on his or her spiritual experiences and insights in life on their journey of faith as they proclaim God's word. I was speaking up at "testimony time" long before I stood behind the pulpit to preach. Now that I do preach from the pulpit, I still incorporate personal testimony. The value of a testimony over a standardized illustration is its personal connection and that little extra unction that comes with relating our own experiences out of our shared faith.

Amos Yong certainly incorporates all of the above elements (Scripture, current issues, testimony), and more, into his preaching. But the distinctive element to which I would call attention is theology. Amos Yong the theologian and Amos Yong the preacher are one. There isn't any disconnect. Obviously, the language and pathos of a theological lecture and of a pastoral homily are decidedly different. Yet the truths are the same. It requires exceptional commitment and skill to weave these timeless verities together into a fabric that can be worn equally well in the sanctuary as in the classroom. But that's precisely what the sermons in this volume do. And, in my opinion, it increases their quality considerably. I think that it is a model that would help many of us preachers, too.

It's really not a new model; but, unfortunately it appears to me to be all-too-rare in this present age. John Chrysostom was easily the most popular preacher of Christian antiquity. He undoubtedly stands out in Christian history as one of the most accomplished preachers ever. Yet Chrysostom's sermons commonly contained knotty or controversial points of doctrine or interpretation. Their content was often heavily theological. Doesn't public popularity and theological density seem incompatible in a preacher? How did Chrysostom manage these apparently polar opposites?

Chrysostom's influence was so immense that he, Basil the Great, and Gregory of Nyssa are together known as the "Three Holy Hierarchs" in the Eastern Church. Although John's thought shared much in common with Basil and Gregory, he far excelled as a preacher. Why? He was

---

6. E.g., Richie, "Spiritual Transformation," and Richie, *Speaking by the Spirit*.

eloquent, yes. But he had "a unique populist flair for making abstruse concepts and complex exegesis accessible to the ordinary folk crowding his church."[7] That appears to be a critical key for his success as a preacher. Although Amos Yong is primarily known as a prolific theologian rather than as a preacher, in his own way I think he reflects the ancient preaching tradition of John Chrysostom. In this vein, Yong's sermons challenge me to reclaim the same in my own preaching today.

Perhaps this issue tugs at my heart more so than it might with some preachers. Through the week I teach historical and doctrinal theology in the classroom of a seminary. On Sundays I preach the gospel in the sanctuary of a little country church. For me these tasks have become two sides of the same coin. In each case I'm endeavoring to faithfully proclaim God's word. Yet I cannot but feel that theological preaching is needed beyond my own situation, outside my particular context, that it is relevant and perhaps even urgent in pulpits across the spectrum of denominations and diverse ministries.

I admit that when I first attempted to preach theology in a congregational setting I made a serious mistake. I tried to deliver a theological lecture in sermonic style. It didn't work. No one, including—especially— me, enjoyed it. That isn't what Amos Yong's sermons do and that isn't what I'm advocating. Yong relates the biblical text to a theological theme as he translates it into a homiletical format suitable for laity consumption. The terminology and the tone of these sermons are not only directed toward the audience; they are determined by the audience. Yet systematic depth and sophistication are evident throughout.

On a pragmatic note, pastors are always looking for good preaching material. Rare indeed (if existing at all!) would be the pastor that hadn't at least occasionally struggled with finding just the right topic for next Sunday morning's sermon. Again, I suggest theology can serve as a major resource for preaching. Historic Christian thought provides a rich reservoir of theological themes that can inspire and inform preaching—making it better, and broader, preaching. The preacher who studies Christian theology will never be at a loss for sermon material. Most good Christian theology arose out of the needs of the people of the day and time. Often those needs still exist in the "average" Christian's life today.

If I might again draw on my own experience, I've found additional benefits to preaching the Bible theologically. It is delightful and

7. Kelly, *Golden Mouth*, 62.

transformative for the preacher him/herself. Regularly preparing and preaching sermons can be hard work. It certainly is time-consuming. Even though sermon preparation and delivery is a labor of love for most preachers, it can be demanding and tiring. Much of the week pastors pray, study, think, and pray some more in anticipation of Sunday. Then Sunday comes and goes. And it starts all over again. The process alone can be mentally exhausting and emotionally draining. No wonder so many pastors endure recurring bouts of burnout.

Yet preachers also know the delight—the sheer joy, the outright exhilaration—when the word of God comes alive to us in our personal study time. There's an indescribable thrill. One works with enthusiasm and excitement. He or she anticipates Sunday keenly. The delivery itself becomes infused with fresh energy. This delight in preaching God's word is one of the factors that make preaching the favorite activity of the pastorate for many of us. It happens for me most often when I study the Bible directly and deeply with theological insight aimed at pastoral application. Further, I experienced it when *hearing* Amos Yong's Easter sermon on "Resurrection Life for the Perplexed, Terrified, and Unintelligible" from Luke 24:1–12 as referenced above. I also experienced the joyous delight of *reading* God's word theologically through the sermons of Amos Yong in this volume.

Not only have I discovered that reading, preaching, and hearing the Bible theologically can be delightful, it is frequently transformative as well. In Yong's Easter sermon, he addressed the "burning hearts" of Luke 24:32. He passionately affirmed the Holy Spirit's life-changing power experienced through personal encounter with the risen Lord and Savior, Jesus Christ. Centuries earlier, John Wesley's *Journal* related how his own heart was "strangely warmed" as he listened to a reading of Luther's Preface to his commentary on Romans at a meeting on Aldersgate Street. Imagine it! Wesley's heart was transformed by the fire of the Holy Spirit while listening to *theological* commentary. Isn't it deliciously appropriate that evangelicalism's great revivalist/theologian had a transformative experience as he heard God's word from the pen of Protestantism's great reformer/theologian? Pastor, preacher, has your heart burned within you as you heard/read/preached profound theological truths from God's word? Mine has. And it has always made a life-changing impact on me.

Like most pastors reading these words, and certainly like most others who have preached frequently over a long period of time, I've developed my own basic approach to sermon preparation and delivery. First (well, after prayer!), I do an exegetical study of my text. Second, I turn to commentaries and other aids to cover what I may have missed. Third, I identify key themes that stand out. Fourth, I think through how it applies to/in my congregation. Finally, I organize my thoughts around what I've learned thus far as I move toward actual delivery. Briefly, these are a few steps I've found helpful over the years in preparing a minimum of two sermons and a Bible study on a weekly basis. What I learn from Yong's preaching example is how to more effectively dispatch preaching duties with an emphasis on theological preaching.

Early in my preaching career (I had only preached about half a dozen times) I spoke at the Church of God in Morristown, Tennessee (my home church at the time) from Romans 12:1–2. At that time I primarily used the King James Version, especially in preaching.

> I beseech you therefore, brethren, by the mercies of God, that ye present your bodies a living sacrifice, holy, acceptable unto God, which is your reasonable service. And be not conformed to this world: but be ye transformed by the renewing of your mind, that ye may prove what is that good, and acceptable, and perfect, will of God.

As I recall, my title was something like "Live Worship" and my four points were 1) *Salvation,* 2) *Presentation,* 3) *Transformation,* and 4) *Demonstration.* My general thesis involved the interrelatedness of conversion and the experience of sanctification as lived out in daily Christian life. I thought it went well enough. A few days later my pastor, Earl T. Golden, and I were having a chat. He mentioned that he noticed that I gravitate toward doctrinal preaching. His affirmation and encouragement were deeply appreciated. He shared that in his forty-plus years of pastoral ministry his preaching had usually emphasized life-application. In nearly forty years of ministry myself I came to increasingly appreciate the great need for life-application sermons.

However, I do not always sharply delineate between doctrinal or theological preaching and practical, life-application preaching. As we all know, each sermon may have different aims or objectives. Some aim to instruct, others to encourage, yet others to inspire, and so on. Some sermons are aimed toward sinners (i.e., the unconverted) and some toward the saints (i.e., the converted and church members). Yet I'm persuaded that all sermons should be biblically based and theologically grounded. Therefore, I propose that careful and thoughtful study of Amos Yong's sermons can help even the most experienced preachers accomplish the sacred task of proclaiming the word of God effectively and faithfully.

Amos Yong is well known as an excellent scholar. Perhaps it's not as well known, but he's also quite a good preacher. I'm sure that both scholars and pastors can learn a lot from his homiletic examples. And I predict they will enjoy the process too.

Now may God help all of us preachers be able to utter with apostle Paul the wise and wonderful words of Acts 20:20: "I have not hesitated to preach anything that would be helpful" (NIV). That's certainly my personal prayer. In the name of the Lord Jesus Christ, who together with the Father and the Holy Spirit is worshiped and glorified, Amen.

Appendix: Yong Sermons 1999–2018[1]

1. "The Work of the Mind and Life in the Spirit" (Romans 12:1–2), chapel, 1 College, Houghton, New York, 2 November 2018.

2. "From the Jewish Diaspora to the CSI Diaspora: Grace, Peace, and Abundance," (1 Peter 1:1–2), Church of South India Family & Friends Conference, Cerritos, California, 6 October 2018.

3. "The Last Days of Mission: The Spirit Poured Out on (New) Creation" (Acts 2:17–21), First Baptist Church, Pasadena, California, 22 April 2018.

4. "'Your Sons and Daughters Will Prophecy . . . !' The Millennial Witness of the Church" (Acts 2:17–18), Winston-Salem First Assembly, Winston-Salem, North Carolina, 8 April 2018.

5. "'. . . To the Seven Churches that are in Asia . . .': Betwixt-and-Between" (Revelation 1:4), chapel hosted by Asian Pacific Islander Club, Vanguard University, Costa Mesa, California, 3 April 2018.

6. "'. . . All Who Are in Asia Have Turned Away from Me . . .': Diasporic Discipleship from Asia Minor to Asian America" (2 Timothy 1:15–18), chapel hosted by Asian Pacific Islander Club, Vanguard University, Costa Mesa, California, 30 November 2017.

7. "Divine Host ~ Missional Hospitality" (Psalm 146), chapel, Pittsburgh Theological Seminary, Pittsburgh, Pennsylvania, 26 September 2017.

8. "Namaan as Host and Guest: Hospitality Then and Today" (2 Kings 5:1–19), chapel, Pittsburgh Theological Seminary, Pittsburgh, Pennsylvania, 25 September 2017.

---

1. I preached regularly from 1983 to 1999 but unfortunately did not keep accurate records of such sermons for this period.

9.   "Made for Thinking! The Life in the Spirit and the Intellectual Life" (Luke 10: 25–29), Alphacrusis, Sydney, Australia, 16 August 2017.

10. "Empowered for Thinking! A Spirit Filled Life of the Mind" (Luke 10:25–29), Hillsong College, Sydney, Australia, 15 August 2017.

11. "The Powers Within, and the Powerful Reign of the Holy Spirit" (Mark 3:19b–35), Landeskirchliche Gemeinschaft *jahu*, Biel, Switzerland, 25 June 2016.

12. "Hearing and Obeying the Many Voices of the Lord's in Our Generation" (Acts 2:1–13), Pentecost International Worship Centre, Dansoman, Accra, Ghana, 13 November 2016.

13. "Life in the Spirit and the Intellectual Life" (Luke 10: 25–29), Pentecost Theological Seminary chapel, Gomoa-Fettehe, Accra, Ghana, 9 November 2016.

14. "Life after a Knockout: The Holy Spirit on the Rocky Road" (Acts 7:54—8:1a), The Barn at Evangel Temple, Springfield, Missouri, 25 September 2016.

15. "When Lightning Strikes!" (Luke 10:17–24), Bethel Church, Glendale, California, 18 September 2016.

16. "Adventures with Jesus: Moving in the Spirit" (Gospel of Luke), First Evangelical Church Glendale, annual retreat, California Baptist University, Riverside, California, 1–4 July 2016.

17. "Light in a World of Darkness: Pentecostal Witness and Missional Existence to and from the Ends of the Earth" (Acts 13:44–48), One Mission Society annual conference plenary, Indiana Wesleyan University, Marion, Indiana, 25 June 2016.

18. "Bringing the Kingdom: The Church-Unifying, Culture-Changing, Cosmos-Shaking Work of the Holy Spirit as Our Inheritance" (Ephesians 1:13–14), Arise City Summit 2016, University of South Florida, Galleria, Florida, 3 June 2016.

19. "Between Jerusalem and the Ends of the World (Acts 6–8): Crossing Cultures in the 1st and 21st Centuries," Annual "Go Conference," Mount of Olives Lutheran Church, Mission Viejo, California, 30 April 2016.

20. "Following Jesus in the Power of the Spirit" (Luke 4:14–21), First Evangelical Church, Glendale, California, 24 April 2016.

21. "The Life in the Spirit and the Life of the Mind" (Luke 10: 25–29), Foursquare National Education Symposium, Life Pacific College, San Dimas, California, 1 March 2016.

22. "The Gift That Serves the World" (Luke 2:22–32), Restoration Church, Norfolk, Virginia, 6 December 2015.

23. "Thanksgiving—Past and Future" (Acts 28:11–15), Bethel Church, Glendale, California, 29 November 2015.

24. "Mission in Translation" (Acts 2), Presbyterian Church of the Master, Mission Viejo, California, 4 October 2015.

25. "On Earth as in Heaven: Guests, Hosts, and the Holy Ghost" (Luke 1:26–38), The Foursquare Church Northwest District Fall Conference, Faith Center, Eugene, Oregon, 28 September 2015.

26. "Radical *Ruach*: The Wind and Breath of Ordinary Liberation" (Exodus 15:8–10, 31:3, 35:31), Aloha Foursquare Church, Aloha, Oregon, 27 September 2015.

27. "'That's My Son! . . . That's My Dad'! Fathers, Sons, and the Mission of God" (Matthew 3:17; 26:39; 27:46, 50), with Aizaiah G. Yong, Winston-Salem First, Winston-Salem, North Carolina, 21 June 2015.

28. "Praying in the Spirit: Apostolic Prayer in the 21st Century" (Acts 1:14; 28:8), Christian Reformed Church Prayer Summit, All Nations Christian Reformed Church, Lake Terrace, California, 13 April 2015.

29. "Reconciliation: Heads-Hearts-Hands and Jews-Samaritans-Others" (Luke 10:25–28; Acts 2:5–11), Chapel, Life Pacific College, San Dimas, California, 24–25 March 2015.

30. "Plundering the Egyptians—Apostolic Style" (Acts 7:20–22), Wycliffe College Chapel, Toronto, Canada, 11 March 2015.

31. "God's Servant among the Nations" (Matt. 12:15–21), Fuller Theological Seminary, Pasadena, California, 25 February 2015.

32. "Caring for the Lord's Vineyard" (Luke 13:6–9), Chapel, Ambrose University College, Calgary, Alberta, 12 February 2015.

33. "Heads-Hearts-Hands: The Call to a Spirit-Filled Life of the Mind" (Luke 10:25–28), Latin America Bible Institute, La Puente, California, 9 December 2014.

34. "Back to the Future: The Wilderness before the Kingdom" (Luke 1:41, 80; 3:1–6), Faith Center, Eugene, Oregon, 13 October 2014.

35. "Back to the Future: The Wilderness before the Kingdom" (Luke 1:41, 80, 3:1–6), Theophilus Church, Portland, Oregon, 13 October 2014.

36. "Both/And—Jesus and the Spirit beyond Nazareth" (Luke 2:1–7, 4:14–21), opening plenary message, Foursquare Northwest District Conference, Spokane, Washington, 7 October 2014.

37. "The Voice/Breath in the Wilderness: Heralding the Spirit-Empowered Life" (Luke 1:41, 80; 3:1–6), Summit Church, Spokane, Washington, 6 October 2014.

38. "David, the Holy Spirit, and Us: Reading Scripture with the Apostles" (Acts 1:15–16), International Christian Fellowship, Stockton, California, 26 July 2014.

39. "Spirit-Empowered Parenthood: Mothers and Fathers Full of the Holy-Spirit" (Luke 1:5–7, 39–45, 57–80), Bethel Chinese Assembly of God, New York City, 13 July 2014.

40. "Pentecostal Teaching and Learning: On the Education of the Spirit" (Acts 2:1–21), Regent University School of Education chapel, Virginia Beach, Virginia, 9 July 2014.

41. "Praying with the Apostles: Then and Tomorrow" (Acts 4:23–31), Great Bridge Presbyterian Church, Chesapeake, Virginia, 22 June 2014.

42. "'. . . For All Who Are Near and Far Off . . .': Pentecost from Jerusalem through Manchester, Georgia, to the Ends of the Earth" (Acts 1:8, 2:37–39), A House of the Living God, Church of Jesus Christ, Manchester, Georgia, 8 June 2014.

43. "Who Are the Christians? The Nature of the Church" (Acts 11:19–26), Great Bridge Presbyterian Church, Chesapeake, Virginia, 25 May 2014.

44. "Preaching, Teaching—and Learning—into the 29th Chapter of Acts" (Acts 28:30–31), Winston-Salem First, Winston-Salem, North Carolina, 18 May 2014.

45. "On Colts, Cloaks, Crowds, and Cobblestones: Anticipating Easter!" (Luke 19:28–40), The Rock Church, Virginia Beach, Virginia, 13 April 2014.

46. "From Holy Ghost to Holy Spirit: Living the Spirit-Filled Life" (Acts 5:26–32), Wheaton College chapel, Wheaton, Illinois, 4 April 2014.

47. "From Jerusalem through Cincinnati and Beyond: The Promise of Love Is for You, for Your Children, and for All Who Are Far Away" (Acts 1:8, 2:37–39), People's Church, Cincinnati, Ohio, 30 March 2014.

48. "Unpredictability, Fragility, Volatility: On (Not) Knowing Where the Wind Blows" (Acts 16:6–10), Regent University School of Divinity chapel, Virginia Beach, Virginia, 13 January 2014.

49. "For All Who Are Near and Far off" (Acts 2:37–39), Gereja Bethel Indonesia, GLOW Fellowship Centre, Serpong, Indonesia, 28 July 2013.

50. ". . . For All Who Are Near and Far Off . . . : From Jerusalem through Jakarta to the Ends of the Earth" (Acts 1:8; 2:39), International English Service, Jakarta, Indonesia, 28 July 2013.

51. ". . . For All Who Are Near and Far Off . . . : From Jerusalem through KL to the Ends of the Earth" (Acts 1:8; 2:39), Calvary Church, Damansara Heights and Kuala Lumpur, Malaysia, 20–21 July 2013.

52. "A New Pentecost! The Spirit's Leading to the Ends of the Earth" (Acts 1:6–8), First Assembly of God, Kuala Lumpur, Malaysia, 14 July 2013.

53. "Guests, Hosts, and the Holy Ghost: Apostolic Mission Down Under in the 21st Century" (Acts 1:8), Wesley International Congregation, Sydney, Australia, 7 July 2013.

54. "From Azotus to Auckland: The Gospel to the Ends of the Earth" (Acts 8:39–40), Titirangi Baptist Church, Auckland, New Zealand, 30 June 2013.

55. "Guests, Hosts, and the Holy Ghost: Apostolic Mission in the 21st Century" (Acts 1:8), Eugene Faith Center, Eugene, Oregon, 23 June 2013.

56. "Guests, Hosts, and the Holy Ghost: Triune Mission from Theophilus to the 21st Century" (Acts 1:1–5), Theophilus Church, Portland, Oregon, 23 June 2013.

57. "Apostolic Question and Angelic Counter-Questions" (Acts 1:1–11), Christian Life Community Centre, Abbotsford, Canada, 12 May 2013.

58. "Acts 28 and Beyond" (Acts 28:23–31), Regent University School of Divinity chapel, Virginia Beach, Virginia, 6 March 2013.

59. "Calling All Prophets and Teachers . . . !" (Acts 13:1–3), Regent University School of Divinity chapel, Virginia Beach, Virginia, 26 February 2013.

60. "Looking Out for #1!?" (Matthew 20:17–28), Great Bridge Presbyterian Church, Chesapeake, Virginia, 3 March 2013.

61. "New Wine for a New Year" (Acts 2:13), Västerås Pentecostal Church, Stockholm, Sweden, 6 January 2013.

62. ". . . For All Who Are Near and Far Off . . . : The Witness of Love from Jerusalem through Winston-Salem to the Ends of the Earth" (Acts 1:8; 2:39), Winston-Salem First, Winston-Salem, North Carolina, 2 December 2012.

63. "Awakened! Transforming Sleep into Action—for Eutychus and Us" (Acts 20:7–12), Evangel University, Springfield, Missouri, 2 November 2012.

64. "Saved from Shame and Stigma: Shortness of Stature and the Gospel in a Disabled World" (Luke 19:1–10), United Theological Seminary, Dayton, Ohio, 17 October 2012.

65. "Saved from Shame and Stigma: Shortness of Stature and the Gospel in a Disabled World" (Luke 19:1–10), Central Woodward Christian Church, Troy, Michigan, 23 September 2012.

66. "How Will This be?" (Luke 1:26–38), International Christian Fellowship, Stockton, California, 7 July 2012.

67. "To the Ends of the Earth: Romanian Pentecostal Power in the 21st Century" (Acts 1:6–8), Vestea Buna, Bucharest, Romania, 24 June 2012.

68. "Graduation in the Footsteps of Elijah: A Spirit-Filled Commissioning" (2 Kings 2:7–16), Commissioning service and address,

Institutul Teologic Penticostal din Bucuresti, Bucharest, Romania, 24 June 2012.

69. "When It Seems as If God has Turned His Face: The Spirit of Holiness, the Power of the Resurrection" (Matthew 27:45–50; Romans 1:1–4), Bethel Church, Glendale, California, 20 May 2012.

70. "Spirit-Filled Motherhood: Elizabeth as Exemplar" (Luke 1:39–45), International Christian Fellowship, Stockton, California, 12 May 2012, and North County Christian Center, Castroville, California, 13 May 2012.

71. "When It Seems as If God has Turned His Face: The Spirit of Holiness, the Power of the Resurrection" (Matthew 27:45–50; Romans 1:1–4), Indonesian Assembly of God Church, Redlands, California, 22 April 2012.

72. "A New Pentecost! The Spirit's Leading to the Ends of the Earth" (Acts 1:6–8), Church on the Hill First Assembly of God, Redlands, California, 22 April 2012.

73. "When It Seems as If God has Turned His Face: The Spirit of Holiness, the Power of the Resurrection" (Matthew 27:45–50; Romans 1:1–4), Grace Bible Church, Irvine, California, 21 April 2012.

74. "The Spirit Helps Us Live for Christ" (Philippians 1:19), Logos Evangelical Seminary chapel, El Monte, California, 18 April 2012.

75. "A Love that Changes that World!" (Song of Songs 8:13–14), Faith Assembly of God Church, Pasco, Washington, 14 April 2012 [Aizaiah and Neddy Yong's wedding].

76. "The Spirit of Holiness, the Power of the Resurrection" (Matthew 27:45–50; Romans 1:1–4), Point Loma Nazarene University chapel, San Diego, California, 11 April 2012.

77. "The Spirit of the Resurrection: From Chaos to Cosmos" (Matthew 27:45–50), Full Life Christian Center, San Francisco, California, 11 March 2012.

78. "When It Seems as if God Has Turned His Face . . . !" (Matthew 27:45–50), International Christian Fellowship, Stockton, California, 10 March 2012.

79. "Saved from Shame and Stigma: Shortness of Stature and the Gospel in a Disabled World" (Luke 19:1–10), Rosemead School

of Psychology chapel, Biola University, La Mirada, California, 14 February 2012.

80. "The Glory and Honor (of the Finns) in the New Jerusalem" (Revelation 21:22–27), Finnish Christian Fellowship, Whittier, California, 4 February 2012.

81. "Loving My Neighbor? You've Gotta Be Kidding!" (Leviticus 19:15–18), Union Theological Seminary, New York City, 27 October 2011.

82. "In the Days of Caesar: Pentecost and the Redemption of Empire" (Luke 1:5–7; 2:1–7; 3:1–6), Pleasant Bay Church, Kirkland, Washington, 10 June 2011.

83. "Paul's Persuasive Persistence: Pentecostal Power, Philosophy, and Proclamation" (Acts 19:8–11), Regent University School of Divinity Chapel, Virginia Beach, Virginia, 8 March 2011.

84. "To the Ends of the Earth: Pentecostal Power in the 21st Century" (Acts 1:6–8), Beulah Heights University Chapel, Atlanta, Georgia, 16 September 2010.

85. "The Lukan Commission: The Spirit, Im/migration, and the De-Construction of Empire" (Acts 1:6–8), All Nations Church, St. Paul, Minneapolis, 7 March 2010.

86. "Living Beyond the Sanctuary: Living within the Kingdom" (Luke 11:1–13), Great Bridge Presbyterian Church, Great Bridge, Virginia, 24 January 2010.

87. "The Spirit Poured Out on All Flesh: Acts 29 and the Pentecostal Outpouring in the 21st Century," North Central University First Things Last Lectures, Minneapolis, Minnesota, 17–19 November 2009.

88. "Fervency: St. Paul and the Passion of and for God" (Romans 5), Annual Retreat for Bethel Chinese Assembly of God, New York City, St. Mary of Providence Center, Elverson, Pennsylvania, 5–7 September 2009.

89. "Indispensable Body Parts" (1 Corinthians 12:20–25), Church of God, Knoxville, Tennessee, 16 August 2009.

90. "Through You, All the Peoples of the Earth Will Be Blessed!" (Acts 3), Yoido Full Gospel Church, Seoul, Korea, 22 May 2009.

91. "Hitchhiking Hellenist 2" (Acts 7:58—8:1), West Ridge Community Church, Pittsburgh, Pennsylvania, 1 March 2009.

92. "Post-Election Euphoria or Depression? Where Is the Holy Spirit in All of This?" (Acts 1:15–26), Christian Life Church, Middlesex, New Jersey, 9 November 2008.

93. "Who Are We Staying and Eating With? Christian Hospitality Today" (Luke 24:28–32), 6 July 2008.

94. "Resurrection Life for the Perplexed, Terrified, and Unintelligible" (Luke 24:1–12), Easter Sunrise Service, New Harvest Church of God, Knoxville, Tennessee, 24 March 2008.

95. "The Spirit and the Renewal of the Mind: Receiving (Luke's Reading of) Eternal Life" (Luke 10:25–28), Regent University School of Divinity Chapel, Virginia Beach, Virginia, 10 March 2008.

96. "Globalization, Immigration, and Exiles: Captivity or Opportunity?" (Jeremiah 19:1–9), International Student Christian Fellowship, Old Dominion University, Norfolk, Virginia, 11 November 2007.

97. "Worship in the Economy of God" (Acts 2:42–47), First Assembly of God, Kuala Lumpur, Malaysia, 17 September 2006.

98. "A 'New Thing' for a New Year" (Isaiah 42:1–9), Cedar Road Assembly of God, Chesapeake, Virginia, 1 January 2006.

99. "From Ephesus to Crystal, Minnesota: A Sermon Inspired by Olivet Baptist Church" (Ephesians 1:1 and passim), Olivet Baptist Church, Crystal, Minnesota, 31 July 2005.

100. "Passion, Pathos, Power: God and the Renewal of Creation" (Revelation 4–5), Word of Grace Baptist Church, Minneapolis, Minnesota, 26 June 2005.

101. "My Mother Taught Me: Mother's Day Sermon" (Hebrews 11:24), Olivet Baptist Church, Crystal, Minnesota, 8 May 2005.

102. "'Poured Out from on High': Pentecostal Vocation and Higher Education" (Isaiah 32), Valley Forge Christian College Chapel, Valley Forge, Pennsylvania, 18 April 2005.

103. "The Politics of Exile and Homecoming: The Challenge of Nehemiah for Evangelicalism Today" (Philippians 2:5–8), Olivet Baptist Church, Crystal, Minnesota, 17 April 2005.

104. "An Ordinary Day with Jesus—Week 2: Jesus in Our Everyday Relationships" (Matthew 22:36–40), Olivet Baptist Church, Crystal, Minnesota, 16 January 2005.

105. "Things They Carried" series, "Carried by Our Memories: The Good, the Bad, the Redemptive" (Acts 22:2–7; Philippians 3:3–11), Olivet Baptist Church, Crystal, Minnesota, 27 June, 1 August, 8 August 2004.

106. "Sunday School: The Corporate Memory" (Psalm 136), Word of Grace Baptist Church, South Minneapolis, 25 July 2004.

107. "Remembering the Past I: Israel, Our Nation, the Church, Our Church" (Psalm 136), St. Luke's, Fairbault, Minnesota, 4 July and 11 July 2004.

108. "Enoch Walked with God, and . . ." (Genesis 5:21–24), Hastings, Minnesota, 23 May 2004.

109. "Melissa Surface," Funeral Sermon (Revelation 21:1–6), Moses Lake, Washington.

110. "David and Absalom" (2 Samuel 14–19), Olivet Baptist Church, Crystal, Minnesota, 16 November 2003.

111. "The Precious Cornerstone: In Zion and in Hampton, Iowa" (Isaiah 28:14–22), First Baptist Church, Hampton, Iowa, 19 October 2003.

112. "Probing Stories Told by Jesus: The Good Samaritan" (Luke 10:25–37), Olivet Baptist Church, Crystal, Minnesota, 17 August 2003.

113. "The Holy Spirit and the Arts" (Exodus 31:1–11; 35:30–35), Word of Grace Baptist Church, Minneapolis, Minnesota, 22 June and 29 June 2003.

114. "Memorials: Truth, Lies and Christian Identity" (Matthew 28:11–20), Olivet Baptist Church, Crystal, Minnesota, 25 March 2003.

115. "Blood and Bones: Disability and the Power of the Spirit" (Luke 24: 36–49), Calvary Baptist Church, Hastings, Minnesota, 27 April 2003.

116. "Biblical Perspectives on War and Peace," Olivet Baptist Church, Crystal, Minnesota, 9 February 2003.

117. "Out of the Mouths of Infants . . ." (Matthew 21:14–17; Psalm 8), Grace Baptist Church, Grantsburg, Wisconsin, 12 January 2003.

118. "Pentecost and the Christian Mission" (Acts 1:8; 2:1–21), 1st Baptist Church, Forest City, Iowa, 19 October 2002.

119. "Overcoming the Fear of Death" (Hebrews 5:7—6:3), Olivet Baptist Church, Crystal, Minnesota, 6 October 2002.

120. "God with Us II: Pentecost" (Acts 2:1–13), Olivet Baptist Church, Crystal, Minnesota, 11 August 2002.

121. "God with Us: On the Incarnation" (Philippians 2:1–8), Olivet Baptist Church, Crystal, Minnesota, 4 August 2002.

122. "Spirit of (the) God(s)?" (Genesis 41:37–45), Word of Grace Baptist—14 July 2002, and Litchfield 1st Baptist—7 July 2002.

123. "Contending with the Spirit of the Lord" (Genesis 6:1–4), Litchfield 1st Baptist, Word of Grace Baptist—14 July 2002 and 7 July 2002.

124. "After the Dedication" (1 Kings 9:10–14), North Isanti Baptist, North Isanti, Minnesota 30 June 2002.

125. "Sent Forth with the Ways and the Presence of the LORD" (Exodus 33:12–16), Olivet Baptist Church, Crystal, Minnesota, 23 June 2002.

126. "What Kind of Father is This?" (Luke 3:23), Father's Day, Riverwood Baptist Church, Minnesota, 16 June 2002.

127. "Building the House of the Lord" (Ezra 1:1–4), Riverwood Baptist Church, Minnesota, 9 June 2002.

128. "The Kingdom of God Is in the Midst of You"? (Luke 17:20–21), Isanti Baptist, Isanti, Minnesota, 19 May 2002.

129. "What Is an Asian Pentecostal Doing in Minnesota?" (Acts 2:1–13), Asian Chapel, Bethel College, St. Paul, Minnesota, 10 May 2002.

130. "Now You See Me, Now You Don't . . . : Revelation and the Darkness of God" (Exodus 19; Hebrews 12:18–29), Olivet Baptist Church, Crystal, Minnesota, 28 April 2002.

131. "Remembering the Lord through the Supper" (1 Corinthians 11:23–26), First Baptist Church, Forest City, Iowa, 3 February 2002.

132. "Prevailing Prayer" (Genesis 32:22–31), Olivet Baptist Church, Crystal, Minnesota, 6 January 2002.

133. "Magi from the East: Matthew and the Gospel to the Gentiles" (Matthew 2:1–12), First Baptist Church, Forest City, Iowa, 25 November 2001.

134. "Faithfulness—Divine and Human" (Jeremiah 35:1–11, 18–19), First Baptist Church, Forest City, Iowa, 28 October 2001.

135. "Remember, O Lord . . ." (Psalm 137), Parkview Baptist Church, Black River Falls, Wisconsin, 14 October 2001.

136. "Remembering the Past, Anticipating the Future" (Psalm 136, Hebrews 12:1–2), Harvest Home Celebration, First Baptist Church, Augusta, Wisconsin, 30 September 2001.

137. "The Acts of the Holy Spirit: Pentecost and God's New Work" (Acts 2), Park Assembly of God, St. Louis Park, Minnesota, 19 August 2001.

138. "Enoch Walked with God, and . . ." (Genesis 5:21–24), Olivet Baptist Church, Crystal, Minnesota, 29 July 2001.

139. Pentecost and God's Reconciling Work" (Acts 2:1–4), Northaven Baptist Church, St. Paul, Minnesota, 15 July 2001.

140. "Remembering . . . on Memorial Day" (Joshua 4:1–7), Olivet Baptist Church, Crystal, Minnesota, 27 May 2001.

141. "Loving the Lord Your God with All Your Mind . . ." (Mark 12:28–34), Bible College of Malaysia, Kuala Lumpur, Malaysia, 3 May 2001.

142. "The Resurrection and the Life" (Luke 7:11–17), Easter Sunday, Jessup Bible Fellowship, Waterloo, Iowa, 15 April 2001.

143. "Tempted beyond What We Are Able?" (1 Corinthians 10:1–22), Olivet Baptist Church, Crystal, Minnesota, 1 April 2001.

144. "A New Beginning" (Genesis 8:13–22), First Baptist Church, Augusta, Wisconsin, 7 January 2001.

145. "Listening to All the Voices of Advent" (Matthew 2:16–18), Blaine Baptist Church, Blaine, Minnesota, 26 November 2000.

146. "Baptists on the Road to Emmaus" (Luke 24:13–35), First Baptist Church, Fergus Falls, Minnesota, 8 October 2000.

147. "Striving with the Spirit: Insights into the Life of the Spirit from the Book of Genesis" (Genesis 2:7; 6:3; 7:15–22), Oak Hill Baptist Church, Oak Hill, Minnesota, 20 August 2000.

148. "Jesus the Bread of Life" (John 6:25–70), International Christian Fellowship, Stockton, California, 5 August 2000.

149. "Freedom in the Spirit" (Galatians 5:13–26), Word of Grace Baptist Church, South Minneapolis, Minnesota, 2 July 2000.

150. "Go to Bethel and Sin?" (Amos 4:4–5), Bethel Chapel, St. Paul, Minnesota, 8 May 2000.

151. Richard Garcia Funeral Service, Assembly of God Church, Moses Lake, Washington, 30 March 2000.

152. "The Nuclear Family: Lifestyle and Ethical Issues" (Genesis 12; Hebrews 11:8–10), Calvary Baptist Church, Roseville, Minnesota, 6 February 2000.

153. "The Whos, Wheres, Hows, and Whys of Following After Jesus" (Matthew 26:6–13), Olivet Baptist Church, Crystal, Minnesota, 9 January 2000.

154. "Y2K: Woe or Redemption" (Revelation 8:13; 11:15–18), Fergus Falls Baptist Church, Fergus Falls, Minnesota, 28 November 1999.

155. "New Beginnings" (Revelation 7:9–17), New Beginnings Christian Fellowship, Mansfield, Massachusetts, 21 November 1999.

156. "Behold I Come Quickly" (Revelation 6), Humboldt, Illinois, 14 November 1999.

157. "Jesus at the Center of Y2K" (Revelation 5), Olivet Baptist Church, Crystal, Minnesota, 7 November 1999.

158. "Behold, I Come Quickly . . ." (Revelation 4), North Isanti Baptist Church, North Isanti, Minnesota, 31 October 1999.

159. "Four Part Series: Believing in and Living according to Word and Spirit I: 'Hovering over the Waters . . .': Word and Spirit in Creation" (Genesis 1:1–5; 2:4–7), June 1999.

Bibliography

Albrecht, Daniel E. *Rites in the Spirit: A Ritual Approach to Pentecostal/Charismatic Spirituality.* Journal of Pentecostal Theology Supplement Series 17. Sheffield, UK: Sheffield University Press, 1999.

The Apostolic Faith. Los Angeles: 1906–8.

Bartleman, Frank. *Azusa Street.* 2nd ed. With an introduction by Vinson Synan. Alachua, FL: Bridge-Logos, 1980.

Carwardine, Richard. *Transatlantic Revivalism: Popular Evangelicalism in Britain and America 1790–1865.* Westport, CT: Greenwood, 1978.

Chan, Simon. *Liturgical Theology: The Church as Worshiping Community.* Downers Grove, IL: InterVarsity, 2006.

Cho, Youngmo. *Spirit and Kingdom in the Writings of Luke and Paul: An Attempt to Reconcile These Concepts.* Milton Keynes, UK: Paternoster, 2009.

Crabtree, Charles T. *Pentecostal Preaching: Empowering Your Pulpit with the Holy Spirit.* Springfield, MO: Gospel Publishing House, 2003.

Finger, Thomas N. *A Contemporary Anabaptist Theology: Biblical, Historical, Constructive.* Downers Grove: IVP Academic, 2004.

Forde, Gerhard O. *Theology Is for Proclamation.* Minneapolis: Fortress, 1990.

Gause, R. Hollis. *Living in the Spirit: The Way of Salvation.* Rev. and expanded ed. Cleveland, TN: Pathway Press, 2009.

Holm, Randall. "Cadences of the Heart: A Walkabout in Search of Pentecostal Preaching." *Didaskalia* 15, no. 1 (2003) 13–27.

Kelly, J. N. D. *Golden Mouth: The Story of John Chrysostom: Ascetic, Preacher, Bishop.* Grand Rapids: Baker, 1995.

Killinger, John. *Fundamentals of Preaching.* Minneapolis: Fortress, 1984.

Kim, Eunjoo Mary. *Preaching the Presence of God: A Homiletic from an Asian American Perspective.* Valley Forge, PA: Judson, 1999.

Kim, Matthew D. "Asian American Preaching." In *The Art and Craft of Biblical Preaching,* edited by Haddon Robinson and Craig Brian Larson, 200–204. Grand Rapids: Zondervan, 2005.

Lakoff, George, and Mark Johnson. *Philosophy in the Flesh: The Embodied Mind and Its Challenge to Western Thought.* New York: Basic, 1999.

Leoh, Vincent Beng. "Ethics and Pentecostal Preaching: The Anastatic, Organic, and Communal Strands." PhD diss., The Southern Baptist Theological Seminary, 1990.

Liardon, Roberts. *The Azusa Street Revival: When the Fire Fell*. Shippensburg, PA: Destiny Image, 2006.

Lischer, Richard, ed. *The Company of Preachers: Wisdom on Preaching, Augustine to the Present*. Grand Rapids: Eerdmans, 2002.

Long, Thomas G. *The Witness of Preaching*. 2nd ed. Louisville: Westminster John Knox, 2005.

Martin, Lee Roy, ed. *Toward a Pentecostal Theology of Preaching*. Cleveland, TN: CPT, 2015.

Martin, Lee Roy, and Mark L. Williams, eds. *Spirit-Filled Preaching in the 21st Century*. Cleveland, TN: Pathway, 2014.

McClendon, James Wm. Jr. *Biography as Theology: How Life Stories Can Remake Today's Theology*. Nashville: Abingdon, 1974.

Millard, Bart. *I Can Only Imagine*. Nashville: Thomas Nelson, 2018.

Neville, Robert Cummings. *The God Who Beckons: Theology in the Form of Sermons*. Nashville: Abingdon, 1999.

———. *Preaching the Gospel without Easy Answers*. Nashville: Abingdon, 2005.

Niebuhr, Reinhold. *The Children of Light and the Children of Darkness: A Vindication of Democracy and a Critique of Its Traditional Defence*. Reprint; New York: Charles Scribner's Sons, 1960.

Noll, Mark A. *The Scandal of the Evangelical Mind*. Grand Rapids: Eerdmans, 1995.

Oliverio, L. William Jr. "An Interpretive Review Essay on Amos Yong's Spirit-Word-Community: Theological Hermeneutics in Trinitarian Perspective." *Journal of Pentecostal Theology* 18, no. 2 (2009) 301–11.

Parsons, Mikeal C. *Body and Character in Luke and Acts: The Subversion of Physiognomy in Early Christianity*. Grand Rapids: Baker Academic, 2006.

Payne, Leah. *Gender and Pentecostal Revivalism: Making a Female Ministry in the Early Twentieth Century*. Christianity and Renewal: Interdisciplinary Studies. New York: Palgrave Macmillan, 2015.

Powery, Emerson A. *Spirit Speech: Celebration and Lament in Preaching*. Nashville: Abingdon, 2009.

Ragoonath, Aldwin. *Preach the Word: A Pentecostal Approach*. Winnipeg, Manitoba: Agape Teaching Ministry, 2004.

Richie, Tony. *Speaking by the Spirit: A Pentecostal Model for Interreligious Dialogue*. Asbury Theological Seminary Series in World Christian Revitalization Movements, Pentecostal/charismatic Studies. Lexington, KY: Emeth, 2011.

———. "Spiritual Transformation through Pentecostal Testimony." In *Knowing God in the Ordinary Practices of the Christian Life*, edited by David Sang-Ehil Han and Jackie David Johns. Cleveland, TN: CPT, forthcoming.

Robeck, Cecil M. Jr. *The Azusa Street Mission and Revival: The Birth of the Global Pentecostal Movement*. Nashville: Thomas Nelson, 2006.

Samuel, Josh P. S. *The Holy Spirit in Worship Music, Preaching, and the Altar: Renewing Pentecostal Corporate Worship*. Cleveland, TN: CPT, 2018.

———. "The Spirit in Pentecostal Preaching: A Constructive Dialogue with Haddon Robinson's and Charles Crabtree's Theology of Preaching." *Pneuma* 35, no. 2 (2013) 199–219.

Schmit, Claytom J. "Manuscript." In *The New Interpreter's Handbook of Preaching*, edited by Paul Scott Wilson, 394–95. Nashville: Abingdon, 2008.

Smith, Robert Jr. "Call and Response." In *The New Interpreter's Handbook of Preaching*, edited by Paul Scott Wilson, 297. Nashville: Abingdon, 2008.

Thiselton, Anthony C. *The Two Horizons: New Testament Hermeneutics and Philosophical Description*. Grand Rapids: Eerdmans, 1980.

Trask, Bradley. "Pentecostal Preaching and Persuasion." In *Foundations for Pentecostal Preaching*, edited by James K. Bridges, 169–90. Springfield, MO: Gospel Publishing House, 2005.

Trementozzi, David. *Salvation in the Flesh: Understanding How Embodiment Shapes Christian Faith*. Eugene, OR: Wipf & Stock, 2017.

Turner, William C. Jr. *Preaching that Makes the Word Plain: Doing Theology in the Crucible of Life*. Eugene, OR: Cascade, 2008.

Vondey, Wolfgang, and Martin W. Mittelstadt, eds. *The Theology of Amos Yong and the New Face of Pentecostal Scholarship: Passion for the Spirit*. Global Pentecostal and Charismatic Studies 14. Leiden: Brill, 2013.

Webb, Joseph M. "Without Notes." In *The New Interpreter's Handbook of Preaching*, edited by Paul Scott Wilson, 429–31. Nashville: Abingdon, 2008.

Whitehead, Alfred North. *Process and Reality*. Edited by David Ray Griffin. Revised and corrected ed. New York: Free Press, 1979.

Wolffe, John. *The Expansion of Evangelicalism: The Age of Wilberforce, More, Chalmers, and Finey*. Nottingham,. UK: IVP, 2006.

Yong, Amos. "American Political Theology in a Post-al Age: A Perpetual Foreigner and Pentecostal Stance." In *Faith and Resistance in the Age of Trump*, edited by Miguel A. De La Torre, 107–14. Maryknoll, NY: Orbis, 2017.

———. "Apostolic Evangelism in the Postcolony: Opportunities and Challenges." *Mission Studies* 34, no. 2 (2017) 147–67.

———. "The 'Baptist Vision' of James William McClendon, Jr.: A W.esleyan-Pentecostal Response." *Wesleyan Theological Journal* 37, no. 2 (2002) 32–57.

———. *The Bible, Disability, and the Church: A New Vision of the People of God*. Grand Rapids: Eerdmans, 2011.

———. "Creator Spiritus and the Spirit of Christ: Toward a Trinitarian Theology of Creation." In *The Work of the Holy Spirit*, edited by Jeffrey Barbeau and Beth Jones, 168–82. Downers Grove, IL: IVP Academic, 2015.

———. *The Dialogical Spirit: Christian Reason and Theological Method for the Third Millennium*. Eugene, OR: Cascade, 2014.

———. *Discerning the Spirit(s): A Pentecostal-Charismatic Contribution to Christian Theology of Religions*. Journal of Pentecostal Theology Supplement Series 20. Sheffield, UK: Sheffield Academic Press, 2000.

———. *The Future of Evangelical Theology: Soundings from the Asian American Diaspora*. Downers Grove, IL: IVP Academic, 2014.

———. *The Hermeneutical Spirit: Theological Interpretation and the Scriptural Imagination for the 21st Century*. Eugene, OR: Cascade, 2017.

———. *Hospitality and the Other: Pentecost, Christian Practices, and the Neighbor*. Faith Meets Faith series. Maryknoll, OR: Orbis, 2008.

———. "The Im/Migrant Spirit: De/Constructing a Pentecostal Theology of Migration." In *Theology of Migration in the Abrahamic Religions*, edited by Peter C. Phan and Elaine Padilla, 133–53. Christianities of the World. New York: Palgrave Macmillan, 2014.

————. *In the Days of Caesar: Pentecostalism and Political Theology*. Sacra Doctrina: Christian Theology for a Postmodern Age series. Grand Rapids: Eerdmans, 2010.

————. "Informality, Illegality, and Improvisation: Theological Reflections on Money, Migration, and Ministry in Chinatown, NYC, and Beyond." In *New Overtures: Asian North American Theology in the 21st Century—Essays in Honor of Fumitaka Matsuoka*, edited by Eleazar S. Fernandez, 248–68. Upland, CA: Sopher Press, 2012; originally published in the *Journal of Race, Ethnicity, and Religion* 3, no. 2 (2012) [http://www.raceandreligion.com/JRER/Volume_3_%282012%29.html]

————. "Persevering through 1 Peter." Hermeneutics BI107 thesis. Scotts Valley, CA: Bethany College, 1984.

————. "Poured Out on All Flesh: The Spirit, World Pentecostalism, and the Performance of Renewal Theology." *PentecoStudies: An Interdisciplinary Journal for Research on the Pentecostal and Charismatic Movements* 6, no. 1 (2007) 16–46.

————. "Proclamation and the Third Article: Toward a Pneumatology of Preaching." In *Third Article Theology: A Pneumatological Dogmatics*, edited by Myk Habets, 367–94. Minneapolis: Fortress, 2016.

————. "Reading Scripture and Nature: Pentecostal Hermeneutics and Their Implications for the Contemporary Evangelical Theology and Science Conversation." *Perspectives on Science and Christian Faith* 63, no. 1 (2011) 1–13.

————. *Renewing Christian Theology: Systematics for a Global Christianity*. Images and commentary by Jonathan A. Anderson. Waco, TX: Baylor University Press, 2014.

————. "Salvation, Society, and the Spirit: Pentecostal Contextualization and Political Theology from Cleveland to Birmingham, from Springfield to Seoul." *Pax Pneuma: The Journal of Pentecostals & Charismatics for Peace & Justice* 5, no. 2 (2009) 22–34; reprinted in *The Spirituality of Fourth Dimension and Social Salvation: Studies on Dr. Yonggi Cho's Theology*, edited by Mun Hong Choi, 163–88. Journal of Youngsan Theology Supplement Series 1. Gunpo City, South Korea: Hansei University Press, 2012.

————. "The Spirit and Proclamation." Three parts. *The Living Pulpit* 24, no. 2 (2015) 20–38.

————. *Spirit of Love: A Trinitarian Theology of Grace*. Waco, TX: Baylor University Press, 2012.

————. "The Spirit Poured Out: A (Pentecostal) Perspective after Pentecost," in Guido Vergauwen, o.p., and Andreas Steinbruber, eds., *Veni, Sancte Spiritus! Theologiesche Beiträge zue Sendung des Geistes/Contributions thélogiques à la mission de l'Esprit/Theological Contributions to the Mission of the Spirit – Festschfit für Barbara Hallensleben zum 60. Geburtstag*, Studia Oecumenica Friburgensia 85, Studienzentrum für Glaube und Gesellschaft 7 (Münster: Aschendorff-Verlag, 2018), 198–210.

————. *The Spirit Poured Out on All Flesh: Pentecostalism and the Possibility of Global Theology*. Grand Rapids: Baker Academic, 2005.

————. *Spirit-Word-Community: Theological Hermeneutics in Trinitarian Perspective*. New Critical Thinking in Religion, Theology and Biblical Studies Series. Aldershot, UK: Ashgate, 2002.

————. *Theology and Down Syndrome: Reimagining Disability in Late Modernity*. Waco, TX: Baylor University Press, 2007.

————. *Who is the Holy Spirit? A Walk with the Apostles*. Brewster, MA: Paraclete, 2011.

———. "Zacchaeus: Short and Un-Seen." In *Christian Reflection: A Series in Faith and Ethics—Disability*, 11–17. Waco, TX: The Center for Christian Ethics at Baylor University, 2012. http://www.baylor.edu/ifl/christianreflection/index.php?id=92612; reprinted as "Short, Saved, and Un-Seen: Zacchaeus and the Invisibility of Disability in the Bible." *NCC* [National Council of Churches, India] *Review* 84, no. 9 (2014) 510–17.

Yong, Amos, and Dale M. Coulter. *Finding the Holy Spirit at a Christian University: Renewing Christian Higher Education*. Grand Rapids: Eerdmans, 2019.

Yong, Amos, and Dale M. Coulter, eds. *The Spirit, the Affections, and the Christian Tradition*. Notre Dame, IN: University of Notre Dame Press, 2016.

Scripture Index

Subject Index